"A 'trial through fire' book filled with valuable lessons learned along the way. Bill Farr shares his insights into the complicated world of personality and love. A concise and refreshing perspective, surely meant to help you grow, a little less painlessly, along the way."
-DR. NIVEA BRIGGITTE CALICO, MD
PSYCHIATRIST

"This book gives an understanding of how your perfect partner could be right beside you and what you do that prevents your relationship from working."
- HARRY PAUL, SHAMANIC HEALER & LIFE COACH, SHAMANHARRY.COM

"An honest, provocative book that goes right into the core of dating. If you're looking for your match, this is a must have book for you! Bill Farr offers insight into dating failure and success, and shows how achieving harmony is possible. More pleasure, less pain – aren't we all hoping for that."
- NATALIYA NOZHAROVA, LIFE COACH, M.A. IN SPIRITUAL PSYCHOLOGY, AUTHOR, "THE HEART'S DIARIES" (PUBLISHED IN BULGARIAN)

The
POWER of
Personality Types
in Love and

Relationships

The POWER of Personality Types in Love and Relationships

Build a *Great* Relationship
with the *Right* Partner
and Stop Wasting Time
on the Wrong One

BILL FARR

Books may be purchased by contacting the author at:

Info@theartofunity.com

Cover Design: Gaelyn Larrick
Interior Layout and Design: Julie Csizmadia
Publisher: Enlightened Heart Publications
Editor: Claude Hall

Library of Congress Control Number: 2013938400
ISBN-10: 0989337707
ISBN-13: 978-0-9893377-0-0

Enlightened Heart
PUBLICATIONS

TABLE OF CONTENTS

DEDICATION

When I was in third grade my teacher told my mother, "When your son finally does learn to read, he will never be smart enough to work in a field that requires extensive reading or comprehension." Lucky for me that was not something she was about to accept. Thank you for the monumental efforts to help me do all the things only you seemed to know I was capable of, such as reading. I dedicate this book to you Mom, and to all the mothers who refuse to accept anything less than what they know their child can achieve. For my father and the incredible amount of work that he endured so that his children would have an education. I love you both.

ACKNOWLEDGEMENTS

What a joy it has been writing and sharing this work with so many inspirational people who have shared their lives and encouraged me to create this work. Words cannot express the gratitude I have for their efforts including my teachers, friends, clients, those who worked on this book, and those just passing in and out of my life that have inspired me equally in its creation. For those who have given me their trust and allowed me to delve into their lives and relationships with the hopes of finding happiness, I hope I helped and inspired you as much as you have me.

For Breck, my teacher and friend, thank you for introducing me to this concept and so many others that have changed my life for the better. For Alan, thank you for the many lessons and inspirations you have given me, most of which I probably made as hard to give as they were for me to receive. Your lessons provide endless payback.

Special thanks to all those who have shared and inspired me to develop this concept into what it has become including: Joey S, Mike M, Johanna P, Pamela Z, Andrea H, Laura Z, Nela, Marge, Andrea R, Charles G, Natalia M, Rachel M, Cindy, Earl, Raf, and Consuelo. Thank you for your trust and all that I've learned from you.

For Claude Hall, every writer should be lucky enough to have you as their editor. I hope you know how much you inspire all those who come into your life.

For all those who come to this work on the path to finding happiness. I send all my love, support, and the best energy I have to you in hopes you achieve all that you hope for and more.

ABOUT THE AUTHOR

Bill Farr is a wellness coach, an instructor in various forms of martial arts and meditation, a former kickboxing champion and professional Argentine Tango dancer. As a consummate student Bill has studied with well-known Western psychology teachers as well as Buddhist monks, South American Shaman, Chi Gong masters, Grand Masters of martial arts and other prominent teachers. He now travels worldwide teaching the principles in this book as well as meditation and wellness. His concepts are designed to help people become healthy and united in mind, body, and spirit in order to prepare themselves to find their perfect mate as well as a path to fulfillment and higher consciousness. The focus is on developing compassion, understanding, and respect for each other based on important differences, existing in both intimate and professional relationships.

PREFACE

As with anything in life, relationships have rules as well as consequences. In a committed relationship, there are rules. In a recreational relationship, there are consequences. Everyone's heard the alarmingly high rate of divorce today, and those numbers do not reflect the also alarmingly high percentage of unhappy marriages. Often a relationship fails because the participants don't have a full understanding of the rules. I used to think of rules as binding, but I now realize that they are freeing because they replace consequences. Without them, we experience suffering and chaos. I'm not saying you always have to follow the rules, but it's important that you know them.

Imagine a football game in which neither team knew the rules, but were only told that they need to score touchdowns. They would make mistakes on how many players should be on the field, boundaries, when to play or not, possessions, etc. Their few successes would be sheer coincidence. Without agreements on certain rules, there is no purpose, nothing to strive for, and the game would be very uninteresting. Once collaborating teams know the rules of the game well, they then have an opportunity to successfully break or bend them.

It is the same with coordinating personality types. Once you know your characteristics, and who can match most harmoniously with you, then you know what to look for. If you know them well you can have success with any type, knowing the consequences as well as how to act and what to expect during a disagreement. There are also times when you need to exit ongoing relationships with people because your nature does not coincide with their nature. This is not that they are bad and you are good or either is wrong and right, but just that you are not naturally harmonious together.

Many people have lost their ability to express their emotions. They have been hurt in the past from bad relationships, including with their parents. Moving forward they feel a relationship is going to be hard, so they endure bad circumstances to avoid being alone instead of waiting for a person who truly inspires them. Instead of operating with passion, many relationships operate on autopilot. They are not conscious why they react the way they do, why they chose the partner they are with, and why they can't seem to make a relationship work harmoniously. Instead of making choices to maximize pleasure, many of their choices are made simply to avoid pain, often drawing the realization of their fears to them like a magnet. Unfulfilling relationship choices such as this can be minimized when a person knows what they can naturally offer in a relationship, and what to look for that will complement their personality. Knowing the rules will bring back the emotional intelligence needed to approach a relationship successfully because the rules can explain why past relationships have been so difficult. This new approach helps a person to regain hope in a different outcome and create new relationships under different terms.

My Story

I began my process of self-discovery because I wanted to stop suffering so much in relationships. I realized that I inadvertently hurt the ones I love the most, and vice versa, and I wanted that process to stop. If our intention is not to hurt the ones we love, then why does it happen so often?

One of my first advisors asked me what I thought of my parents' relationship. He had me take their relationship and break it down into parts—conversation, financial, emotional, physical, affection, love and their expression of it—he then asked, what did I want to emulate? I told him I wasn't interested in recreating any of those categories for my own relationship. He explained that their relationship trained me how to be in a relationship, and if I didn't want to recreate theirs, then I would require retraining. If a person *does* want to recreate their parents' relationship on all those levels, then they need to find someone whose ideas match theirs. Everyone else needs to be taught, counseled, advised, coached and learn what they want, instead of what they do not want; and so began my training. Learning to move from disastrous relationships to healthy ones led to the insights in this book that I've been able to share with people, helping them to improve their relationships or create healthier ones.

Many people have subconsciously convinced themselves that they can't make it in a relationship because their parents couldn't. After years of internalizing their parent's emotional struggle, when an argument comes up in their own adult relationship, they assume things are going to look just like their parents did. This fear creates a self-fulfilling prophecy that often forces the relationship to implode even when things are going smoothly.

The good news is, with simple awareness, this prediction does not come true. Although people often have similar characteristics as their parents, they don't always accept the same things their parents do. They also do not offer the same things, and they don't like the same things. So as they mature, they will have different interactions, but they may still need some guidance not to create an equivalent, sometimes toxic relationship. This is why many people are frightened at the prospect of marriage. They are fine being in a relationship, but the idea that they might create the same bad situation as others they know, such as their parents, scares them out of the long-term commitment. The better option is to identify and face their fears and learn how to overcome them so they don't plague every relationship going forward.

I have made many mistakes while striving to find my happiness. As an "Entitled," I have been in relationships with women who were wonderful "Supports," and I lost them because of my pathology, not realizing how right they were for me. I have also attracted the wrong partners and spent my time trying to make those relationships work, instead of dealing with my fear of being alone. I've experienced problems in many relationships, because I did not realize I was dealing with different personality types.

For example, I was with a "Selfish Entitled", who, in agreement with her type, was not interested in doing much for me. Anytime she did do something, I had to hear what an incredible favor she had done for me for the next week, even for something as small as making dinner. After we broke up, I then found myself with a "Blind Support," not realizing the incredible differences in their personalities. One of the many ways I went wrong was thinking I had learned from my mistakes in the previous relationship; I wouldn't let her do the smallest task for me, such as making me a meal, because I didn't want it to be thrown back in my face. This took away a simple, yet joyful experience of offering a supportive gesture to the one she loved, typical of her type.

Also, as part of my problem, I did not realize that I was an Entitled masquerading as a Support a lot of the time, especially in the beginning of many of my intimate relationships. As an Entitled, this was setting up deceptions that would be revealed as my relationships proceeded. I began to feel as if I wasn't meant to be in an intimate relationship at all.

I was raised with an older sister, very close in age, who is "Selfishly Entitled." So for me to spend time with her, things pretty much went her way or not at all. If I wanted to do anything with her, I had to give her support. I looked up to her greatly, so as unnatural as it may have been for me, I played the Support role. Only after years of studying psychology and different personality types did I figure this out about myself. I only acted Entitled when I was around other Supports, or when an Entitled pushed me too far. For the most part, I waited for other Entitleds to step up, instead of taking any leadership myself, while hiding any agenda I may have had. This happened because of insecurity and low self-esteem. This obviously set up a lot of unfulfilling intimate relationships with the partners I chose. I could not figure out why I was failing in so many relationships, with women I cared about and who I knew cared about me.

It was only through working on my issues with professionals that prompted me to realize that the problems I was having in every relationship stemmed from me. I was unknowingly acting as a type not natural for me, combined with choosing personality types not suited for me. Once I figured this out, everything started coming to me more easily. The struggles I had and frustrations in communications started becoming much clearer to me. I was working twice as hard to get along and get what I wanted from people by deceiving myself and not choosing my relationships wisely. I am not a doctor or psychiatrist, but a coach, working with people in business and personal relationships to improve their lives and discover happiness. I don't pretend to be an expert on relationships, I'm not even sure that exists, but someone who has transformed from choosing partners that could have never worked for me to someone who now consciously chooses harmony in my approach to all relationships. This is a concept I have been able to share with others who have had success as well. My hope is that the explanation of the personality types in this book gives others the same insights I've had, allowing for more harmony in relationships. More ideas for couples to find harmony and individuals to find unity within themselves can be found at *www.TheArtOfUnity.com*

INTRODUCTION

A person's temperament and type influence harmony in relationships more than gender, age or social background. People have basic differences in their communication styles, emotional needs and modes of behavior. Once we acknowledge and understand these better, we can understand one another and create happier relationships together. Without understanding these differences, people will have difficulty effectively fulfilling the needs of their partners and finding contentment together, and they will continue to rely on luck in whom they choose for their next relationship. This book combines the psychology of personality types, as well as the psychology of why people choose the person they are with. Before developing a bias about the categories, it is highly recommended to start by taking the profile in chapter eight before reading on. The Profile is a questionnaire that helps you to discover which type you are. (It can also be found at *www.TheArtOfUnity.com*)

Can Your Relationship Last?

In order to be in an emotionally healthy relationship, one must have many things: *acceptance, affection, appreciation, approval, attention, comfort, encouragement, respect, security, and support.* Call them the "Essential Ten." If this does not sound like the relationship you had with your parents, or that they had with each other, then you need to make a conscious effort to offer these, and you will probably need to learn how. That list can be overwhelming. In fact, if you think back to when you met your partner, did you take time to think if you would get these things from him or her, or did you just find him or her attractive? Or were you mostly impressed with his or her confidence in speaking to you, or maybe even just their good career? Now you know why there is such a high rate of divorce.

It has never been easier to meet someone than in modern times, but for the same reasons, it has never been harder to stay with someone. For people to stay together *happily*, it requires some work. The beautiful thing about love is that, despite the high rate of divorce and unhappiness, people still believe eternal love and happiness is possible. They ignore the statistics, the majority of unhappily married friends and family, and optimistically enter a relationship and get married, thinking they will be the exception and create an endless romantic bliss. However, the same people do not carry this same optimism into the relationship once it has started. Instead they bring their shame, fears, insecurity, baggage, and past abuses in to the relationship. These could include self-righteousness, pride, the idea that they could find someone better suited for them, anger, contempt, lack of trust, and other highly destructive qualities.

The good news is that eternal lasting happiness and love is possible. In order to have it, you just have to offer into your relationship the "Essential Ten," qualities mentioned earlier. People often wonder, since we all want a happy relationship, why we don't naturally offer these good qualities to the ones we love. Simply put, we were not taught to. In fact, most of us were taught the exact opposite. We are also sensitive to the fear and risk associated with the vulnerability of love. And we don't look for those qualities in our potential partners. We mostly look for beauty, confidence, a sense of humor, what emotions they make us feel, what fears they will help us overcome, what people say about us as a couple, and many other things that do not matter as much over the course of a healthy long-term relationship.

No matter who you are with, your ability to stay in love and be in love depends mostly on the ability to give up your own selfishness and need to be right, while offering the "Essential Ten" positive qualities. No amount of commitment can change that.

When Sofia first came to me, she told me how great her relationship with Roger was. She was from Costa Rica and Roger was from California, two very different cultures. When they met in her native Costa Rica, it was very clear that she would fill the role of hostess, when he decided to move there for her. When they went to America, the roles switched. For them, it was clear who would be responsible for the other in each situation based on their agreed-upon differences.

Their situation is an example that similarly illustrates the roles of the two personality types in this book. Unfortunately, most people can't differentiate one another's contributions this clearly because they don't seem so obvious until you understand them. In most relationships, the individual personalities are as distinct as the cultures from the different countries Sofia and Roger come from, but most people either refuse to acknowledge this, or try to change the other person. This would be like trying to make a foreigner into a native. Accepting our differences is the key to getting along. Roger didn't expect all of Costa Rica to stop eating rice and beans or speaking Spanish because he went there. He adapted to, and experienced that culture, enjoying its positive and negative aspects, for as long as he was there; the same is true in a relationship with people of different types.

Often people are drawn together by their differences and expect to be challenged or stretched in the beginning of a relationship, however, they lose patience for this after the relationship has progressed. People with opposite types have the potential to appreciate, transform, and improve one another, or they can explode in frustration because of a lack of understanding and inability to relate. Knowing your personality type will give you a better understanding of your actions and reactions within any relationship. This awareness will better show you why your failed relationships didn't work, and how to choose partners more suited for you. It will also bring you further compassion and understanding for those you are currently in a relationship with, allowing for more harmony with them. Many of us have said at one time, "If I did that to you, you would be so angry." The opposite occurs when people of different types know the emotional requirements of their partner and are able to offer those, instead of competing with them.

With the current divorce rate so high, part of the reason people are not getting along is because they are picking people they can relate to rather than people they have a natural tendency to get along with. Love and sensitivity together can either be a threatening, or an incredibly intimate combination. What couples are sensitive to or fearful of, and what they recognize as love directly correlate to their type and knowing them will help bridge the gap to find harmony, especially during times of stress.

Six pillars to establish a healthy relationship:

1. Knowing yourself. This includes knowing how you express and accept love and appreciation. You will learn what you should expect from a partner and what you can offer. (Chapters 1-8)

2. Committing to personal development and growth. This includes giving up self-righteousness and ego for the sake of love. (Chapters 11, 14-17)

3. Understanding the importance of give and take. That is based on what you are naturally capable of giving and what you should get in return. (Chapters 7, 11)

4. Using communication skills to achieve cooperation and understanding. (Chapter 11)

5. Practicing compassion and acceptance, which allows for appreciation of and adaptation to your partner; this comes from understanding your partner's type. (Chapters 11, 16)

6. Recognizing your partner's expression and acceptance of love and what you can do to offer your love to them. (Chapters 11, 14-16)

What Can You Learn from this Book?

All great relationships are comprised of two distinct personality types that work perfectly together. The "Entitled," is the one who, in the majority of time, takes the initiative, the responsibility, and has the vision for the couple's actions. The "Support," in the majority, prefers to support the initiative or vision mapped out by their partner. You will see how the Entitled takes care of the Support, and the Support advocates the Entitled. They consistently do things for one another they may not have done in past relationships, because they fit together like a puzzle. Despite their differences, they have a take care of, and support ratio that meshes well together. While many people outside of this relationship may not get it, these outsiders are often the same people who can't get a relationship to work for themselves. Chinese philosophy of the Yin Yang states that two opposing yet complementary forces lie at the base of how all things work; this model shows how very true this is in relationships that have harmony and points to what is missing in those that don't.

It is important to note that, similar to being right or left handed, both qualities are present in all people, but you naturally lead with one over the other, which the profile (chapter eight) will help you to define. The key is to find a partner who can match with you, allowing for natural harmony together as a couple. There are many things that can get in the way of your true nature, this book shows you how to discover that part of yourself. Once you've done that you can offer it to a partner that has the ability to accept it while fulfilling theirs. After having an understanding for this model and which type you are, with love, it is easy to find this same harmony and contentment with a partner who may not be a natural match for you because you will both know where to shift to accommodate one another.

In the first four chapters, you will learn about the two main categories and their subcategories. Knowing which type you are will help you to know who will complement you in a relationship, and it will also show you why people sometimes feel threatened or fearful. Often people go wrong in relationships when they expect care but do not offer support, or they expect support but don't offer care. This book makes it clear what two people in a healthy relationship can offer, so they are both clear on what they should expect to receive. Among many differences, explained in related chapters, Entitleds are more concerned with accomplishments, while Supports are interested in the intimacy reached during the path. With cooperation, both can be happy. When partners don't understand this, both can be extremely frustrated and end up focusing only on their own needs.

Chapters five and six describe the potential of unhealthy interactions both categories are in danger of. Entitleds are frequently designed with a kind of rocket fuel to motivate them to accomplish their goals. This can set them on their path to pursue their dreams, but they need to be careful not to go on a path in the wrong direction. Entitleds often look ahead to what is next in their future—a quality of leadership—but it can also take them away from living "in the moment."

Unbalanced relationships can also become dangerously unhealthy when the Support becomes self-sacrificing and the Entitled becomes controlling. Supports could make the mistake of hooking up with "false protectors," or could become depressed because they have not found the right partner to follow through on their creative ideas. This chapter, (six) points out the many things Supports need to be careful of.

Chapter seven describes behavioral patterns and why people often think they fall into a category where they don't belong. It shows how to contribute your positive traits and how to avoid acting on your negative ones. There are lists showing the typical pathologies of each category and how they, along with your fears, take part in deciding what category you fall under. They also show what typical behavior you should look out for while under stress. For example, while under stress, typical Entitled behavior is aggressively outward. They blame others, avoid facing responsibility and can utilize "know it all" style fighting. They can be demanding, judgmental and intolerant. Supports go inward, blaming themselves or cross the line to behavior typical of an Entitled, where they won't find any contentment.

In chapter eight, a questionnaire will show you which of the two basic types you are, and what subcategory you also may fall into. If you haven't already, it is recommended to take this profile now before reading further.

Chapters nine and ten discuss what could cause someone to jump the line without realizing they are masquerading in the opposite category natural to them. Explained here is what Masquerading is, how a person in this category acts and why this would occur. This chapter also shows pathologies associated with this category, how to identify them and how a person in this category can get back to their more natural behavior and realize peace. If you have difficulty finding contentment in certain areas of your life, this could be you.

The majority of problems in relationships boil down to communication issues. Chapter eleven shows how to use good communication to save a troubled relationship and make good relationships more trusting and compassionate. Learn here what the different types want when they are anxious, fearful or upset and how they act out to get it.

When my brother was seven years old, he bought my mother a lizard for her birthday. He thought it was the greatest gift because that's exactly what *he* wanted, not realizing she would want something completely different. Often people do the same thing in their relationships. They offer love in the areas that *they* want it, not realizing their partner often wants something very different. Entitleds and Supports often have completely different needs that can easily be met once their partner understands their type. This chapter offers insight into the motives of each type as well as how to get what you want from a person by speaking language specific to their type.

The final part of chapter eleven can show you if harmony is possible in your relationship or if the challenges are too much to overcome. There are rules when in conflict, guidelines on if compatibility is possible, and if you are thinking of separating what to know, based on your situation.

With many communication exercises and guidelines, this chapter, as well as chapter 16, are all a person needs to discover why most problems in relationships occur. It is an essential guideline for people who love one another to keep their relationship new and attractive in the long term.

When two people of the *same* category get together, they have unique challenges to find harmony. Chapter 12, includes how and why two Entitleds can come and stay together, the pathologies involved, and what this relationship will look like. Chapter 13 talks about how two Supports would find themselves together, as well as the problems associated with such a relationship, especially with their decision-making process. These chapters discuss typical problems that occur with two of the same type together and how to overcome them.

Chapter 14 and 15 explain the goal, or the highest level of the categories, called "Reformed" Support or Entitled. These chapters explain how people in these categories think and act with others, especially in intimate relationships. Their unique personality traits are discussed as well as who they accept in their life and how their relationships look in business, friendship and intimate situations; including what they offer and what they receive. There is a list of things to do to evolve to Reform, and why a person would want to.

Chapter 16, *Finding Yourself – The Key to Reform,* describes the way in which people can achieve self-awareness, based on their psychology as to why they are the way they are, and what they can do to reform and become happier in their life and relationships. It has theories that will be ongoing and important to be aware of for successful relationships of any kind.

The chapter includes:

- Finding your pathology versus your nature.
- Finding partners whose nature coincides with yours.
- Identifying defense mechanisms and fears typical of each of the categories.
- Listing different types of fear and explaining their development in childhood, carried over to adulthood, and how they can be recognized and treated.

- How your upbringing and childhood relationships affect what category you fall into and your intimate relationships today.

- Explaining how negative pathologies often keep bad relationships together.

- Defining co-dependence – What it is and how to break out of it.

- Self-fulfilling prophecies and Emotional Prisons – What they are, how to know yours and how to change them.

- Identifying Shame and "Escapes" – What they are and how to find them.

- Discovering how your past affects your relationship and how to keep love alive in the long term.

Once you have a basic understanding of the types, chapter 16 will provide insight about why we experience many of the things in our life we are unhappy about. The lessons learned in this chapter will help to remove many self-imposed limitations people struggle with.

The final chapter (17) shows ways to find balance in your specific type providing ease in your life as well as an opening to create even more harmony with your complementary type. One of my favorite quotes about love is from Jalaluddin Rumi. He said, "Your task is not to seek for love, but merely to seek and find all the barriers within yourself that you have built against it." I hope the theory in this book removes as many barriers for you as it did for me.

CHAPTER 1

ENTITLED

"He's really good looking and romantic, but his best quality is the way he takes care of me. I get a feeling of constant protection from him." This is one of the first descriptions I got about Noah from his fiancée Rachael.

"So why are you here to see me?" I asked.

"Because it feels like he thinks there's something missing in his life, and I'm afraid he's not ready for marriage." She felt his discontent, and it was making her insecure. Rachael's insecurity also made her react with jealousy, a trait not typical of her type. She was unsure if the problems were a result of Noah's issue, or if she was being jealous and controlling. Her instincts were correct, but in reality, the problem had nothing to do with what they were both imagining. What was missing in Noah's life was communication, based on not understanding the differences in their personalities.

Noah seemed to possess all the qualities a woman would want in a man. When I met him, I was curious to know if he was as committed and interested in Rachael as she was in him. He responded enthusiastically, "Yes!" He told me he loved her and was all for a family and marriage with her. I knew either one of them wasn't being honest with me, or we had to go deeper to find the root of their problem.

Noah and Rachael fell into different categories of "Entitled" and "Support," and would benefit to interact with awareness of their differences. Each of the categories has roles in the relationship. But what does all this mean?

Simply put, if someone is "Entitled," he or she thinks of their own vision before thinking of another's. If someone is a "Support," he or she tends to think of other people's needs before their own. In complementary relationships, the Entitled initiates a direction because they have a stronger vision for the couple's actions. The Entitled provides vision, initiative, and follow through for the actions taken in the relationship while taking care of the Support. In return, he or she receives support from their partner for the agreed vision. Each person has a role in this dance of opposing yet complementary forces; and this in no way implies that either has authority over the other. When both partners are aware of their strengths, and consistently offer them, harmony is created. These strengths are often the qualities that attracted their partner in the first place.

The "Benevolent Entitled"

Within the category of Entitled there is a lot of potential for irresponsible leadership and control. Because of this, a subcategory of responsible, healthy Entitleds is called "Benevolent Entitled." A Benevolent Entitled carries all the responsibility an Entitled should such as initiative and accountability. This includes following through on their vision, as well as care and protection of their Supports without controlling them. A subcategory of unhealthy Entitleds, called "Selfish Entitled," is explained further in chapter three.

It is important not to judge any category as better or worse, or which you one would like to be in when trying to figure out your own. You might think of an Entitled person as someone with negative qualities, such as arrogance or self-righteousness.

Though it is possible that an Entitled person could have those qualities (especially a Selfish Entitled), this is not the title's intention. Also, keep in mind that both people in the relationship could be the same, such as two Entitleds together (discussed in chapter twelve).

Vision

Vision can be defined as specifically where a person plans to go in his or her life, career, relationship, etc. If an Entitled and a Support are together, the Entitled holds the vision and leads the path of that vision for the two. The vision can include everything, from the important to the mundane, such as if and when they will be married, where they will go, what they will do, etc. The vision includes the ideas, imagination, and creativity, but most importantly, the planning and execution for the fulfillment of their goals.

For example, in our previous case, Noah had a vision for his career, his relationship and his plan for what kind of a husband he would be. All three were in coordination with one another; however, in Noah's mind, the lack of success in one area was preventing executing the others. Noah had a business selling plants to nurseries. He earned about $50,000 per year, but wanted to expand his business to its full potential, earning over $500,000. His vision included ideas on how it would be done, what extra work would be required and how he would execute this plan; these steps are all necessary for follow through in an Entitled's vision.

Noah was prepared for the extra work, but he was lacking the capital funding to buy more products and hire employees. He had risk projections, detailing possible losses and the time frame. He was ready to take that risk, but this vision did not match the vision he had for his relationship. He was worried about the type of partner he would be during that risk period.

His insecurity stemmed from his vision of himself as a man with money to "take care of," and "protect," his future wife, Rachael. He was worried she would not think he was as much a man if he was working longer hours and not having the same cash flow she was accustomed to. This stemmed from his lack of understanding of her role as a Support. All he had to do was explain his insecurity to her, and she would have made any adjustments necessary to aid him in his vision. That is especially true since it included his vision for their relationship, which she was in agreement with.

Rachael came to me because she thought he was not ready to be married, and she was right, but it was not because of Rachael. Noah was not ready for marriage because he had not measured up to *his* vision of "the man he should be" because his business vision had not yet been fulfilled. Supports are good at feeling another's discontent. For this reason, communication is essential. Without it, a Support will draw their own conclusions, as Rachael was doing, which led to false insecurities.

Don't be misled; Supports also have ideas, creativity, and inspiration, but in order to be classified as Entitled, this vision will need to not only include a plan of action, but also the steps to actually execute that plan. For example, an entrepreneur sees the vision it takes to put an idea into action, and the practical steps needed to continue that action to its success or demise. The vision includes the follow through, as opposed to just the idea. An entrepreneur also possesses a love for the vision, or a strong emotion to have it seen through to its implementation. Noah loved the idea of having more customers, making more money and "building something." Without emotional connection, a "vision" is really just an agenda or idea.

Vision includes passion. For example, someone may have a vision for a relationship, but if they do not have love for the other person, it's just an agenda for them to complete. In business, the Entitled will be passionate about the love for business, money, power, or recognition or for the business itself. The idea is one thing, but the vision that puts that idea to action and continues it on the path is the trait typical of Entitleds. Supports know this; that is often why they will find an Entitled they trust to help them execute their ideas.

The idea of a "vision" does not need to be a grand, change-the-world idea; it could be simple and small as long as there is a strong intention and the confidence to reach fulfillment. It doesn't have to be a completely original concept either, it could be following a path others have walked. As an Entitled, I have a vision to write a book but I didn't invent the idea of writing relationship books. An Entitled's vision makes him or her inventive, ahead of their time, and a forward-thinker, but also those that take leadership and improve on existing concepts.

There are, of course, successful Supports with visionary ideas. Supports are often good with ideas and highly creative, but they often require a partnership with an Entitled to help see their ideas to fruition. With actions towards completing their goal in place, usually set by an Entitled, the Support can get behind fulfilling their idea.

When I consulted for Lorraine, she told me how her accountant husband was leading her to fulfill her dream of having a successful clothing store. It was her idea, but her Entitled husband William and his business experience guided her through the steps: from finding the location, hiring a staff, minimizing risk, to bookkeeping and more. What he provided was the initiative and know-how, but more importantly he gave her the confidence to help her fulfill her goal. Under his vision for the business, she was able to focus on the design of their clothing and attracting clients, to make the most sales within her expertise and interest. His vision and follow-through of her idea was also a way for him to provide care for her.

Protection/Care

The Entitled also provides the protection, or "shelter," if you will. A healthy, or Benevolent Entitled takes care of the Support. The Support feels comfortable under the Entitled's care. That is one of the reasons they enjoy being supportive. The protection given by the Entitled could be physical, financial, career-oriented, advice, or anything the Support perceives as care. An Entitled's care can be defined simply: a Support does not have to be concerned about certain things when they are with the Entitled. That is, they are under their protection, or higher level of experience. Lorraine felt that all would go well for her as long as she followed her husband's vision and business experience. This gave her a feeling of protection under his advice.

A basic example is an employer who offers his employees job security without financial risk. The salaried employee does not need to concern himself with good or bad revenues, debt, gaining or losing clients, insurance premiums, etc. He or she is under another person's care as long as they live up to their defined role supporting the company. The Entitled role could even be the *potential* for protection. Even if it is not obvious to anyone else, as long as the Support finds comfort somehow under the wing of the Entitled, he or she will support them. This care then becomes the responsibility of a Benevolent Entitled in a healthy relationship.

In our first example, Rachael would have gladly cut back on her lifestyle to help Noah in any way necessary to help fulfill his vision of expanding his company. Noah, not understanding Rachael's supportive nature, doubted himself and the relationship. This is the problem with not understanding this model.

The care and protection an Entitled provides can also become unhealthy if it is used to control. There is a big difference between taking care of someone and manipulating, controlling, hindering, restricting or dominating them. An example of these abusive situations would be like Noah manipulating Rachael with money or over the strong emotions he knew she had regarding her desire for marriage. It could also be an employer knowing a business is going to close soon, but not informing the employees in advance. This goes against the proper care of those supporting the company's vision. These are emotions healthy Entitleds are responsible with and not controlling. This is why some people have a negative view of service/support: they are afraid of being controlled. There are Entitleds who suck people dry versus giving them energy back for serving. More on that is discussed in the chapter three, called *Selfish Entitled*. Both "Benevolent" and "Reformed" Entitleds follow through on the responsibilities of this type.

Responsibility of an Entitled

As part of their responsibility, the Entitled must also look into whether or not his Supports are in *service* or *sacrifice*. Sacrifice occurs when someone overextends him- or herself to the point where the Support is diminished. The Entitled should be aware of whether or not they are generating real support, or if it is a masquerade of support because the person offering the support fears losing something. False support will eventually turn into resentment.

A Benevolent Entitled will determine if his partner is happy by questioning their contentment in the position of Support. Are they satisfied with the leadership or care he is providing? This will prevent problems from snowballing. True Entitleds, as leaders, extinguish crisis before they occur, but they also have a take-charge attitude in times of crisis. This is the quality any Support admires the most from Entitleds as part of the protection they receive.

When a person gives support that is above and beyond their comfort zone, that is a good indicator they are feeding a fear or pathology. A *pathology* is a negative behavior pattern that is developed from childhood. It is a person's go-to response, even when it isn't healthy or fulfilling. If the care received comes at a cost higher than the Support is comfortable paying, but continues to support the Entitled regardless, then the Support is there based on a fear or pathology. For example, if an employee stays in a job he seriously dislikes and feels underpaid, but he is there because he is fearful of losing his home, the insecurity or fear forces him to otherwise support a cause he normally wouldn't. This fear should be identified as real or if he is too insecure to find a job he would be more comfortable in.

The same situation is found in relationships. If someone continues supporting an abusive relationship, it could be because of a fear of being alone. Any number of unrealistic insecurities could explain why they would not leave and offer support to a different, non-abusive partner. If the Entitled continues to expect the support that is given under duress, they are subjecting the Support to sacrifice and abuse. This is an example of an Entitled not living up to their responsibility.

It is important not to take this out of context. For the first few chapters we are speaking in general terms, in order to define which partner fits the overall category of Entitled. However, as you have probably realized by now, everyone has qualities of both categories, depending on the situation and the person's expertise. Healthy people move in and out of both categories in different situations.

If we had a panel of professional athletes, politicians and musicians, each would take the authoritative and seemingly Entitled role when their respective expertise was being discussed. This is because, in their respective profession, each holds the clearest vision. This would leave the rest of the panel to support or self-righteously ignore the conversation, because while interacting with an expert in one field, it becomes difficult to masquerade an unreal vision.

A man who tends to be more normally Supportive may choose to be Entitled with his wife when it comes to something simple, such as driving, because he wants her to be safe and he will insist on taking on that role, despite her objection. Similar to being right handed, you have ability and often use your left hand as well but favor the right. It is the same with either Entitled or Support, not only do you have ability in both categories, you also switch in any given situation. The point is to figure out which you use naturally and most often. You might be Entitled at home and in your relationship, but at your job (such as a therapist), you need to take a more supportive role. The point is to identify which you are more than 50 percent of the time in any particular relationship.

The ratios of Entitled versus Support are different in every relationship. One couple might have a ratio with 90 percent Entitled and 10 percent Support, and another might be 60/40 percent Entitled/Support. Once you know all the characteristics, broken down in chapter seven, you can figure out which category you fall into, and whom you will find harmony with most naturally. If you realize that you are an Entitled, to be in healthy relationships, you must act with responsibility towards the Supports in your life.

By the same token, if you find yourself with other Entitleds, in any type relationship, whether business or intimate, you can learn to be aware of their intentions. You can recognize whether or not you are more suited for the responsibilities they are assuming, or vice versa. More on the ramifications of two Entitleds together are detailed in chapter twelve. The most complementary relationships know their roles, their strengths and weaknesses, without judgment. In a beautiful dance of two trained professionals, it is often hard to tell who is leading and who is following. It is the same in a very well coordinated relationship between a "Reformed" Entitled and Support (Chapter 14-15).

CHAPTER 2

SUPPORT

Rachael, whom we talked about earlier, demonstrated many qualities of a Support in her initial meeting with me. One of the things she originally told me was that she wanted to help her fiancé so he didn't worry so much. Now, if you think about that request, she was paying money to see a consultant on how to improve her life and one of her top priorities was how she can help someone else. When I asked her to tell me about her life, she mentioned where she grew up, then went into how she met Noah, and proceeded to tell me a fifteen-minute story about him until I stopped her.

Flustered, she asked, "Why would you stop me just as I'm getting to the end of the story?"

I told her, "Because I asked you about your life, and although your life includes your fiancé, it is not only about him." It never occurred to her she was doing this. I don't find anything wrong with this, but it needed to be pointed out to her. Being more interested in a partner's life is a perfect illustration of a Support.

As a Support, Rachael was not at all concerned with the temporary setbacks Noah thought would bother her, hence the root of their problems. Anticipating problems not typical of her type, Noah was afraid of losing her during the expansion of his business because of not being the "man" he wanted to be, in her eyes. What he didn't know is that those concerns would be more typical of an Entitled partner. Supports are, as the name suggests, more interested in getting behind the ideas, visions, desires, interests and needs of others, than they are of their own.

Supports typically have keen instincts to discover what others are interested in and how to help them achieve, even at the smallest level. This is why many Supports are great "ideas people." They do things for others because it makes them feel comfort and a purpose, not because they feel obligated to. There is a very distinct difference between a waiter or a flight attendant who loves to serve and one who is doing it just because they need the income.

In intimate relationships, a female Support sees the Entitled's vision, falls in love, and supports the man he is going to become; a male Support sees an Entitled woman's vision and loves a woman that has "fire," and will follow through on her plan despite any obstacles. They get behind the path they believe their Entitled partner can carve out feeling a certain care and protection supporting that vision.

Supports are typically more creative because they are not particularly limited by following through on their ideas. Often, they do not think they are going to execute their ideas, so their creative thoughts are not limited by their own ability or the hardship of completion. In contrast, Entitleds often just try to think of things that they can do and how they can accomplish it.

With complementing personalities, I knew Noah was a great match for Rachael, they just needed some refinement. Similar to many couples, a lot of their problems together stemmed from their communication with one another. For example, Noah had stayed in contact with two of his ex-girlfriends from over ten years ago. Although he thought of this as completely innocent and harmless, Rachael was unhappy whenever he heard from either of them. Not knowing how to ask for what she wanted, often she told him what to do from an Entitled standpoint. She needed to understand that she was more powerful from the standpoint of a Support, and he more receptive as an Entitled.

She would tell him, "If you keep talking to your ex-girlfriends, I will call some of my ex's," and, " Maybe you just don't want to get married!" She didn't actually mean that, and worse, she was inadvertently posing a challenge that as an Entitled, would instigate him further. The better way to express what she wanted would be to point out how much she liked his commitment to her and the relationship, and explain that she felt insecure when he spoke to women from his past. This would make his strong qualities of protection for her kick in, as well as triggering the man he wants to be recognized as, increasing the chances of getting what she wanted. This communication hit his target strengths he prided himself on, as an Entitled. More on communication styles specific for each type are discussed in chapter eleven, on *Getting Along Together.*

As mentioned, it is important to be careful of your own value judgment when assessing which type you are. A Support in judgment won't allow themselves to support or be taken care of by anyone. This usually happens after they have been in support of someone unappreciative for an extended period of time. They end the abusive relationship with the idea that they do not want to be with anyone similar to that again and think they can avoid that situation by handling everything themselves. This is a very difficult way to have any personal growth. Without reliance and trust in other people we can never create true friendships, beautiful family dynamics, and certainly not a loving intimate relationship.

Another judgment comes from those who think Entitleds are "smarter," or in a more advantageous position, and want to be in that role themselves. Neither type implies greater intelligence or advantage over the other. Supports who are in a state of judgment rob themselves of their soul's pleasure to support others based on a faulty attempt at self-protection or ego. In this position, a person will remain unfulfilled and never express himself fully or create a great relationship. To free yourself from this position, it will help to learn the traits of a responsible, non-abusive partner worth your support.

When Kim first came to see me she was 38 years old and seemingly Entitled. After a short time, I realized she was only acting as an Entitled because she had been hurt in so many relationships. She had a few boyfriends who were very controlling and because of this, she would not let men offer her any care or protection because she thought this would eventually turn into control; even though this was against her nature. Her confusion was the difference between care and control. She believed that all men are controlling, and her self-fulfilling prophecy drew them to her like a magnet. Because she was so closed off to men and their approaches, only arrogant, aggressive men got through to her. After submitting to their charms, she would break down and find herself with another controlling abuser. She even dated a few unsuccessful men because she thought they didn't have the means to control her, but as she learned, they were able to obtain control over her in areas besides money.

Kim had to look deeper into the source of who she was choosing to be with. Her solution began with taking time off from dating and learning how to differentiate between genuine care and a set-up that started with manipulation leading towards control. We worked on her getting a firm realization of what she offered to a relationship, and what to expect in return. Much of the reason she found herself in the abusive relationships was because she felt undeserving of something better. In her search for a companion, because she was not so good at deciphering what would lead to control, she consulted with people who had a more clear opinion than her. In addition to myself, this included some trusted friends and family. She found that one simple way to tell a man's intentions was if he didn't mind coming to counseling to talk about what she was dealing with, and how it would affect him. That was a good start; it gave her an indication that he was open to work on a relationship, not controlling her. This was an ongoing process of trust for her, as well as an exercise in choosing the right partner.

The "Constructive Support"

To separate healthy from unhealthy Supports, a subcategory called "Constructive Support" is associated with responsible Supports. Part of the responsibility of a Constructive Support is to support only those with consideration of themselves and others, while receiving something in return for their support, even as little as appreciation. A Support moves away from being Constructive when they go from service to sacrifice. The subcategory of unhealthy Supports called "Blind Support" is discussed in chapter four.

Despite their problems, Noah and Rachael are Benevolently Entitled (Noah) and Constructively Supportive (Rachael) towards one another. Kim however, acted as a Blind Support because she continued offering support to partners in relationships that were abusive and controlling.

Service versus Sacrifice

Supports by nature are more selfless, and they have to be careful not to put themselves in sacrifice mode. Sacrifice means giving something up, or having something taken from you, as opposed to serving and offering it willingly. Serving is sharing your power instead of having it taken away. When in service of someone, there is nothing being given up, you will actually feel more like "who you are." As a writer, I am in service of the people reading this book. Symbiotically, we both gain power in the exchange.

The people I studied for information for this book were in my service while I learn from them. In return, I taught them techniques to find harmony in their relationships. In a healthy relationship, for the support received, an Entitled gives power to his Support. In sacrifice, no power is given to the Support. Instead, something is being taken away. The Entitled acquires things from them that are expected, not appreciated. The Support here is more a victim than a partner. A Support in sacrifice is as much at fault as the abusing Entitled.

A Reformed Support never finds him- or herself in this position. When this behavior begins and the Support feels unappreciated, or taken for granted, then communication is in order. If the behavior continues, a Reformed Support will exit the relationship. A Support in sacrifice is often reliving habit-forming events, wounds that occurred to them as children. It could stem from any number of situations, including fear of abandonment or isolation, lack of confidence or fear of not finding another Entitled with a path they believe in. A Reformed Support lives in the moment, serving for enjoyment as they wait for the right Entitled to appreciate their ideas and support.

Greg frequently went into sacrifice with his Entitled wife Victoria because of a deep-rooted insecurity. He equated an intimate relationship with suffering. There was almost no limit to the amount of what she needed him to do. He did not speak up until he was resentful of her endless requests. His life had very little success, or even progress, because he was always trying to please her, thinking if he just would comply with her "one last request," then it would stop. Needless to say, the cycle never ended.

Putting his foot down and having her agree and respect his goals was the start to them reforming their relationship. With a Support that goes into sacrifice, there is no gatekeeper to tell them when too much energy is being taken. The only time the gate is closed is when enough resentment slams the gate shut with the force of a volcano, exploding in anger.

Reforming Sacrifice

"Selfish Entitleds" justify their own behavior and "Blind Supports" justify the behavior of others, especially those who are abusive. As Blind Supports continue to serve those abusing them they might say, "He/she has a great heart" or "If I had a problem I know he would be there for me." Blind Supports try to convince themselves that it is okay to be around an abuser. Let's assume most people have a good heart and will help you if you have a problem, but that is no reason to accept abuse or manipulation from them. Even sociopaths may have good hearts underneath all the pathologies. The bottom line is that Blind Supports settle for less, and Selfish Entitleds expect too much.

The important thing to remember is a time when your service of someone gave *you* energy. If you were to volunteer at a foundation to help less fortunate children, odds are that, even after an exhausting day, you would feel charged spending your time with them. When that same energy is not being received for helping a loved one, employer, friend or family member, a change is necessary, or your service should discontinue until it does.

Connection versus Attachment

Often Supports will accept abuse because they generally carry more fear of abandonment than Entitleds do. Supports are more prone to developing an attachment to people. It is important to be aware of the difference between connection and attachment. Attachment takes you away from yourself. An addiction of any kind is an attachment. It makes you feel not whole when the person you are attached to is not there; it is actually disconnected in many ways because there is obligation present. It is abusive to develop and put attachments on someone; this happens because of fear. When attached, a person expects specific results and is usually led into disappointment.

During a break-up, Supports often suffer greater than Entitleds. This is because they stay in support of the relationship and not themselves. They relive their fears and pathologies set up at a young age and associate those with the current break-up they are suffering from. This is a good time for them to get in touch with their Entitled side, and support themselves and not the one they are separating from. You can share just as much love, spirituality, intimacy, partnership, etc., and not be attached, but connected.

Connection is the healthy discourse between two people in a relationship, whether they are physically together or not. I have strong connections with people I have not spoken to in years. When we do speak, we communicate and express our love right where we left off.

Any bad intentions you hold for someone indicates attachment. This includes controlling them, resentment, anger and any abuse towards them including speaking badly about them. If you find yourself speaking negatively about someone, there is some attachment involved to a result you are unhappy with. This is not connection because you are not accepting of them and compassionate to their struggle but thinking solely of what you want. If they are actually abusive there is nothing to discuss, the relationship should be exited.

If you accept abuse, you are attached based on some fear or pathology. You have dependence on something that is alleviating your fear. An example of attachment is, "I can do whatever I want, and she won't leave because she's so jealous." What the speaker is talking about is an attachment by a pathology, and this is abuse. Connection is true love in your heart with a partner, not just a relationship based on what a person can get from another. Connection also often encompasses the person beyond the relationship and all *selfless* actions done without obligation.

Connection exists where both people are whole and contributing to the relationship but not obligated to one another. It starts with acceptance, appreciation of others, and not taking one another for granted. Of course, they can miss one another a lot, but attachment is associated with suspiciousness, yearning, jealousy and fear during times of separation. When two people attach, rather than connect, the separation is not as clean and will be painful like an addiction. Many of us have experienced the obsession that can be mistaken for love—this is most likely attachment. Drug addicts don't love crack, they are attached to it.

This exists even with material things. Connection means enjoying your possessions, such as driving a comfortable car. Attachment is having your reputation bonded to the need to have a luxury car because you think you are seen a certain way because of it.

Suggestions for Supports in Situations Not Typically Strong Points of Their Type:

At Work
If you feel uncomfortable in group situations or boardrooms, you can practice ways to include yourself and your opinion in meetings by speaking up beforehand. Let people know that you will give your thoughts afterwards. Let people know you work

better when you have a chance to write down and evaluate your ideas. Speak to all parties involved one on one if that is more comfortable than addressing the entire group.

In Relationships

If you are not very expressive with how happy you are with people, make it a practice to leave notes for your loved ones. (This positive communication is important for all types.)

Be clear when talking about the differences in your personalities. Explain to your Entitled partner that you are more sensitive than they are, and you are absorbing more of the negative energy projected in a disagreement. Explain to them that you will appreciate their consideration of this in the way they talk calmly to you and protect you even when they are upset. This is a way to send the message that you will not accept abuse, and is a request for respect.

Entitleds often feel comfortable in the heat of an argument because they feel like they are solving problems on the move and creating a new, better vision for the relationship, while Supports feel that problems are actually being created, not solved. Be clear that you will go on having absorbed the energy of the disagreement, and that at the end of the discussion you would like to point out how you love them, and have them point out how you are loved by them and how conflicts can and will be resolved.

Realize that time in private should be enjoyed whenever possible, and be careful with your fear of abandonment. This means not needing to have someone with you just for the sake of not dealing with your fear of being alone in the world or because your thoughts are not in the present. This could include skipping social events if you find you are there just to quiet the "chatter" in your mind. When socializing, know yourself and how you operate in a group. Be okay with only talking to a few people personally and not having to impress everyone, for that may not be your strength. Don't concern yourself too much with hurting people's feelings about not going to social events if you are going to feel awkward while there, or at least tell yourself it's okay to leave early. If you feel shy at parties or events, set up conversation starters, such as wearing an unusual ring or necklace, hat or outfit. Sitting alone is okay as long as you are comfortable with it. Don't be overwhelmed with how you think you look. A simple smile will attract the type of person that may feel as uncomfortable as you do. Choose your conversations and don't feel that you have to get people to like you; not everyone deserves your support.

CHAPTER 3

SELFISH ENTITLED

As stated earlier, there are different levels of being Entitled. "Selfish Entitleds" are people with extreme Entitlement in almost all cases, meaning they think of what is best for *them* 90 to 100 percent of the time. Selfish Entitleds or "SE's" almost always need to be supported in order to get what they want. Once they see their demands will be complied with, they will offer some form of care, enough to keep the Support going. The only time they offer support is when they want something, or to get "credit" to get support in return. They don't get along well with other Entitleds because they don't usually like any alterations in their visions, ideas or plans.

Mark was eager to meet with me and asked me to adjust my schedule to accommodate him. I thought, *great, he's Entitled.* So far it seemed like a good match for his wife Selma, who had already been consulting with me. It wasn't until he was late for his appointment with no call or apology that I realized he was Selfishly Entitled.

When he entered the room, he started barking out orders at both his wife and me, saying things such as, "I do not want to be here," and "I don't need therapy; I'm just here to help my wife." He went on to say how I needed to tell her to stop questioning him and appreciate everything he's done for her. Fortunately for both of them, I did not comply with his requests. His ideas fit into the category of a typical Selfish Entitled. He wanted to control and manipulate his wife through the threat of taking something away. He wasn't interested in real communication. She was interested in saving the marriage, but mostly she wanted to be happy again. He was stuck in a pattern where he would push away any and refuse any of her requests, and after fifteen years she was finally fed up and ready to erupt.

Selfish Entitleds need to be in charge, and they crave the center of attention. They usually choose jobs, business situations, social positions, and partners that allow them to act entitled. They frequently feel like a victim when they are not in an Entitled position. Models, actors, and people who have been spoiled by beauty or wealth find themselves in this unfortunate position. Their best assets have created a strong liability where they tend to overcompensate for their insecurities. SE's quite often alienate themselves from others because they need things done their way, and exactly how and when they want it. From this position, it is impossible to maintain relationships with healthy Supports, because supporters of SE's don't get much appreciation. Instead, their uncomplaining assistance is just expected of them.

In this book, I've slightly altered the standard definition of Entitled to include everyone who has a tendency to take the initiative and responsibility within his or her relationship. Thinking of yourself before others, a quality of an Entitled, is almost a necessary part of taking initiative and is from where the name is derived. The standard definition of *entitled* refers to someone who thinks they deserve something which most often they do not. This standard definition very much describes a Selfish Entitled (SE). SE is a form of selfishness masquerading as confidence. SE's feel they need to overcompensate with entitlement because they are insecure about the position people have placed them in, or undeserved attention they receive.

For example, a model knows she has always gotten power from her beauty. She is worried that if another, more beautiful than her comes along, she then loses her power. Knowing this, she has to hold on to her power by proving that she deserves it, when she has done nothing to get it, and knows it could be taken away in an instant.

A short man, who is insecure about his height, but thinks he deserves the respect that is automatically given to taller, more muscular men is acting entitled. He feels he's entitled to respect based on an appearance he doesn't have, so he self-righteously overcompensates for that. This type of entitlement requires being a victim in some way. In this case, if he is not getting respect, he feels somehow disrespected or overlooked.

Selfish Entitleds are insecure because they ask for something that they feel at a deeper level they don't deserve, and they feel that it can be taken away from them at any time. Also, once they get what they thought they wanted, they then feel that they should have more. They are always looking for what's next as part of their lack of appreciation. Sometimes it will appear that they are actually getting what they want. On the surface, they seem to have the results of what they are acting entitled to. This could include sex, money, power, or respect. But the truth is they are so worried about losing it, they don't actually have it. This is part of the cause of their lack of satisfaction. Part of becoming reformed is enjoying the moment and being content with what you have and where you are currently.

Motivations

Selfish Entitleds are not born this way. They are created by motivations of fear, insecurity, jealousy or control. These negative motivators can also force them to follow through and take risks to create their vision and see it through. That may have some positive results; however, a more positive motivation such as creativity would be healthier and more satisfying. Control can be exercised in various areas: sexual, power, money, leadership, attention, etc. This need for control is negative and usually destructive.

For SE's, once a goal is reached successfully, contentment is still not achieved. This causes the SE to desire more and more to try to reach some contentment. However, when the path a person takes is misguided from the start, more of the same will never work. Trainers of highly skilled athletes, such as golfers, might have a golfer adjust their stance to move their elbow three degrees in a certain direction. This seemingly small change will make all the difference because it addresses a specific problem in their game. Meanwhile, golfers at a driving range often will only continue to hit the ball harder, thinking they will achieve better results. However, because they are misguided from the beginning, hitting harder with improper form will only create more of what they don't want. This illustrates the life of a Selfish Entitled and how continuing on a negative path only brings more of the same. A total overhaul is needed to find happiness for an SE.

As people evolve or reform, they become more aware of their motivations, especially the negative ones. This includes anything—exercise, career path, friendship, or expressing themselves. If a person exercises at the gym, not for health or self-improvement, but out of fear that their loved ones will leave if they are not in the best shape, then they are being ruled by and enforcing that negative pathology. This negative self-image can lead to further health problems, such as eating disorders, anxiety, questioning people's motives in their lives, or being defensive. More evolved people find motivations outside of pathologies. They *avoid* having negative motivations such as implications (what it says about them), instigations (manipulation by others), or indictment (proving others wrong). They use creativity and inspiration as their motivators.

To start with, a person should choose a goal he or she has a love, or a passion, for. This passion will motivate them through difficult periods when accomplishing the goal is more challenging than anticipated. This can be said for sports, a career, a relationship, or anything a person wants to improve in their life. In the form of a relationship, it might involve becoming the husband/boyfriend or friend you want your loved one to have.

My requirements for Mark to stay in this marriage and improve the situation might seem basic to most, but they scared him to death. The first was that he needed to start showing appreciation and gratitude of his wife Selma and everything she did for him. This was difficult for him because he had spent years manipulating and controlling her into believing she did nothing. To appreciate her and actually let her know she was bringing something to his life would mean he would then owe her something. The resentment Selma built up was so weighty that she had reached her breaking point, and the small fixes Mark had made in an attempt to keep everything status quo were not going to work anymore. He needed to give her real acknowledgement for what she did for him and their children on a regular basis. She would no longer accept his manipulation that she was worthless in order to control her.

SE's have a hard time giving appreciation whether in relationships or the workplace. Often when a person tells a SE they do not feel appreciated, the SE will further try to diminish what the person offers. They do this in order to make them feel that they do not deserve any extra appreciation. It's an attempt to bring them down so that the SE doesn't have to give them anything more than they already are. This is especially evident when someone is asking for something such as a raise. What SE's don't understand is that Supports often only require more appreciation and not more money.

Mark kept saying, "Why should we change now? It has been this way for years." Selma and I painted a new vision for her life, with or without him, which she was now willing to support, even if that meant leaving him. The leverage that would force Mark into change was his money. He was a successful banker and was afraid if she left, she would get a good lawyer, and a divorce would cost him a fortune.

What he didn't realize was that if he worked at the marriage, his own happiness would greatly improve. Looking for ways to show appreciation and gratitude for others always makes both partners happier. Sure, it may have been contrived at first, but similar to how a muscle gets stronger with use, so our sense of appreciation grows when we consciously work at it. Selma found it ironic that the very thing he used to control her, for so many years, was now being used against him. I also explained to him how he was teaching his daughter to find a man just like him and teaching his son that this was how to treat a woman, and they both would probably wind up as unhappy as he was.

Control

Care is one of the important qualities offered by a Benevolent Entitled. Being in relationship with a Selfish Entitled, there is very little care. They are interested in caring for themselves and they expect their partners to do the same, so nobody is taking care of the person supporting. SEs offer control that is dressed up to look like care. So if they are giving money, it is just to maintain what they want. This creates a one-sided relationship.

Selfish Entitleds often have a distorted view of themselves. They have the hardest time identifying themselves as Selfish Entitleds because it takes emotional evolvement to realize they are wrong or have destructive behavior. They don't identify their selfish behavior as hurtful to anyone because they justify it away. Selfish Entitleds can actually justify their actions so much that they think of themselves as Supports! It is not natural for them to offer support, so when they do, they think of it as a greater contribution than it is, and they will even keep a list of all the times they've done so to prove their case, like a balance sheet of favors they've done. They mostly offer support as a means of controlling others, which may be happening at a subconscious level. They offer their resources, material goods or other desirables as a means of having someone in a position where they have to answer to them, or be under their control.

A good indication if someone fits into this category is if a person is offering support and others refuse to accept it, especially if they need it. They don't accept it because they recognize it as a means of control. If a wealthy SE assumes everyone worries about money and they use their money for control, it will be odd for them if a person evolving or reforming doesn't allow the obligation to be placed on them. The SE will feel they have no control over this person and will be very frustrated. They will either investigate where they could take the control, or instigate problems to remove the troublesome person from their lives, which is also a manipulation.

As part of the irresponsible behavior, a controlling Entitled may try to get the person they are controlling to think that they can't do anything without their guidance or vision. They try to make them feel helpless, useless, unintelligent, etc. This is an effort to keep them from being able to escape the Entitled's control, and it should be recognized as a form of abuse. A SE turns their natural talent of leadership into a weapon to manipulate others. In addition to using fear, guilt and shame against people, SE's often create situations that are perfect for them to maintain manipulation and control. They create relationships where their partners, family, friends and/or employees have:

- *Dependence* on them – This could be financial or some other form.

- *Isolation* – SE's cause others to spend time only with them, and deny access to other friends or outlets that could make it easy for the dependent to leave.

- *Obligation* or debt – SE's do things with the intention that the people in their life will owe them something. They often offer things with an implied contract that says, "If you accept this you are agreeing to…"

Nobody wants their independence to be taken away in a relationship. SE's take it away in pieces and present the loss as something that is good for their partner. They take freedom away under the grounds of offering protection. They do things that seem to be a gift but they are really taking away independence little by little and creating dependence on them. A SE man might inspire a woman to quit her job or source of income, quit school, and leave her family or friends—anything that will separate her from her independence.

The opposite—a Reformed Entitled—would be someone who looks to create independence for their partner. They will do what they can to help their partner pursue their dreams. This person knows that if their partner is independent and still with them, still loving them, then the love is true without any agenda of being with them because they are providing something for them.

Part of the reason Entitleds have a need for control is they feel that if they are not in control, life will return to a previous time when they were unhappy, such as a traumatic point in their childhood. This often happens on a subconscious level. In a private session between just Mark and myself, he revealed to me that he felt he didn't deserve Selma, and he feared that she would eventually leave him or cheat on him if he showed any vulnerability. This was in part the reason he found it important to control her. He didn't realize he was well on his way to creating a self-fulfilling prophecy. I practically begged him to share this with her. When he finally did, the two of them broke down. Much to his surprise, his communication made her realize this was the man she loved, giving her compassion to understand his point of view. She started to see him as a little boy with insecurities and feelings she never thought he had. Through this work and mapping out both of their fears and insecurities, they developed compassion for one another and turned their marriage around. Of course they will have to work on this for a long time; it took many years to create such a negative result, so it would take a lifetime of commitment to clean it up. When a need for control is replaced with vulnerability, relationships always improve.

Controlling a partner replaces the lack of control a person experienced as a child, alleviating some of their fear and resentment. The negative past experience does not necessarily have to be obvious abuse as a child. Everyone is sensitive to different things. It could have been simply a critical or judgmental parent.

When evolving a person realizes there are two options: either trust or control. One cannot exist if the other is present. A strong degree of closed-mindedness is also typical of Selfish Entitleds. They prefer to take the role of teacher rather than student and will try and break down any new ideas that come their way. They also equate what they know with the truth. If they learn and agree with a new idea, they will often consider it as their own and speak on it as if they were experts. A person who will not take their eye off their vision of how they think things need to be done closes off many new opportunities to come their way.

Closed-mindedness is also a form of control. A person who is closed-minded is comfortable in familiar surroundings, and uncomfortable anywhere unfamiliar because it can make them feel as if they are not in control. Being open allows the unknown to occur, which may be out of their range of control. Many of the Selfish Entitleds I've been around have some form of OCD as a means of control. For example, it could be as little as needing the papers on their desk to be at 90-degree angles, or having their house spotless. If little details are changed from the way they left it, the feeling of control is lost.

Self-righteousness

One of the qualities of someone in extremes (both Selfish Entitled and Blind Support) is that they are often very stuck in their point of view. This type of focus can help the SE to get what they want, but it also makes it difficult to get along with them. If there is one thing you can say about SE's, it is that they have a strong degree of self-righteousness. It is dangerous to be in a relationship with someone like this because they will go to great lengths to always be right. They are constantly fighting to keep up an image. SE's spend so much time and energy trying to create and maintain a perfect image of themselves that they prefer to damage or lose relationships rather than this perceived image. You will notice SE's lie or manipulate stories to make themselves sound better, thinking they are impressing people. The image they often try to create is that they offer care for everyone around them (which is not true). They feel that apologies or admitting that they are wrong can only get in the way of this image. Their real fear in admitting they are wrong is that they would lose control over those people doing things for them. Often if they do apologize, it is accompanied by so many justifications that it's not worth anything.

One reason SE's are so concerned with appearances is because of their insecurity. Deep down they believe the respect or support they have acquired is false, so if they don't keep up an appearance, they worry it could fall like a house of cards. One of the reasons they are self-righteous is because they are often fighting for something they know they don't deserve; so they have to continue to prove they deserve it. Part of the negative aspects of being a "great arguer" is that you evoke enabling. This occurs because the people around the skilled arguer prefer not to cause a disagreement in which they themselves will be proven wrong by the great arguer. This does not allow a person to become aware of his own pathologies. It takes a more evolved person to recognize the bigger problems behind arguments with partners and loved ones they trust. "Winning" arguments never makes for good relationships.

One of the problems with SE's is that they become very sensitive, because they internalize everything based only on their point of view. They are easily insulted or hurt. When people mostly think of themselves, they take everything personally. Because they do favors with obligation attached, SE's are often waiting for a specific result in return. When the other person doesn't live up to exactly what they want, they become offended and often reactive. Selfish Entitleds often end up in a fight because they are tormented over their perception of what has been done to them.

If you find yourself in this circumstance (Selfish Entitled or not) you need to ask yourself, *do I prefer to stay mad, angry, upset or should I let it go? Should I forgive, reevaluate my motives, forget, and interpret this another way, or dismiss this person from my life and move on?* Ask yourself, *why is it of value to me to stay angry over this?* The answer could be, in the mind of a SE, that if they don't stay angry, they will be further taken advantage of, or lose control over the other person, which is usually just another illusion. Those who choose to hold on to self-righteousness can never hold on to a good relationship. *The ability of both parties to give up their self-righteousness defines a relationship.* It is better to spend more time finding compassion for others, and seeing their point of view, than justifying your own position.

There is justifiable and unjustified Entitlement. An example of justified Entitlement would be the expert in the room demonstrating their expertise. The master of a dojo teaches the class, demands respect by his actions and speech because he has earned that right and everyone there agrees on this. In almost all cases, Selfish Entitleds are unjustified because their behavior includes an arrogance to overcompensate for what they feel they do not deserve. There is no martial arts master that feels he does not deserve the position of teacher. They know the work they have done and are justified to act on it. Generally, if you are the only one who believes you deserve to act entitled to something, then it is unjustified. If everyone else thinks you deserve it, it is justified entitlement. Selfish Entitleds are almost always unjustified in their entitlement because they act as if they are in their area of expertise when they are not.

Part of what made Mark fit the category of Selfish Entitled is that he thought he was justified in treating people any way he wanted. He was inconsiderate to his wife, children, and coworkers—even me. Their sessions together began to unwind the years of manipulation and cover-ups he had created to get his wife to believe she was nothing. In some of our communication exercises, Mark realized that he never listened to Selma. He waited until she finished speaking so he could tell her what to do, a trait typical of SE's. One of the things that turned Mark around into a man interested in genuinely working on his marriage was that he realized he had learned this behavior from his father, who was "also miserable," as he described, and didn't want to repeat his mistakes. As hard as it was to change the direction of his thoughts, his motivation was for his son not to suffer the same consequences. This is what I call evolution; that is, not passing on the same negativity you received from your parents to your children. He realized he had become the exact man his father was, a man he hated.

In our private sessions without Selma, Mark described his father as a man who never treated him or his mother well, but was always critical and judgmental of them. No matter what Mark accomplished in his life, his father would somehow diminish it, telling him he should have done better. Listening to his description of his father, it was immediately apparent to me that Mark was very similar to him, and to my shock he did not realize any similarities even after I pointed them out. Days later he came to me with a "revelation," that he was exactly his father, and feared his son was headed for the same fate. Mark actually thought that criticizing his son for everything he did encouraged him to succeed.

"I just want him to be better than everyone else his age." He was surprised when I told him everyone wants that for their children. He literally didn't think that other people wanted as much success for their sons as he wanted for his. He only got it when I explained to him that success was what his father wanted for him. He realized his son was on the quick track not only to treating women poorly, but to hating him too. He realized he needed a complete reevaluation of his family values and communication style. Further evidence of this would happen as he was starting to show his wife appreciation in front of his son. He was thanking his wife for a wonderful job she did taking care of the house, and his son was shocked.

Mark's son even asked, "What's wrong with you two?" The idea that appreciation of his wife appeared as "something wrong" showed Mark how important it would be to unwind the effects of the horrible pattern he had created.

Critical and Judgmental

Often the victim of critical parents, Selfish Entitleds follow the same path, doing exactly the same thing to themselves. *It is often the same weapons that were used against a person that they use against themselves and others.* Of course, most times this is occurring at a subconscious level. In Mark's case, because his father was critical and judgmental of him, he developed the same pattern. This goes for most abuse people project, including physical, verbal, mental, sexual and more.

It is difficult to be in a relationship with someone critical of themselves for many reasons, some obvious, some not. For one, they enter a vicious cycle that starts with being critical of themselves, causing them to assume other people are equally critical of them for the same reasons. This then causes anxiety and resentment against others that they have to overcompensate for and this makes them unnecessarily defensive.

If a person is self-critical about their body image—for example, someone who is overweight—they assume others also think of them as overweight. Anytime someone glances at their body, they assume that person is thinking they are fat, because that's what they think about themselves. Now, anyone who thinks everyone who looks at them is judging them and calling them fat is obviously going to be anxious about it, making them irritable and resentful of others.

Next, their partner might ask something innocent such as, "Why are you going to wear those pants tonight?" and the resentment volcano erupts, without either party realizing why they are in an argument. This is one of many reasons it is hard to even be friends with a person who is self-critical. For this reason, look to see where you are critical of yourself and realize how you are sensitive to others in this area. Then you will lower the risk of turning simple communications into potential fights.

Being self-critical adds to the discontentment of who a person is, and anything they have achieved, is not enough, because of a need to always be at the next step. This is one reason why SE's are rarely, if ever, concentrating on enjoying the moment. They are always comparing and competing with others at a level they consider just "above" where they are. People who compete with everyone need to put others down to make themselves feel better. They also compare themselves to a vision of where they want to be, causing them to feel inferior in their current position. Because of this, they rarely truly feel successful, condemning their current life. The lie they tell themselves is that once they get to their next goal, they won't feel that way anymore.

It is similar to a dog chasing its tail. Often the very mechanism that has generated their need and vision for success is exactly what fuels their unhappiness and discontent. This causes them to be irritable, short tempered, frustrated, angry, and anxious; certainly not someone leading a blissful life despite any perceived success. SE's have a hard time recognizing their own successes, accomplishments, talents, or skills, and they find it difficult being comfortable where and who they are. Recognition and appreciation of this will bring ease to their lives. They often have externally "successful" lives in their chosen profession. This also makes them feel it is okay to judge others. However, they are almost always unhappy at the core because they are more critical of themselves.

Having been criticized, SE's are under the misconception that a "smarter" person is critical of others. They judge everything based on how they would have done it "better." This causes them to have almost exclusively unhealthy relationships, because no relationship can be healthy where one person is constantly criticizing the other or themselves. It is perpetually negative and abusive. It also demotivates the people closest to the person from doing anything because they don't want to be criticized, just the same as self-criticism demotivates self. Criticism is like adding weight to a person's back. It may be okay for a while, but eventually it breaks them.

Of course self-criticism affects both Entitleds and Supports. In order to release the criticism, look at what "escapes" you have in place in order to allow you to accept it. For example, when someone criticizes you, what do you do? Instead of telling them to stop doing that, and actually putting a stop to it, do you go and have a drink, get angry and leave the house, smoke a cigarette, play video games, or choose something else that takes you out of the situation, or relieves your frustration?

Ask yourself: Why is this environment of accepting criticism okay for you? Is it something you are used to from your childhood? Usually when you accept an uncomfortable situation, it echoes a familiar feeling you recognize from the past. That is because you had no choice but to live in this environment, such as your parent's house. Do you expect this discomfort in any relationship you will be in? Why and how have you accepted it and allowed it to go as far as it has? If you are critical of yourself or others, you need to realize that you are unhappy. You have been using criticism for years, and unhappiness is where it has gotten you. Try approval: that is, approval of yourself and others. Every time you want to point out something negative, give yourself or the other person approval for something instead. Trying this for just thirty days will change a relationship.

As abusive as Selfish Entitleds are, they often attract many friends, or at least acquaintances. Often the people around the

SE's are nice people, because a SE won't be around another person that is abusive, or who needs to be the center of attention, unless they need something from them. SE's are also very adept at finding people who can't say no to them, people who are non-confrontational. If you find yourself identifying Selfish Entitleds in your life, and if they have no desire to reform, it is advisable to exit the relationship.

If you feel you are locked in and cannot exit, then learn from the experience. What is it you have in your pathology that you manifest that allows these people to come into your life? Do you have a victim mentality? An example of this is a woman who thinks she will only find a man who cheats. It is likely that as a result, this is all she will find. Keep in mind the ego wants to be right, so if you feel you deserve to be abused or in toxic relationships, even at a subconscious level, then your ego will manifest that.

When you are in an abusive relationship, there is something you are trying to re-create from your past. Some pathology is present. When you discover what that is, in many cases you can release the toxic relationship with little or no pain or regret typical of a break-up. You will have the realization of how bad this was for you and want to run from it. Holding on to the pathology or fueling it won't get you what you want anyway. Time and history will prove that to you. Be aware of your tendency to search for a toxic pattern when starting future relationships. SE's have a very difficult time with Reforming Supports (and of course vice versa). This is because SE's often look to find what a Support worries about and alleviate that as a form of manipulation (disguised as care). Reforms are working on their fears and will not let the fear be used against them.

Here are some triggers to tell you when you are with a Selfishly Entitled person:

- People who cause you to ask yourself, "Am I crazy?" when they make illogical moves.

- People who make other people feel bad with small digs.

- People who consistently make you feel bad about yourself.

- People who tell constant small lies so you don't know where you stand on an issue with them.

- People who always pity themselves and their childhood or situations, but never extend that compassion to anyone else in a genuine way. They might even turn every situation around into how they have suffered more than someone else. Keep in mind that self-pity can often masquerade as being sweet or compassionate to a Blind Support.

- People you feel insecure about introducing to others, because they are unpredictably negative, and you don't know what they may do or say. If they can't control themselves for an introduction, this is a problem.

- People who are constantly interrupting you to the point that you feel that very little or nothing you say is being heard.

- People who are always nice when they need something, but may be hard to find when it's the other way around.

- People whose other qualities include an inflated sense of self-importance, need for admiration, extreme self-involvement/self-interest and lack of empathy for others.

- People who complain about the things in their life to those that wish they had them. An example is a person who complains about having two homes to a person who wishes they had one. A wealthy person complaining about how traveling so much affects them, etc.

- People who speak about themselves in the third person.

- People who self-stimulate through creating conflict, drama or turmoil. These people usually have to stimulate their brains any way they can. They often create their own problems just to solve them, and try to worry others with this. Be careful of conflict-seekers, they look for ways to keep their brain stimulated with no consideration the well-being of others.

Once you recognize that someone is Selfishly Entitled, be aware of their potential for abusive behavior. Until they make a serious change, often with the help of a professional, negativity is about the only result of a relationship with them. A Selfish Entitled who claims to want to change is not enough. That could be a manipulation to get what they want. When in conflict, the Selfish Entitled has to admit they are wrong. This shows they want to change and an awareness of self-righteousness. Not admitting wrongdoing only fuels their pathology, making them worse. All the justification and dealing with the torment associated with their pathology and lying takes an incredible amount of energy, leaving not much left for any kind of happiness for yourself, or for a good relationship.

This model (Entitled and Support) can be used in many different ways. Understanding the nature of people allows you to not be sensitive to their actions. When I meet someone who is totally selfish, I immediately realize they are either having a really bad day, or are Selfishly Entitled; then I expect negative interactions from them. I don't try to change them. It would be like getting upset at a dog for wanting affection, or getting mad at a cobra for wanting to bite you. It is their nature. If you are not okay with that nature, don't put yourself in that situation. That is why people have dogs for pets and not cobras. When I discover someone is Selfishly Entitled, my plan almost always is to avoid them as much as possible.

Another reason it is difficult to have a good relationship with a SE is they often don't have good abilities to notice the clues in the body language of others, such as facial expressions, mannerisms and voice inflection. They are not good at listening, or paying attention to others' needs. Often SE's do not notice when someone they are with is bored, angry, uninterested, or in a hurry, unless it is painfully obvious.

If you are Selfishly Entitled, recognize your closed mindedness, discontent and self-righteousness. If you want to evolve, realize one of your complaints is that you are always in the company of people not as smart as you and instead appreciate them. Realize that much of the fun, or good experiences you've had, have been through spontaneity or being open for something new. Look for friends who can inspire you and let them lead as if you are a Support, without being frustrated with them and their decisions.

Normally, Selfish Entitleds are doing only what they want to do, and if you are with them, you have to go along; which, in this case, is not leading. It's forcing someone's hand. On a given day, a five year old may be temporarily leading what goes on in the relationship with his parents, but that is not real leadership. That is the other person giving in to avoid confrontation.

Real leadership requires organized thought, attention to feed-back and care for others. Real leadership is pro-active, and is not dominating. SE's are normally so busy getting/taking what they want to the point of gluttony that they often leave Supports unavailable to continue supporting them. They burn them out and leave them with no energy. That is the opposite of leadership.

Typical Qualities of Selfish Entitleds:

- Devalue others' feelings, opinions, accomplishments or ideas.

- Have a hard time letting go of anger or a fight even after they get their way.

- Humiliate people in public or do not have awareness of time and places for certain things.

- Blame others for problems, lack of success or anything negative in their life, and their lover for all the problems in their relationship.

- Are overly critical of others.

- Get annoyed easily.

- Are controlling, intimidating, threatening, dominating, and inconsiderate to others needs.

- Any extreme jealousy or possessiveness is Selfish Entitled.

- Are always ready for confrontation. (This could also be a quality of Supports Masquerading as Entitled.)

- Have to win every time or justify why they didn't.

- Belittle others and their accomplishments or happiness.

- Make you feel you are walking on eggshells.

- Possess Jekyll and Hyde personalities. (They have to be super nice some of the time to get away with extremely destructive behavior.)

- Accuse others of being selfish every time they don't jump to their every command.

- Lie and manipulate stories to make themselves always look like a hero, or prove they have done something remarkable or that they are a really good person.

- Pursue what they want despite the impact on others, even to the point of abuse.

CHAPTER 4

BLIND SUPPORT

A Blind Support is supportive in more than 90 percent of all instances. They often go against their best judgment supporting people or ideas because of a fear that if they do not, they will lose something. No one is born in Blind Support or even Selfish Entitled—they become that way due to pathologies. Their often subconscious pathologies are fueled by fear of abandonment, isolation, insecurity, feelings of worthlessness or undeserving, and an inability to get over failure in their lives. These fears are set up at an early age and carried forward to adulthood. Often Blind Supports find themselves in a position of supporting anyone Entitled that comes their way, regardless of whether or not they have any clear vision. Their neediness often puts them in a position to be taken advantage of. This pattern is difficult to break, and it often takes many painful circumstances to create an awareness of how they find themselves repeatedly in that position.

They have a hard time saying no to anyone. When questioned, they will tell you of the few circumstances in which they said no. They use these rare occasions to prove that saying no is easy for them. They find themselves in many abusive relationships, and because of their self-fulfilling prophecies, they can't find a means of escape. They might think they cannot get out of an abusive marriage because of children or finances. They justify their actions by saying, "all men cheat," or "all women are bitches," so, "why leave one bad relationship to find another one?" "He/she is better than the last guy/girl I was with."

In Selma's case, discussed earlier with Mark, in some way this was true. When she started with me, she was so unhappy in her marriage and her life that she couldn't see a way out. We worked to repair her marriage because if she were to leave, the same situation would reoccur in any other relationship she would create. She had to learn to put her foot down, and it started with her most difficult case, her husband Mark. She also had to do the same with her parents, children and friends. I had to coach her on how to do this with grace, and not just explode at people. Her resentment was so high, she would wait until a full-fledged argument broke out. There are simple times to say no and she, similar to most Blind Supports, did not do so nearly as much as she should. Anytime she told him no, he railroaded her with so many objections that she either just complied with him, or exploded in anger. Not surprisingly, Mark first refused to come to meet with me to work on their issues. Desperately wanting a change Selma finally thought about her leverage rather than her need to please him; he was persuaded to come after she contacted a divorce attorney.

Even before he came in I knew Mark was Selfishly Entitled. Anyone who lays down for other people in the way that Selma, and most Blind Supports do, would only attract a Selfish Entitled. No Reformed Entitled would continue to be friends or intimate with someone who would allow themselves to be abused. Blind Supports actually draw out the worst in Entitleds. A Reformed Entitled would not remain friends with her while she accepted such abuse from her spouse, or they wouldn't allow it to continue.

Often friends of people in abusive relationships have asked me, "What does he have that keeps her from leaving?" The answer is found not in what the abuser is offering but more in what the abusee is lacking. That is, their own lack of self-confidence or low self-esteem. They don't think they can create a better situation for themselves.

Blind Supports always find a reason to justify accepting abuse. Because of commitments or bills, they can't stop working for an abusive employer. Because of guilt, they can't stop accepting abuse from their parents, siblings or friends. They relate the guilt to having a conscience and concern for others, and use it to make what they call "rational" decisions. Usually once they finally put their foot down, the Entitleds around them have an easy enough time manipulating them right back into the same situation. These abusive Entitleds (almost always Selfishly Entitled) use any number of weapons against them, such as guilt, aggression, abandonment, finances, blame, criticism, physical threats and more. All are manipulations fueled by ego and fear. The soul screams to be released from this, knowing a life of subjection is not its purpose, and that it can easily find a way out when properly executed. This is why Supports are often discontent and scattered. Supports crave leaders and someone to take charge, but they need to be sure they are being taken care of as well. They need to make a conscious effort to look for a person who offers both drive and care.

People are positively surprised with what they can accomplish when they get the Selfish Entitleds out of their lives. Everything turns out better for them. They come into their own leadership and realize they have been wasting so much time for so many years putting energy into someone who cannot be satisfied.

Relationships

Blind Supports are not great in relationships because when someone lends support to everyone around them, their primary relationship is diminished. They feel guilty if they don't assist their parents, friends, boss, coworkers and anyone else in their life that wants something from them. Because of the lack of balance, they become worn out and irritable and build resentment instead of expressing their frustrations. They are often in intimate relationships with a person that none of their friends like, which drains their energy while they try to please everyone until they are forced to choose between them.

Selma was close with her mother, who was also Selfishly Entitled and, not surprisingly, did not get along with Mark. Selma eventually had to minimize contact with her mother because she was asking too much, forcing Selma to choose between her and her husband. This is often the dilemma of a BS (Blind Support - pardon the obvious negative BS connotation). People become accustomed to pushing them around so much, they don't get any allowance to say no. Selma had a lot of friendships years ago, but now has trouble holding on to them because few people can get along with Mark. Her one lasting friendship was very limited because Selma refused to hear anything negative about Mark from her. BS's have a hard time accepting advice that speaks against the person they are supporting, such as a friend or parent telling them they should not allow their spouse to treat them in such a way.

Balance

All healthy relationships have an even exchange. Both parties should receive as well as offer something to the other. There are simple ways to identify relationships that are out of balance. The easiest symptom of dysfunction is when you are afraid to confront your partner regarding something you are unhappy about. Healthy partnerships welcome the expression of unhappiness felt by either side. If you are fearful to express yourself, then that is an indication your partner has little or no concern for you. This is also an indication that they are providing something that you are afraid of losing, and you are dismissing your own unhappiness to receive it, even if the trade-off is just companionship.

You can also find a lack of balance in relationships that you have in place solely because you think the person will alleviate some fear. For example, if you are in a relationship that provides financial protection, and you are unhappy, but you fear that if you leave you will lose some material comfort, such as your house, then this relationship will obviously have imbalances based on this person knowing they can take advantage of your fear. This could be a work relationship, intimate relationship, friendship or any relationship that is providing you something you fear losing. It could even be the fear of being alone, or just the desire to be liked by the other person.

Another imbalance occurs in a relationship in which the Blind Support thinks the other person is offering care, when in reality they are not. These are usually more obvious to those around the Support. This could be a case where an employer is offering a minimal amount of money to an employee with the promise of more but he never delivers, or relationships where the Entitled claims they will provide something the other wants but never actually does. It's like waving a carrot in front of a donkey.

The Supports in these abusive relationships often think, *if I ever needed anything they would be there for me.* These are the kind of relationships people find in their lives when they blindly support anyone. If you find yourself identifying with any of these examples, or constantly having to convince yourself that a person loves you, make a list of exactly what value the people in your life bring to you. Not perceived value, but what they actually contribute. This may reveal a lot.

It is in our nature as humans to receive and Blind Supports deny this instinct too often. They never find contentment because the people they serve always want more from them causing them to feel on edge. Because BS's are insecure, they do not mount a sufficient defense when their well-being is threatened or are not cared for. They often accept requests they will later build resentment for, rather than face the conflict of saying no. They seldom set boundaries on helping others, so it becomes a never-ending cycle without appreciation, draining their energy.

Blind Supports have an incredible pessimistic side to them. They fantasize about being swept off their feet or people magically realizing their incredible qualities and giving them unconditional love and acceptance, however, in reality, they expect and prepare for the worst. Their psyche tells them they will get scarcity, rudeness, emotional abandonment, or unfair treatment and this is what they accept. The difference between their fantasy and reality causes further resentment and erupting anger. Seeing your lover clearly for who they are, what to expect, what to give, and requesting what you would like to change is a good way to break away from this model.

Blind Supports invest too much into another person's life, especially at first. They idolize people and imagine their life with them to be a dream. They often indulge in a fantasy about the person they are intimate with because they desire the predictability and security they didn't feel as a child. They accept poor treatment because they are afraid to lose the security they think they have in the relationship. They even fantasize about love at first sight and will project that on someone who doesn't deserve or reciprocate it, causing an obsession.

Blind Supports tend to take breakups hard because they are supporting the relationship, or the fantasy of their "perfect" mate, and not themselves. Polar extremes (BS's and SE's) are prone to cheating and being cheated on, as well as other dishonesty. They cheat because they often put a new potential lover in this position of greatness, and they lie because they do not want to lose their current partner. And because they expect so much, their resentment is often double what it would normally be.

This is especially true at the end of a relationship. BS's often have intense anger and resentment because their partner did not live up to the expectations they put on them. The anger is aimed toward their partner as well as themselves for continuing to accept mistreatment. They trusted in the wrong person, who actually showed them signs that they were the wrong person since the beginning, yet the Blind Support thought that they would inspire them to change. It's like a person playing with a hungry lion and not expecting to get bitten, then having anger when they are. It is a matter of knowing what to expect from people based on what they have shown you.

When a Blind Support feels the possibility of rejection, or oncoming abuse, they will often work to obtain the attention they crave, or win the person back. When the other person grants them the attention they wanted, or gives some love, the BS will feel as if they are incredibly lucky to have this wonderful person in their lives, regardless of the abuse of the past.

For example, when I was a child, I used to ride on a teeter-totter with my sister. She was older than me and I idolized her. She would often wait until she was on the bottom and I was on the top and then jump off quickly, so I would come crashing down on the other side, which she found quite humorous. Begging her to stop, and wanting so much to gain her acceptance, I would go on the teeter-totter with her over and over again. On the rare occasion she let me off without hurting me, I would thank her a million times, telling her what a wonderful person she was, just because she didn't hurt me. This is how many people act in their adult life. When they are expecting to be hurt, confronted, or abused, and they are not, they create a false idea that their partner is wonderful for them, when in fact the opposite is often the truth.

Blind Supports often think putting up with abuse or negativity is a sign of love for their partner, and that they are providing insurance for them not to leave because the Entitled will then feel indebted to them. This does not work with Entitleds because they don't accept obligations like Supports do.

As stated earlier, Selma was the victim of a Selfishly Entitled abusive mother. She put many pressures on Selma as far as what kind of woman, mother, and wife she should be. No matter what Selma did, it was never enough for her mother. Her mother imposed herself in every aspect of Selma's life. Selma's Blind Supportiveness was created in part by her mother. Her mother raised her to live in fear of a man leaving her, or not being good enough for him in some way because she would be a failure as a woman, or a mother. Although her mother may have had good intentions, she had an insatiable need to control her daughter in every way possible. Selma allowed this even into her adulthood, which further fueled her mother's behavior. People will only push as far as they are permitted to, or the relationship will come to a halt. We did important work trying to discover why Selma would allow this. We needed to uncover the fear that was causing her to accept the negative behaviors. Once the fear is brought to light, it is, in effect, like turning the light on in a dark room. Even if the rate of illumination is slow, awareness will change a person who is seeking happiness.

Women Finding Themselves in Sacrifice or Blind Support

Women can be drawn into Blind Support because of parental or social pressures. This is happening less frequently now than in years past, as women are working, supporting themselves, and gaining more social and cultural independence. However, advertising in our current culture is often designed to keep women within a certain body type, wearing certain clothes and makeup to promote their sexuality, and having certain skills, like cooking for attracting "Prince Charming." Women without this perfect body type, makeup, hair, clothing, or career might feel the pressure to be more supportive, or accept a certain amount of abuse in order to start, get, or maintain a relationship. Parents often still put pressure on their daughters to find a man, get married and have children before "it's too late." Having career responsibilities on top of that might cause women to put themselves more in a sacrifice mode, or masquerade as Supports at first, in order to ignite a relationship. This can create a perfect storm for acceptance of abuse.

Relationships can find themselves in unsaid or unconscious agreements. These may include agreements such as, "I'll please you if you don't leave or cheat on me," or, "I'll accept your abuse if you love and accept me," or, "I'll worship you if you just tell me you love me." Women in these situations need to let go of their fears by getting in touch with their security, independence and self-confidence and learn about codependence, outlined in chapter 16, *Finding Yourself.*

Men

A similar circumstance can happen to men for cultural reasons, and others, such as guilt. There are, for example, men raised by single mothers who accept the guilt for their fathers leaving. If the mother is constantly speaking negatively about men or is domineering, she could cause guilt in her son just for being a man. The son could then get in a relationship with an abusive, domineering woman, sacrificing his own needs because of the guilt associated with being a man. The next step in the vicious cycle is that he should just accept it, or leave and be like his father, whom he often hates whether he has met him or not. Like the typical Blind Supports, they will often be overly compassionate or accepting. They may tell themselves they had the abuse coming to them (justifying), or that they are just misunderstanding their partner.

These boys of single mothers are also forced to learn about masculinity from their mother, while finding independence from the mother; whose job is typically to provide nurturing more than independence. Single mothers who have had bad experiences with men—and often single mothers have—will project that on their sons consciously and subconsciously in many ways. The sons are often even taught to accept abuse because "that's what a real man does, instead of leaving." It is often difficult for these children not to carry guilt, and go into sacrifice with women as an adult. The daughters of single mothers, from men who left or were abusive, are prone to either being abusive themselves or find men that are abusive. They accept the abuse because they are afraid the man would leave them, like their mother's situation. The unchecked imbalance within the person's childhood promotes for the same situation in their adult life.

When Selma had realized why she was in the situation she was in, we had the challenge of unwinding the results of her fears that had been in place for many years. She had to make it very clear to Mark that she would no longer accept abuse that she had accepted for almost twenty years. As you would imagine, he was very resistant. The first thing she needed to get comfortable with was telling him "no." She also needed to "stick to her guns," so to speak, and have confidence that after she communicated what she wanted and what she was no longer going to accept, she would follow through and expect it to happen. If not, she would have to exit the relationship, further facing her fears head on.

Reforming

As a Blind Support, the first step to reform is identifying abuse and putting a stop to it, and if this cannot be accomplished, exiting the relationship is recommended. This will be difficult because the people in a BS's life have become accustomed to getting what they want and they know just how to manipulate them. This includes best friends, siblings, parents or spouses. The BS needs to be ready to potentially lose them, at least for a short period of time. The consequence in not doing this is continued unhappiness, guilt and abuse. One of the first manipulations a Selfish Entitled will do is put an end to their relationship to see how the BS handles that. Under the circumstances, that is the best thing for the BS. The Selfish Entitleds, however, are so needy they will return as soon as they want something.

Blind Supports are dealing with two core confusions. One is the difference between service and sacrifice, and the other is care and control. When true service or support is offered to someone, both parties become empowered to fulfill their roles and both receive positive energy. When a person is in sacrifice, their energy is drained, causing a loss from the experience. Sacrifice occurs when someone has gone too far to serve another. Those who are served should reciprocate by giving care in the form of protection, such as financial, physical, or emotional care or something that makes the Support feel *happy* to serve. This care can take a negative turn to control, which is an abuse the Blind

Support either doesn't notice or accepts, not recognizing it as abuse. Blind Supports often have a lack of trust in themselves, and they don't feel they deserve any better. Blind Supports have accepted control their entire lives and actually seek people looking to control them and will apologize, accept abuse, or move into sacrifice to avoid confrontation. This is not genuine support but an effort to alleviate a perceived threat.

Avoiding conflict sets up more turmoil rather than less as resentment builds up. In our example, Mark complained about everything, and Selma chose to accept it instead of making a conflict. She didn't realize that it was only getting worse as the years went on. We teach other people how to treat us by what we accept, and what we don't accept. Conflict-phobics teach that it is okay to walk all over them and that there are no consequences for misbehavior. Other examples of this are parents who give in to temper tantrums, or a person who acquiesces to a bully to avoid being hurt. Avoiding minor conflicts eventually creates major ones.

To escape anxiety, often BS's become engrossed in other people's lives. This often causes more anxiety and resentment because ultimately they have no control or say in another's life. When they are in an intimate relationship, it becomes like a drug. They are so unhappy with their own life that they use the other person for their own happiness. On an emotional scale, they often operate at either a one or ten, meaning they either explode in anger, depression, or are non-communicative. Not speaking your mind when your emotions are at a six will cause this.

When they do finally speak up, they often masquerade as an Entitled until they have some acknowledgement of what they are asking for. They do this because they think they need to over-compensate to get what they want. They also often masquerade as an Entitled after an intimate break-up as a form of protection in order to prevent someone new from treating them abusively again. This is unnecessary and takes away from their nature and happiness. The real solution lies in learning to deal with the fear of confrontation. Speaking up in smaller matters, and allowing for their own emotional expression, will help them to acquire the much-needed balance in their lives.

A Blind Support building resentment is unhealthy for many reasons. First, the resentment itself eats away their energy and happiness, but it is eventually accompanied by self-criticism and passive aggressive behavior. The passive aggressive behavior is often designed as instigation to get the other person to ask, "What's wrong?" This can all be avoided by simple communication. Because BS's are not good at communicating, they often expect their partners to read their mind. When they don't, more resentment is added. It's challenging to reform from this because when Blind Supports start expressing themselves, they often have a lot of resentment built up and they have never had to express their feelings before. They need to get in touch with their own needs specifically and express them. For them, this has never been done from a place of calm with much success. Normally for a BS, it is done in explosive anger, so practice and developing a feeling for what they want and what they deserve is necessary.

Neediness

In order to reform, Blind Supports need to learn that neediness is a repellent, especially to those who are reformed. The only people who recognize and attract neediness are other needy people. If you find yourself with a needy person, reflect by looking into your own fear of abandonment. The way out of neediness is through finding yourself. The only way to do that is to be alone. It can start with small doses, but requires practice.

Losing the insecurity means knowing what assets/qualities you possess and what you bring to the lives of others.

Neediness and a person putting themselves in sacrifice is an escape and will never bring any contentment. From this position, the Blind Support needs to be aware that neediness is a form of giving up their own freedom to the needs and moods of others. This goes against their own well-being, and it is impossible to find the strength necessary to discover and pursue their path when always seeking something outside of themselves. Nothing but temporary happiness will be found from this place. Anyone in this position should strive to seek more independence.

Their neediness also causes codependency and identifying themselves based on what others think of them. Issues of low self-esteem or low self-worth *cannot* be cured by someone else's opinion, no matter how strong. This is what Blind Supports attempt to do, but this only make the problem worse. Too much importance is placed on the opinion of their partner. In this case, the other person is usually far from reformed enough to have that responsibility. Getting temporary satisfaction from low self-esteem by relying on the opinion of others is like using drugs to cure problems. Recognizing this dysfunction is the first step in the process. More on codependence is discussed in chapter 16, on *Finding Yourself.*

Enabling

Often codependence is a product of enabling. Enabling is the action or non-action that allows someone to continue in destructive behavior. Enabling comes in many forms and should be recognized as abuse against the person being enabled as well as against the Support (enabler), and to the people around them. There are, of course the obvious, enablers—partners of alcoholics, gamblers, physical and mental abusers, or chronically unemployed people without motivations. Enabling also occurs in much subtler ways.

When someone is continuing a behavior that does not behoove him or her or the relationship, and the other person is aware of this and doesn't express their dissatisfaction, they are enabling this to continue. It is as subtle as not saying no to inappropriate behavior. There would be no abusive Entitleds without an enabling Support. When Supports are unhappy with certain behavior and do not communicate that, this is enabling. The enabler's intentions are often out of love, motivated by fear of confrontation. They might be trying to help, protect or give someone what they want. However, enabling is often what allows a small problem to grow into an addiction or makes an addiction worse. By not expressing disagreement early on, or forcing it to stop, the person being enabled doesn't have to face consequences for their actions. For Blind Supports, denying their own needs might seem easier at first, but in dealing with Selfish Entitleds, a BS will soon realize they are giving them license to do what they want to further take advantage of them. They soon find themselves in the very difficult position of putting a stop to an established routine.

In an obvious example, by giving a gambler money for their debt they can continue to gamble, not needing to face the losses. Less obvious examples can be as simple as not telling a child to brush his teeth for fear of a confrontation. In not stating when someone is being abusive to another, this is enabling and also has the potential to eventually turn against them. There are many BS's that wouldn't put up with obvious abuses like drugs or physical abuse, but they will put up with emotional abuse without confronting it. The different limits lay in various levels of what is acceptable, but they all enable something that someone more evolved wouldn't stand for. Reformed Supports do not enable any behavior detrimental to the people around them, even at the cost of the relationship. They use their support to enable positive behavior.

For over ten years Selma listened and accepted Mark complaining about everything she did. "Dinner was awful." "Why did you take the kids there?" "Why would you wear that dress?" "This house is a pigsty." He learned that she would accept his negative energy and attempt to accommodate his endless desire to find fault with everything. This is a classic example of enabling someone in his or her misery. It was an accepted habit of his that he had learned from his father. It took a lot of work on both their parts to overcome it.

Enablers adapt to, ignore and even fuel unbecoming behavior. Once someone recognizes themselves as a Support, he or she should look to see if there are any circumstances in which they enable others to behave in ways unbecoming to themselves or others. Enabling usually starts with the inability to say no. Blind Supports operate from a fear of disagreement often with people they respect and love. There comes a point when the BS identifies the confrontation as worse than giving the person what they want. Then, at a later point in time, drastic confrontational action is needed stop the negative behavior, and this effort is not within the Blind Support's abilities, which is why the Selfish Entitled has purposefully chosen them to begin with. This includes even more extreme cases where the female BS is being beaten and won't have the male SE arrested for it. This is the worst of both core confusions mentioned earlier, care versus control, and service versus sacrifice.

As a Support, if you look at all the abusive relationships you've encountered, you'll notice most can be traced back to a smaller circumstance where a simple "no" would have diverted a negative snowball from building, or have ended an abusive relationship. Moving forward, instead of continuing to encounter these relationships, a respectful "no" can remedy being caught up in the same circumstance. It is important to realize that not saying no is making a choice to be unhappy or even miserable for the sake of pleasing others, leading to more abuse. Yes, this may cause disagreements, and even could end certain relationships, but it prevents larger disagreements in the future and abusive relationships. There is also no better way to stop a loved one from going down a path of continued negative behavior or addiction. Setting limits is a good place to start, but you must be firm and not allow yourself to go back on them. If you cannot do this, recognize yourself as an enabler and seek outside help and guidance. The Entitleds being enabled are codependent and cannot function in their behavior without enablers. As stated, every Selfish Entitled finds enablers to support their pathologies even in the subtlest ways. When their behavior becomes so destructive that they can no longer find enablers, they are forced to make changes towards reform.

Once you realize you are enabling someone in any way, look to see the benefits you are receiving for the enabling. It could be that you don't feel that you have the ability to accomplish your desired goals, so you take on someone to enable, using them as a scapegoat in order to distract yourself from trying. I worked with a struggling actor. Over time, we came to discover he had a strong belief that he could not make it as an actor. His benefit of enabling his wife was complex. She, Selfishly Entitled, was very busy as a partner in a start-up finance company, and she needed his help in many areas with regard to her business and personal affairs. Enabling her forced him to miss auditions, arrive late to meetings and left him little time to hone his craft. Her constant need for him to be in never ending service to her, and the desire to be a good husband was the perfect scapegoat for him *not* to succeed as an actor. All abusers need someone to abuse, but there is often a reason why the reverse is also true.

The interesting thing about Blind Supports is that, generally, similar to Selfish Entitleds, they are not good listeners. They spend a lot of time defending/justifying themselves and their actions. Bearing in mind that they will support almost anyone who speaks to them with any type of authority, they have to spend a lot of time interpreting the things that people say to them differently than what is actually being asked of them. This happens because their sensitivity has them in a constant state of worry. This is also part of being on a one or ten in the emotional scale as opposed to having balance. Blind Supports should attempt to seek balance in their life. I always recommend meditation as a means to calm the constant anxiety they feel.

Typical Qualities of Blind Supports:

- Apologize for their feelings.

- Let go of their dreams, ideas or goals for another person's needs.

- Walk on eggshells, hoping not to make anyone mad, especially the Entitleds they support, or just live in fear not to upset them.

- Accept blame for everything, but secretly build resentment and are afraid to express that until they are about to explode.

- Become out of touch with their anger, aggression and power. That is why they blow up when expressing it at all.

- Allow others to control them.

- Give up their own interests and friends because of the lack of compatibility with the Selfish Entitled they are supporting.

- Experience constant anxiety, low self-esteem, and bouts with depression.

- Apologize frequently, even for things that are not their fault.

- Feel insecure to ask for what they want.

- Feel sorry for themselves instead of taking action to change their situation.

- Don't receive much acknowledgement because they don't ask for it.

- Mirror the person they are with emotionally. (They are happy when their partner is happy, or sad when their partner is sad.)

- Have poor judgment of whom to trust, and support those not good for them.

- Justify the actions of others, including dangers they put them in.

- Tend to be *overly* accepting, compassionate or understanding.

- Lose energy wondering what people are thinking of them.

- Crave sympathy.

- Lie to seek approval. (This is a quality of a Selfish Entitled as well.)

- Are self-indulgent and often don't take care of themselves. (They often have many escapes, including junk food or sweets.)

- Are anxious often, trying to get everything right. Have a constant need for reassurance, and always second guessing themselves.

CHAPTER 5

PITFALLS TO ENTITLED

Entitleds by nature are frequently designed with a kind of rocket fuel to motivate them to accomplish their goals. This can set them on their path to pursue their dreams, but unfortunately, it can also set them on a path in the wrong direction. Having too much rocket fuel can weigh a person down or be the cause for a blow up.

Demotivators
— Not Having an Obtainable Vision
Entitleds are inventive and look ahead to what is next in their future by nature. This is a quality of leadership, but it can also take a person away from living "in the moment." Appreciating their current life situation and what they have now will help Entitleds to avoid depression caused by comparing their circumstances to where they would rather be.

Entitleds must also learn to focus on visions that are in the realm of possibility. They have to avoid reaching so far they can't find a path to their goal. Without possibility or optimism to spur them towards obtaining a goal, pathologies such as jealousy, depression and anger become stronger, leading to abuse of others. To avoid this, Entitleds must appreciate the successes they have already accomplished, while looking forward to the next plausible vision, or breaking larger objectives into more easily obtainable goals. I am not suggesting they should not dream big or out of the box. I am always a proponent of innovative ideas and inventions. I am suggesting that, once someone has a dream, they should break it into smaller, obtainable increments.

If you recognize yourself as an Entitled, but have no obtainable vision, or are not gaining any support, or have a tendency to abuse others in order to get it, then reassess your goals. Keep in mind, if an Entitled is not given the right to make any decisions, or is constantly told he is wrong, he will become resentful. Entitleds should avoid these situations. Once an Entitled feels fulfilled with his own vision, he can take better care of others around him. Often if someone doesn't think they can achieve success, they set their goals too high and sabotage themselves from the start. These are the responsibilities of reforming/responsible Entitleds.

—Procrastination

Many factors could cause a breakdown in the natural path of a person's vision. For example, children of abusive or critical parents often become procrastinators, or have a hard time finishing projects because that will open them up to criticism; something they experienced growing up and will subconsciously attempt to avoid. Procrastination, fears, and insecurity directly conflict with an Entitled's vision. This is why it is important to evaluate your motives. You may be carrying fears set up at a young age.

Self-awareness allows you to work through the fears from childhood that have been carried into adulthood. Focusing on these issues moves them from a subconscious level. Someone suffering from these negative feelings of self-worth finds it difficult to believe that others, whom they perceive to be not as smart as they are, could have more success and happiness. They don't realize they are sabotaging themselves and denying their full potential. Their competitive nature can then result in a loss of confidence, insecurity, irritability and critical judgments of others, which doesn't actually work to make them feel better. This often leads them to a need to prove themselves: their assumption being that other people think they are a failure. This is a very poor motivator.

It is also important not to blame others for your lack of follow through concerning your vision. This lack of responsibility is another trait Entitleds need to be aware of. Blaming others creates a constant, convenient scapegoat for the Entitled, and lets them avoid any leadership responsibility they have. Many of us have met people who are quick to tell everyone it is their spouse, or kids or boss's fault why they haven't succeeded to the level they would have otherwise. Convenient scapegoats such as these are often caused by a strong fear of failure.

—Too Much Concern with Cultural Status (or Other False Motivators)

Because Entitleds need the attention of others, they can become too concerned with what other people think of them. They may be stuck in unhappy or unhealthy career or relationship choices, and focused on the importance of material things such as a car, clothes or house they cannot afford. While these things are not bad in and of themselves, an Entitled's main motivation should not be other people's opinions of them. An Entitled trying to rebel could end up choosing a relationship or career that the people they perceive to hold power over them won't like. By trying to take another route to prove they aren't motivated by what other people think of them, or prove they won't be told what to do, they often end up sacrificing their contentment.

The natural path for a soul's motivation is found with inspiration and creativity. Any time someone tries to prove something, their irresponsible behavior motivation is based on ego. This can be a case of a Support masquerading as an Entitled or an Entitled with a false or insecure vision. I say false because the vision is based on the pathology, not what the person wants to accomplish in their life. Whenever someone is resolved with who they are, whether short/tall, skinny/fat, gay/straight, a minority or WASP etc, it no longer becomes an issue. It is only when they try to hide their nature that it becomes a problem. When someone thinks they have to prove something to the world, it is often accompanied by arrogance.

—Jealousy

Entitleds are competitive and often envision themselves ahead of others in their peer groups. Although Entitleds have the potential to motivate, they could easily have an unhealthy comparison of other successful people instead of using them for inspiration. Unless inspired by peer group successes, one Entitled comparing himself to another could react with jealousy, depression, anger or self-criticism, slowing himself down further. Strong Entitleds have strong vision, but they need to realize each vision has steps, and they must be mindful to "walk before they run." The idea is to follow the steps along the path of the plan, rather than just envisioning the end result not yet obtained.

Judgment of Being Entitled

Often I encounter people who are adamant that they are not Entitled. I never claim to be perfect in my assessment of people, but when I think someone is Entitled and he or she is dead set against the idea, it seems their judgment of what it means to be Entitled is getting in the way.

I always ask them, "If you are not Entitled, then exactly who are you supporting?" I also have them give me the exact circumstances of their support. They often tell me of how they offer support all the time, but nobody is smart enough to take it from them. This is because the people they are offering it to recognize the control or obligation attached to their support. Or they tell me of situations where they have paid for something or helped someone that was really a benefit to themselves in some way. Either way it is not actual support, but more like a barter or trade. This kind of support is often found in Selfish Entitleds. When a person is judgmental about a trait from either category, it is usually because they don't like something typical of that category that they see in themselves. This is an unhealthy reaction. This person won't do anything to avoid or refocus their negative or limiting qualities typical in that category and often won't know the positive qualities that should be enhanced.

Even though these people have a negative view of being Entitled, they still expect to be served. They also assume others in Support want something from them because they can't relate to someone who selflessly thinks of others. That is where their judgment of Entitled comes in. They don't think they deserve support for "no reason" or believe that Supports really want to serve. These people can be argumentative, sarcastic and moody. This can also create a vicious cycle of never getting what they want and never having any genuine support, which leads to bitterness.

A client of mine named Thomas worked in venture capital. He brought investors to companies who needed money. He had done well for a couple years, but he had not made any substantial money in ten years. Since then he had many problems with his wife Angela, who had a job in advertising. Angela wanted to leave her job and have children, but she did not feel comfortable with the risks he was taking with their money. Thomas believed he was the Support in the relationship and Angela was Entitled.

He thought this because, as he put it, "Angela criticizes everything I do and never supports anything." From what I could see, Angela was the more supportive in the relationship and was looking for him not to risk their resources so they could start a family. Anytime she asked him about what he did, he would get mad at her and start a fight. That is no way to generate support from someone. Because he kept insisting he was a Support, I asked him for some examples.

"I've been paying her bills for over ten years," he said. I explained to him that if that were true, in his case it was care and not support.

"I don't support her because she does not do anything for me to support," he told me. A statement such as that suggests a marriage near hopelessness. My first step to creating change was to get Thomas to admit he was not happy. When he admitted that, we worked out a new plan of action for them as a family based on his old way not working. The new plan started with a new approach to him making money because his last plan had not resulted in any income in over ten years. Angela agreed to support him in developing a company he had been preparing to present to investors. He began working at a smoothie chain in order to understand this business that he was interested in opening.

They worked on communication exercises where she didn't seem to criticize everything he did, but actually took a real interest in his work and offered help or advice, where it was warranted. This was already at the essence of her conversations with him in the past; she just needed to change her style of communication with him, and learn to differentiate between areas where she could make a difference and those where she should just listen and encourage. Thomas was difficult to break down, but what this model did for both of them was show the areas each of them were most effective in. It allowed them to concentrate on the positive qualities of the different types I believed they were. (These communication exercises and positive qualities are mapped out in Chapter 11, *Getting Along Together*.)

The point is, both possessed a strong vision—his in business and hers in family. Because he would not admit he was Entitled, getting along became very challenging for them. Their visions were not in opposition to one another, but poor communication and inability to execute them had created a situation where neither could be happy. Thomas thinking that he wasn't Entitled was bad enough, but insisting that he was supportive was delusional.

Our sessions allowed him to see Angela was trying to support him, but he would not let her. Running from the relationship would not have helped either. Without admitting he was Entitled, he would most likely find himself in a very similar relationship if they decided to split up. She knew there was a way for them to find happiness again together, and it meant him making a big change. His smoothie chain became successful with Thomas at the helm, and he opened more stores within one year and continues to expand. She had a baby boy eighteen months later, and they are both more happily pursuing their path together.

Abuse

A person with critical parents learns from a young age that being responsible for the things they do can have negative consequences and leave them open to criticism. A reaction to this could manifest itself in adulthood as someone who always blames others, not accepting responsibility for their own actions. This can be especially true regarding actions that result in others' pain or upset. Entitleds need to realize what actions constitute abuse. Any action, intention, expectation or any level of discomfort posed against someone can turn into abuse.

Entitleds don't have a problem seeing abusive behavior in others, but they don't turn the same lens on their own actions. Instead, Entitleds spend their time creating reasons why their abusive or irresponsible action was warranted. They tend to justify their behavior based on their intentions. If their intent was not to hurt anyone, then a person's apparent sensitivity is no fault of theirs. The process gives them a reason to continue the behavior that negatively impacts others. Entitleds should become aware that any justification they make is potentially meant to cover up abuse.

Most Entitleds see themselves as good people despite any actions they have taken negatively against others, so they can easily cover up abuse. Reformed Entitleds discontinue the abusive actions and use their creativity to find healthier ways to express their intentions in order to get what they want. Awareness of when you are justifying a bad behavior allows you to identify how you could have been more considerate. Ask yourself how you would feel if a person displayed that behavior with you. Justification excuses a negative action, preventing the process of learning and gaining knowledge from an experience. Recognizing where you are reckless, irresponsible and selfish as an Entitled is the key to becoming a Reformed Entitled.

The people whose first reaction leads to abuse were often abused themselves. This is usually one of the causes for their need for control. Holding on to pain and fear causes suffering in your life and the lives of people around you, especially those you love. This type of control is usually laced with a lack of trust, lack of forgiveness and dishonesty. Abusive Entitleds often confuse fear and respect. Not knowing how to inspire respect, they try to create fear. When they feel they lose respect, they resort to abuse. Their fear often causes them to strive for great success in their field. It drives them not only to want to control, but also to avoid being controlled.

An important part of releasing negative, abusive patterns is understanding the effects of the abuse on others. The other part is understanding where your pathology developed, how you were hurt and how to forgive. The most important part is then finding how you have benefited from going through that experience. What have you gained from it? How can you now use it to create instead of destroy? Some of the most successful therapists have in their past been molested, beaten, or addicted to drugs or alcohol, etc. The most evolved individuals use the worst experiences in their lives to help others who have suffered the same abuse. Part of evolution is not wanting other people, especially loved ones, to go through the same pain that you went through.

Pitfalls in Relationship

An Entitled could find themselves in an unhealthy place where they are not attracted to a Support because of their different nature, but at the same time, they won't allow another Entitled to take care of them for fear of being controlled. This Entitled says they wish their partner would take more leadership, but as soon as they do, they criticize them for it. When they meet someone who does take leadership, they cross paths with them constantly. It's logical to ask, if they don't get along with other Entitleds, why not go for a Support?

There are questions to ask yourself to see if this could be the root of many of your frustrations: Do you feel you have to take something that is out of control or unpredictable and control it?

Is having something that is sane, not dramatic, easy, or "normal" not enough for you? Think about why that may be. Is it that you were not taught as a child what relationships should look like? A healthy relationship should be cooperative and fluid, with an understanding of each other's needs while giving up selfishness.

An Entitled who can't get along with another Entitled intimately, and also lacks respect for a Support, is like someone who wants company in their car, but does not want anyone in the passenger seat and won't let anyone else drive either. A lack of understanding of who to choose to fit your personality causes frustration and anxiety towards relationships and makes people lose patience easily. These people are not fulfilled in what they have, and they are also not sure what they want. Once they get something, they don't appreciate it and immediately move on to the next thing they want. They move from one thing to the next, trying to find external satisfaction. One of the purposes of this book is identifying where you are, becoming responsible in that role, and finding complementary relationships.

When Dania came to me she was approaching forty and wanted to be married and have children. A single and successful Vice President of a technology company and an Entitled herself, she wasn't attracted to any of the Supports she met because she "didn't respect them for not standing up for themselves." She wanted a man to take charge, but when they did, she began to feel as if she was being controlled. She didn't want to give up her career, but she felt as if she was losing time to have a family.

I advised her to be completely honest about her feelings with the men she dated. The best way to build trust is through honesty. She had to tell the Supports she dated she wanted them to stand for something, and the Entitleds about her fear that she felt they would eventually try to control her. This gave them both an opportunity to put forth their intentions. This also created a space for the men to realize her fears and how she was confronting them. If they were not prepared to support her vision, they could back out early, and nobody's time was wasted. I believed a strong-willed, confident Constructive Support would be the most harmonious with her type and awareness of her own Entitlement would help her to realize this. Once you know the categories, you can operate from a place of higher awareness and identify the people you could have a long-term future with.

In order to reform as an Entitled, you need to first identify your fears. After that, you can identify how these fears have created your pathologies and to be aware of them as they come up. This will help to release them for a more positive path. Let other people be right and use your past challenges to contribute to others. Identifying and eliminating the negative people in your life will also help. Recognize abuse and never accept it or give it. Refocus to avoid "needs" you have outside of living in the moment. Release the need to always get to the next step and instead enjoy where you are currently. More on this is in the chapters 14-15, about reforming.

CHAPTER 6

PITFALLS TO SUPPORT

Supports have a natural tendency to want to help others accomplish their goals and put others before themselves. This makes them vulnerable to accepting abusive people into their lives.

Choosing Who to Support

Knowing you are a Support, you must look into your pathology and see if the trust in your Entitled's protection is false. Do you have a history of hooking up with false "protectors"? Is a fear of abandonment present because one of your parents left, or mentally checked out, while you were at a young age, predisposing you to hold on to someone who is not actually taking care of you? Are you repeating old patterns to try and re-create and relive the pain of a parent checking out?

If you feel unsatisfied in a relationship, make a conscious effort to identify what "protection" or "care" you are receiving from the person you are supporting. Then ask yourself, is the support you give to them an equal exchange? If they are providing you with financial care, are the bills they pay or the things they buy you worth your time, energy and support? Is this care genuine, or are they just buying you off, like a payment rather than actual care? Do they "over" buy or pay for things in order to make up for other abuses they provide? More importantly, are you with them because you are afraid of being alone?

Supports Walking Away from Abuse

I have counseled many people going through break-ups, and the people who have the most difficult time are those who have dependency based on fear of abandonment. Supports typically attach themselves to relationships more than Entitleds because they base their definition of themselves on being part of a relationship rather than on their individuality. Supports often immerse themselves in the life of the Entitled, while the Entitled has less of a tendency to do that. Therefore, the Support is typically hurt more in a fight or a breakup of the relationship. Typically, Entitleds have an easier time creating new visions without the partner; they can imagine their life without their partner more easily, and they can follow through on their ideas more easily. This is why it is important, as a Support, to be aware of just exactly who you are supporting, especially in an intimate relationship. If it is someone that is careless and irresponsible with the relationship, you should evaluate how getting involved in their life can be hurtful to you. To prevent repeating negative patterns, be aware of the mistakes that you have made in prior relationships and why.

Awareness is the first step in not finding yourself with the same type of abuser. Instead of beating yourself up for accepting abuse after you get out of an abusive relationship, learn from the mistake. This doesn't mean you should become defensive. Early in prior abusive relationships you probably saw signs you ignored, furthering you down the unwanted path. Moving forward, don't look out for, or in a sense anticipate, the signs to appear again, but don't ignore them. The reason I say not to look out for them is because then it will become part of your self-fulfilling prophecy. There is no way to better find the same problems you've already faced than by looking for them again.

Instead, create an Entitled vision of what you do want in order to avoid repeating mistakes. Imagine the opposite of what it is you do not want in order to get started. Looking for problems is like walking around with armor all day: you may be more protected, but armor cuts down on agility; it prevents the real you from being seen and anything genuine from getting in. Carrying resentment or fear of a previous Entitled partner who was controlling and not trusting any other Entitleds can put you in this unhealthy place. In order to have a healthy relationship at this point, the Support would have to have faith in a new Entitled, or completely change their personality *to be* Entitled (that would be, masquerading as an Entitled). Unless you were masquerading as a Support in the first place, this won't bring you any long-term fulfillment. To avoid dating the same "wrong" type repeatedly, find out why you are attracted to this type of person. Part of the design of this book is to create awareness of why Supports find themselves with this type, how to recognize them and what is the more complementary type for you.

When Supports find a relationship coming to an end by someone else's choice, they may have thoughts about what could they have done differently, or why were they rejected. It is typical for Supports to think of how they could have better offered support in the relationship. In the breakup of a toxic, destructive relationship, or even just one where the couple cannot get along, this is not a good place to be. This would be a good time for that Support to get in touch with their Entitled side. They should look at where the Entitled was in their own life and his or her vision. It could be that the Entitled was not happy along their path and felt the need for chaos in their life; unfortunately, a loved one is usually the first option. Supports often accept the shame for the other person. Look at the situation and see if you are really at fault, or if the relationship was just not right.

Supports are often too hard on themselves and wrongfully accept the blame others are responsible for. In many relationships, I see Entitleds that create dramas, exit it as if problems in the relationship were not their fault, taking no responsibility, and move on; whereas Supports spend a lot of time rethinking and reliving these past connections instead of creating new ones. Of course, any fight is the responsibility of both parties; however, both not taking responsibility, or either taking all of it, is equally as bad.

Blind Supports can be escapist. In trying to escape their own lives, they can become entrenched in someone else's life, causing dependency. And like any other escape (substance abuse, etc.), running from or ignoring the pathology can only make it worse. This is because the more you run from your soul's preferred path, the more discontent or unhappy you become. Without living your own life, you can create addictive relationships and like other addictions such as drugs, once you leave them you find yourself in as bad or worse a position than before you started. Blind Supports resist any reform out of fear of what it will cost them. With no awareness of being in sacrifice, Blind Supports often are with Selfish Entitleds that are fueled by putting them in sacrifice. This can grow to the point that the Entitleds have Supports believing they can't think for themselves and need to consult the Entitled before doing anything. If you recognize you are a Blind Support, be aware of who you allow in your life with this need for control and avoid them before this type of abuse starts.

Supports play further into this by relying on the Entitled to manage their fears. This is a mistake many Supports make. When offering support to someone, the idea is to accept their care but not have them take over your fears. This will leave the Support in an uncomfortable position if they find themselves back on their own. To avoid this, they allow themselves to fall further under the control of the Selfish Entitled.

There are many premises in which people accept abuse. Often a Blind Support accepts abuse, or sacrifice, in the beginning because it is of some benefit to them. A simple example is a female Support who may accept abuse from her husband in order to have the right to spend his money. Another premise for accepting abuse is so the Support has an excuse, for not realizing success in another area. A male Support may accept abuse from his wife in order to use her as an excuse to why he is not successful in his chosen profession; her constant distraction and need to be taken care of are his excuse for his lack of success.

Abuse could be accepted and traded as credit to be entitled in some other area, or to cause a distraction from some other pain. A Support may accept abuse from a sibling to avoid dealing with the pain of not being happy in their career; so the abuse from a sibling is a drama they have to tend to instead of looking for another career. There are many possibilities why someone will accept abuse. If you are unhappy in a situation, the key is to become aware of where you accept abuse and what benefit it is to you.

In our example of Selma and Mark, Selma accepted the abuse for a series of reasons. To start with, she had a fear of being on her own. She did not know how she would make money, or where she would live. She formed the habit of accepting abuse, and it spiraled out of control. In the beginning, she wanted to be a good wife, and she desperately wanted to be a mother. She found someone who was also ready for a family and had the resources to provide for one. With these perceived benefits at risk, she was afraid to say no to him about anything.

Her situation also stemmed from her thinking that she deserved the abuse, or better stated, that she was unworthy of a better life.

A Support also has to be careful not to get caught up in other people's stress. Blind Supports can often find themselves completely caught up in situations they have no control over. Knowing you are a Support, this is something you constantly need to check, especially with immediate family members, including your spouse and children. This typically doesn't happen to Entitleds to the same degree. They do not think of themselves as attached to other people's situations. Often Supports, especially Blind Supports, will relate the hardships of other people's lives as if they experienced it themselves. They have an ability to empathize and experience other people's pain to a fault. A Blind Support should make it an exercise to not take on another's pains and to be mindful of this with the people they find themselves supporting. Entitleds know who to call when they need sympathy, or someone to feel badly for them. This often includes them "dumping" their negative energy on a willing Support. Supports need to realize that they accept people's energy, so they need to be aware and make a choice which energies they accept. They should choose positive energy. They should make an effort to enjoy people's successes more than just their failures.

Similar to getting caught up in other people's stress, Supports can also find themselves drained of their energy by taking responsibility for the happiness of the people around them. So, if an Entitled is not happy with the restaurant they are eating in, they could project their negative energy on to the Support they are with in order to make them feel guilty for not being as uncomfortable as them. It could be anything: discomfort in sickness, work related stress, etc. Entitleds often want the Support to "jump in their boat," so to speak. As a Support, be aware when you accept this. A good indicator is when you feel as badly or as guilty as someone else is feeling for their mishap. Unreformed Entitleds know who will accept this and will try to use it as a manipulation against them. It is important to identify any Entitled who uses guilt to get what they want. They will drain your energy in order to make themselves happy and will still never be satisfied. Support like this moves into the realm of sacrifice and is of no help to either party. A good indicator of this is someone who is always telling you what they want and complains when they don't get it. Someone who does this often will offer favors or "care" with obligations attached.

As a Support, when you want to make someone happy, you should receive energy in return for working to make them happy. If not, then communicate that you do not feel you are being taken care of in your support of their happiness or goal. You might also let them know that they are making it too hard on you to support them. This is a very difficult awareness to come to because if the self-deluding behavior exists, it probably started at a very early age. The Supports who try and please everyone have the most risk of this, especially when supporting different people with opposing objectives.

An example of this could be an overbearing parent the Support wants to keep happy and an intimate partner who doesn't get along with the parent. The important thing for the Support to do is to choose what will make the Support happy and decide from there. Second, the Support must not accept any form of guilt from the party that is not getting what they want. This will be very odd for the Entitled, having always gotten what they want from the Support, and will cause them to become more aggressive in their communication.

Reformed Supports are clear about who their primary relationship is, and any Reformed Entitled will understand and appreciate knowing. For example, reformed or evolved parents would never expect their adult child to choose them over their own spouse. The spouse is the primary relationship and must be the recipient of the primary support. Often Supports have many demands—spoken or unspoken. These are occasionally expressed in a meek and needy way, instead of directly stating what they want, because of fear of confrontation. When they do express themselves, they often overreact with shouting because they don't know how to express themselves forcefully without rudeness. This mode of expression has to change if they want to be clear who they are supporting to avoid this situation. Supports also have to be aware of how caught up they get when two other people they love are fighting. They should realize it is not their fight and take an Entitled position of thinking of their own well being, not to absorb their energy. They should not get involved in a battle of other's egos.

Supports are more prone to being manipulated by guilt and need to be aware of the destruction and unhappiness guilt can cause in their lives. Guilt could cause a Support to stay in an abusive relationship based on feeling badly about leaving. Obviously Entitleds have guilt as well, but typically they still take actions that are in their best interest as opposed to making decisions based on the guilt. The guilt in this case is nothing more than a feeling that they use to tell themselves that despite doing what they consider wrong, they are still a good person. It's an empty motivator, as opposed to creativity or genuine support for a valid cause. Guilt as manipulation never works against Selfish Entitleds. It's hard to make someone feel for someone else when they only think about themselves. Because they use it so naturally, a Selfish Entitled will immediately recognize it as manipulation. Knowing they are prone to guilt and it being used against them, Supports should be aware of where and how guilt motivates them. Upon realization, Supports should make a firm communication that this manipulation will no longer be accepted.

Justifying Abuse

As Entitleds justify their own actions, Supports typically justify the abusive action of others. In addition to excusing others, they often push disagreement or abuses against them "under the rug" without seeking resolution. Excusing others, justifying their intentions, and overlooking when others take advantage allows abuses to continue. This process takes a lot of time and energy in the suppression and resentment stages. By abuse, I mean any type of negative action, unrealistic expectation or any level of discomfort used against someone.

Supports who accept abuse often fear the unknown or the unfamiliar. They choose a familiar path they do not enjoy over an unfamiliar one, which they feel they have no control over and may be worse. If you are unhappy, focus on redirecting your fear toward the discomfort of the (familiar) abuse, rather than the unfamiliarity of being without your abuser. If you are in an uncomfortable position, more of the same offers no improvement. Although it may be difficult at first, leaving your comfort zone will improve your life, as long as you don't allow the same situation to happen over again. As a Support, trust that continued changes will be a path to happiness until you get what you want.

Although a Support might want out of an unpleasant situation, often they won't do anything until it's far down the road of abuse. This coordinates with the part of them that is better at coming up with ideas than follow through. So although they might have creative ideas to get out of the unhappy situation, they might be too insecure to follow through on them out of fear of creating something worse. If you find yourself here, it is a good idea to jump the line to get in touch with your Entitled side until you are away from the abuse. You must temporarily think of yourself and your own protection and where you want to be. Escaping by using drugs, alcohol, TV or even household chores, to avoid making the change will keep you from your path to happiness.

Setting boundaries are helpful but it is justification that allows you to not do anything to change when someone crosses your boundary. You find yourself explaining why they really didn't cross the boundary because, "they were upset," or "you need to be more understanding," or "he really loves me," etc. This justification renders your boundary useless and allows for more abuse.

Reformed Supports should trigger themselves to react when they start excusing other people's actions. In this way, they become aware of potential abuse. While on the way to reforming, at the very least, weigh what value accepting the abuse brings you. If you find it too challenging to exit yourself from the situation, then determine if what you are receiving is of greater value than the cost of the abuse. This awareness will, at some point, force you to realize the abuse comes at a higher price than your ego's desire for the perceived gain. Making that big change will sometimes make things feel initially worse before they get better. This is what makes it difficult to face the change. For this reason, it is important to have vision beyond that initial discomfort.

To move away from accepting continued abuse, ask yourself these questions:

- *What do you do as a Support to avoid follow through?* The answer could be your ***Escape***. (Drinking, drugs, gossiping, watching TV, video games, reading, etc., anything to avoid taking action.) It could be that you convince yourself that you are not equipped for change. You may build your fears so big that you convince yourself the abuse is a better situation. Escapes then allow people to tolerate abuse, unhappiness and discontent in relationships, work and life.

- *How do you escape?* Escapes are mostly subconscious, meaning you are so accustomed to doing them that you don't realize you are. Escapes dumb down the effects of unhappiness as well as the motivation to change it. A good indicator of being involved in an escape is if you don't like to be quiet or alone. An escape can be anything used to consistently divert your attention from changing an unpleasant situation. If you are unhappy and are not doing anything to make changes, then they are prevalent. Being conscious of them is a way to turn that energy towards change. The answer to finding your escape lies in what you find yourself doing instead of thinking about the discomfort or change. Sit quietly in your thoughts, especially if you feel anxious. What you instinctually want to do to avoid your own thoughts will tell you what your escape is. It could be anything from drinking to getting involved in someone else's life.

- *What convenient distractions do you use to prevent yourself from doing what you think may be your path?* This is similar to an escape, but tends to be more like an excuse as to why you can't have the life you wish you could. This could be anything, including taking care of the very person that is abusing you.

- *How do you convince yourself that you cannot follow through on an idea?* What insecurity is holding you back? If that (usually false) insecurity wasn't there, how much different would your life be?

Modeling someone who makes great changes in their life could be helpful. Yes, you may see them struggle at first, but once they get what they want you notice their happiness.

Fear of Abandonment

It is a good bet that if you are in an abusive relationship, your acceptance of it can be traced back to your childhood. Your parents (or someone in a caretaking role) most likely abandoned or disconnected from you either emotionally or physically. Examples would be that you were ignored or actually left alone, short or long term, and have a fear of that happening again at some level. A parental figure practiced taking their love away, even if it was for good intentions, and you struggled to get it back, either through entertainment, crying, tantrums, etc. This fear is there now as an adult, often in the subconscious, causing you to not want to leave what little love you feel from your relationship, despite the abuse.

This can even be traced to a fear of not belonging or unworthiness based on our cultural need to have a partner, or an unworthiness of receiving real love. The point is to investigate what is keeping you attached to an unhealthy relationship. When you realize you are impossibly trying to relive and heal an old wound from a primary relationship, it is possible to walk away from the abuse with little or no scar tissue. More on fears is discussed in the chapter 16, *Finding Yourself.*

It is also a matter of working on your own attachment issues and fear of loss. You must have an awareness of what you are attached to and dismantle the attachment. Dismantling your attachment will release the fear of losing something. If you are not attached, you cannot be abandoned. It is quite possible to love and have connection with no attachment. Releasing expectations is the start of this process.

The fear of abandonment often manifests itself in a need for control for Entitleds versus neediness for Supports. The Support allows the Entitled to take control when they are using the Entitled to alleviate fears or insecurity to make them happy. Anytime someone places his happiness on another person, the absence or loss of that person will force him back into an insecure state. This is where control or manipulation can occur. This creates codependence, also discussed in chapter 16, *Finding Yourself.*

Fear of Expressing Anger

Supports often mask their anger out of fear of what they might do or say, or how they might hurt the person they feel they should support. In the case of a Support, often their ego tells them to quiet their frustration, when in fact they should stand up for themselves, as opposed to the Entitled, whose anger is often caused by the ego. This stems from a Support's fear of confrontation.

To explain further, when Supports are not expressing their anger, frustration, or rage, it bottles up and becomes resentment and possibly bitterness. This negative energy builds up inside a person and causes suffering or physical illnesses and also leads to enabling. Once identified as a Support, a person should realize when they are doing this and express themselves in some way. If you are biting your tongue and building resentment over something your boss does, communicate to him or her your problem instead of suffering. If that is not yet possible for you, then keep a journal. Often writing the frustration can help alleviate some suffering, but mostly it gets that energy out of your system. This is also a way to turn that resentment into ideas that can lead to the inspiration you need to make changes.

Without some expression of these negative emotions, larger eruptions of depression, despair, powerlessness, hopelessness, fear, insecurity, guilt, or jealousy will occur. Pushing the emotion down and away suppresses a valuable indicator of a necessary change. Responsible Entitleds know their Supports have potential for this and should check in with them to make sure resentment is not building.

Supports who do not speak their mind also have trouble taking a stand. They often find it easier to appear as if they don't have an opinion. Sometimes without backing up an Entitled, it is hard for them to have a strong opinion that is either black and white. Some Supports also have a difficult time self-motivating because without strong follow through, they do not see enough possibility. These Supports do not feel complete unless they have an Entitled to get behind. Even the successful Supports I have spoken with often didn't achieve their success until they found the right partner to firmly guide them, or keep them motivated towards a goal. Without the Entitled, Supports can feel dull, without direction, unlike themselves, and often not clear on their purpose. In this situation, a trusted Entitled is a good person to go to for help in putting together a vision of what you want, plan a schedule for follow through, or partner with to help you execute your plan. The other option is to get more in touch with your Entitled side and confidently follow through, starting from the result you want and work backwards.

Another reason to choose wisely who to support is that person will assist you in meeting your own needs. As a Support, you probably accomplish more when you are with a partner that you can, not only support, but can also be accountable to. Choose those whom you will be eager to support and who will expect you to be accountable to what you do and say.

Supports should be aware of being a "guest" in life. Having qualities of both Entitled and Support within them, often people move from being a guest to a "host" in different situations. A Support can often find himself or herself a constant guest. This means they don't initiate anything unless someone else does. They can be timid, not going after what they want, not pursuing desires, and accepting what is dealt to them, rather than going after it themselves. This is another example of why it is important to choose responsible Entitleds for your life and to watch where they are leading you. Supports should decide how often they find themselves having the energy and actions of a guest and how content they are that way. Would they prefer to be a host? If so, they should move into an Entitled role slowly until they are more comfortable setting their own goals.

CHAPTER 7

HOW DO I KNOW WHICH ONE I AM?

The idea here is not to cure or even fix "problems," but to point out motivations. Minor adjustments in motives, along with a focus on compassion and trust, can create more happiness. Because a person's worst quality is often tied to their biggest contribution, people can move from Blind Support or Selfish Entitled to Reformed, just by using that trait to help others. Someone suffering from an addiction to drugs can turn that around in a relatively short time and profoundly help others get off drugs. Instead of using their addictive personality for drugs, they can replace that with the addiction for helping others off of drugs. A person of extreme greed can suddenly have a change of heart based on an incident in their life and become a philanthropist, giving away the fruits of their former greed.

It can sometimes be hard to tell which category a person is because many people can move freely through all of them. Emotional factors such as a person that is always full of negativity, mentally escapes, with the wrong partner, or in discontent can hide a person's true self. The important thing to discover is where you are most of the time and where you stand compared to the person you spend most of your time with. The good news is, if you are having a hard time figuring it out, it is not super important to know exactly which category you are. Yes, that may be odd to hear, but it is more important to know the positive, contributing qualities that you have from either category and heighten those while avoiding any negative or unwanted ones.

To keep it simple, do you prefer to be the center of attention (Entitled), or do you prefer someone else to be the center (Support)? Do you like to be the leader (Entitled)? Or would you prefer to help see someone else's leadership and get behind them (Support)? Once you've established that, you can monitor your behavior to see which of the subcategories you fall into.

Many clients I have consulted initially think they are the opposite type of what they actually are, especially the very unreformed (Selfish Entitleds or Blind Supports). This usually occurs when people are judgmental against a category or of themselves. For example, Selfish Entitleds think they are actually supporting people when they are not: the little support they give is actually a manipulation to receive support. The Supports consider the smallest entitlement they possess, usually exercised during a time of self-protection, more encompassing than it is.

A Selfish Entitled or Blind Support may have a lot of changes to make for harmony in relationships, but they won't know it unless they first know who they are. The idea is to be open to anything. If someone suggests you fall in a different category than what you think, then consider it by reviewing the positive or negative characteristics listed below. There is no good or bad category, the best place to be is what feels most natural to you.

You also can't be okay with who you are until you know who you are not. If you think you are a leader and you're not, you will be constantly arguing with other leaders' ideas to prove yourself, when you could be having more positive interactions by contributing with your ability to support another leader's vision. This is the standard definition of entitlement–the idea that you deserve something you don't. This will always diminish a person's best qualities.

It is also important to recognize the period of life a person is in. At twenty years old, a person might be Selfishly Entitled, move to Benevolent Entitled at thirty years old, Reformed Entitled at forty years old and Support at fifty or sixty to solely support their children or grandchildren. So the point is not to lock yourself into a category, but to be the most evolved you can be in any given situation and notice where you land. This creates awareness and allows you to decide what you are lacking and who most complements you in any relationship.

Important events in a person's life also help them to fall into their most comfortable role. An event such as parenthood could make a person interested in being supportive in every aspect of their life, having gained compassion for others. The loss of a parent, or an older sibling, could force a person to take the lead, thus creating the start of them having vision and following through with it.

In order to find out which category you are, you need:

1. *An ability to honestly disassociate your actions from your intentions without justification.* You may think you are helping someone, but actually you are hurting them. This happens when we intend to do one thing, but our actions prove to be completely different. An example of this is someone who treats people poorly but believes he is teaching them a lesson. Or a person who is working to make a lot of money to seemingly

support his wife, but in reality he is trying to control her.

2. *An ability to let go of your desire to only have the positive qualities you think of in each category.* People may think Entitleds are inconsiderate and do not want that, others like to think of themselves as leaders, so they want to be Entitled. Some think Supports are nicer; others think Supports are suckers. All ideas of what you want should be put aside in order to assess which type you currently fall under.

3. *To abandon judgment over which category you would like to be in.* People often avoid a category because they don't like someone in that category and do not want to be thought of "like them." Just because two people are in the same category does not mean they are going to be alike.

4. *No ulterior motives for being a part of one category.* If the person you love is in one category, you may want to find yourself in another. Also be aware if you feel others will judge you if you admit to a certain category.

5. *A desire to make changes for the better based on awareness.* If you are too afraid to make any changes in your life, it will be difficult to notice anything that can be improved. This is self-protection.

After you know your type, you will know what to expect of the people in your life and can be honest about what they can expect from you. It is also important to keep in mind that we are all made up by percentages. A person might be 60 percent Support and 40 percent Entitled. That means in different situations, she could fall on either side, but six out of ten times she will be supportive. The important thing to know is which side you fall on in various situations. So if you normally operate 60 percent Support in an intimate relationship, then you would be well matched with someone who is 60 percent Entitled intimately. While in matters of career, you may need more support from others to fulfill your vision. In a perfect dance, the roles switch quickly and easily between partners without question of respect. The purpose of this book is to make you aware of who you are and who your partner is, so that you can adjust well into your respective characteristics, creating more harmony.

General Characteristics

Support:

- Very creative, especially working with someone else's goals or visions.

- Show interest in hearing the opinions of others, generally great listeners, very observant of others' needs. (Supports have a much better attention span for conversations outside of their general interests than Entitleds do.)

- Are more prone to sacrifice personal needs for the happiness of another, put others before themselves, submit or serve others.

- Take on the problems of others, loyal to a fault.

- Can be needy, or find it challenging to find direction when alone, or just not motivated unless in support of another.

- Are more prone to be abused emotionally or physically, or controlled.

- Are more prone to have a fear of abandonment than Entitleds.

- Are not good liars (You must be honest about this trait, because good liars often say they aren't, and this is actually a sign of being Entitled. Supports, however, have the ability to lie for others they are supporting, but not for themselves.)
- Prefer to share special occasions with one person or a select few, rather than a big celebration. (Often Supports wonder why Entitleds could become suddenly energized during a party, while Supports may be opposed to even attending.)

Entitled:

- Possess strong vision, including follow-through for goals.
- Are innovative, inventive and see things other people are not easily able to.
- Desire dominance in relationships. This could be expressed through being protective or leading, as well as a need to tell others what to do or being controlling.
- Need to have their own needs met first before they care for others, even if the other is emotionally upset.
- Possess the ability to lie to attain a personal goal when necessary. This is in line with thinking of themselves first.
- Have a harder time acknowledging people or thanking them. (This is not exactly typical of all Entitleds, but if it is present, it usually indicates Entitled.)

General Behavioral Traits:

Support:

- **Positive** (At their best)
  - ► Creative.
  - ► Helpful.
  - ► Concerned for others before themselves.
  - ► Loyal.
  - ► Always thinking of ideas that will benefit others.
  - ► Good at nurturing relationships as opposed to initiating them.

- **Negative** (At their worst)
  - ► Needy.
  - ► Loyal to a fault.
  - ► Easily manipulated.
  - ► Hard time getting motivated for themselves.
  - ► Enablers.
  - ► Co-dependent.

Entitled:

- **Positive** (At their best)
  - ► Innovative and goal-orientated. (Entitleds are the people who look at something and say, "I can do that better." They make improvements in business, sports, entertainment, and politics and keep things competitive in all aspects of life.)
  - ► Take care and protect others in some way: financially, physically, and/or emotionally.
  - ► Risk takers, including calculated risk takers.

- Leaders, motivators and influencers.
- Execute - Make ideas into reality.
- Influential, take charge, speak up and make sure they are heard.
- Initiate and build relationships.
- Stay focused on the goal despite obstacles getting in their way.
- Take control and make decisions.

- **Negative** (At their worst)
  - Short temper, no patience.
  - Defensive.
  - Have a hard time being happy/content where they are: looking to what is next, or where they "should" be.
  - Lack trust in other's abilities. They feel as though they have to do everything themselves.
  - Take credit for other people's lives. ("If not for me, he would be nothing.")
  - Sarcastic or put others down.
  - Controlling.
  - Manipulating.
  - Easily justify negative action to avoid guilt.
  - Not good listeners.
  - Critical.
  - Blame others for their mistakes.

Pathologies and fears often shape what category a person will be in. They get in the way of a person being able to discover him- or herself and their true nature. Anxiety, jealousy, resentment, anger, low or too high self-esteem, all alter our character. For example, suppressed anger can eventually blow up, or create constant frustration, causing a Support to act more Entitled. Insecurity will cause an Entitled to act more supportive, or more needy of others.

Entitleds don't mind supporting their partner more often than natural as long as respect is given in return. By the same token, Supports will take the lead for their loved ones more often than otherwise when in love. This is especially seen in parent-child relationships. You should also base your assessment of yourself during times of normal circumstance, not when you want something from someone, or are emotional about a situation you are in. For example, if you are angry about your relationship, it is common to jump the line from Support to Entitled for self-protection or out of fear. If someone thinks they are being abused, it is common to leave the role of Support and become more Entitled in order to protect themselves. If someone is promising you everything you desire for your vision, you could jump the line from Entitled to support them. Also, if an Entitled is thinking someone they love is going to leave them, or they are going to lose something important, they could temporarily jump the line to Support.

Typical Pathologies

Not all Entitleds or Supports have these qualities, but if you do, then typically you would fall into that category. If you already know you fall into one category, then become aware which of these is typical of you.

Support Typical Pathologies:

- Fear of abandonment or isolation.
- A need to have people think they are nice.

- Lack of follow through.
- Accepting of others' guilt and other negative energy.
- Tendency to be manipulated or controlled.
- Often unexpressed negative emotions.
- Depend on others to manage their fears.

Entitled Typical Pathologies:

- A need to have people attracted to them or think they are powerful in some way.
- A need for recognition. (More than just acknowledgement)
- A need to look smart—a "know it all."
- A need to be the center of attention.
- A need to have drama in their lives. (Often the drama is there so they can solve a problem.)
- A need to control others and avoid what they perceive as being controlled at all costs.
- Jealous (Of course this could be both, but it is more naturally an Entitled behavior.)

The negative characteristics are not here to beat yourself up with or place blame on anyone else, but to point out important aspects to be aware of. For example, if you suspect you are an Entitled and possibly like to show that you are very knowledge-able, this awareness points out a conversation you could have with yourself such as:

"Since I am more an Entitled than a Support, I know that when learning something new, my ego doesn't like to be a beginner. I'm deciding not to let that get in the way of learning new things. I'm not going to be argumentative or speak over someone who knows more

about a subject than I do. When they are finished speaking, I will absorb what they said, think about it and then speak."

Because every person is unique, not every quality within a category will match up. Difficult circumstances will change which type you fall into. Although I mentioned earlier to assess your type under normal emotional circumstances, it may help to think of how you react in a high-pressure situation such as an emergency. Think of yourself in an emergency situation with another person you are partnered with. Which one of the two of you will take the lead? Which one of you will freeze up and wait for the other's direction/reaction? The emergency could of course be in a business situation where your finances are threatened, or a more life-threatening scenario. The person with slower or stand still reaction is usually the Support. Entitleds typically will begin to put their body in motion, have instinctual anger and take action to overcome the problem at hand, even if their solution is not a great one. With this, as well as all of the test questions, the important thing is to think about how you are and avoid imagining how you would like to be.

Siblings

Often the younger of the siblings will take the opposite role of the older. So if the older is Entitled, then the next one will be a Support. This happens often because they spend so much time together, and the older sibling conditions them to that type. If the older is Entitled and the younger wants to play or stay with them, then they will force the younger to be supportive of that. If the older is supportive, then naturally the younger will become accustomed to getting their way and continuing that behavior. In families with more than two children the pattern breaks and can go either way. But if two are often in one another's company, then the pair will often be one Entitled and one Support.

128

The irony is that as they get older, often the Entitled sibling has problems with the Support's chosen partner. I say ironic because the Entitled had a part in creating his or her sibling as a Support. Then, when the Support naturally finds another Entitled to be their intimate partner later in life, the Entitled sibling resents that partner for leading the Support sibling, or possibly taking advantage of them. This resentment is typical of two Entitleds competing for the same Support. It also goes deeper in that the one Entitled sees much of what they don't like in themselves in the other Entitled. They need to realize their sibling is a Support and in order for them to find fulfillment, they'd prefer the vision of an Entitled partnered with them.

If both siblings are Entitled and not reforming, they could have a lot of competitive resentment towards one another. If one has a great Support as a partner, the other Entitled could resent them for getting what they want from someone else and their relationship in general. In this case, these siblings need to recognize what they both require as Entitleds and respect the other's desires and good fortune, realizing these in no way hinder their own.

Masquerading

The upcoming chapters on masquerading (9, 10) show how insecurity or fear will cause someone to cross the line and continuously act in a category that is not natural to them. There are also cases where someone receives an overwhelming amount of support, forcing them to masquerade as Entitled if otherwise not. This could happen in the case of someone who is very good looking or the child of a powerful or rich person. Even though they are "Entitled," what's missing in the masquerade is the strong vision, follow through, and genuine care of others. The masquerade causes a serious lack of contentment.

Other examples of masqueraders are people who actually prefer to take the lead, but just are not confident enough to do it (Entitled masquerading as Support). Or they take the lead because they feel that it is what they are supposed to do, but would really rather support someone else (Support masquerading as Entitled).

— Masquerading in the Beginning of a Relationship

At the beginning of a relationship, it is sometimes difficult to identify which category someone belongs to because quite often the roles are reversed. In a period of initial lust or wanting something from another, people sometimes act with the opposite behavior than is natural to them. This is the "best behavior" stage. We all have experienced people acting one way in the beginning of a relationship as opposed after they feel more comfortable a few months later. Entitleds can act very supportive and Supports can act very Entitled. It is not necessarily a lie. Entitleds genuinely feel supportive toward the person they are attracted to, but at some point their entitlement demands a turn-around.

The reason Supports could act Entitled initially is because they might have a history of being hurt in relationships, so they get an attitude of defense or protection that could come off as being Entitled.

Their attitude could be, "I'm not going to fall for that one again." But their supportive nature will eventually make a turn-around. They also could be acting Entitled because they want to attract someone Entitled, so they try to come off like that as a way to relate. They might see an Entitled as someone with a "higher" social value, so they try to sell themselves that way.

For both Entitleds and Supports, this initial turn-around behavior is especially prominent in abusive relationships. This is why it is important to act in your nature from the beginning so that you can see how the other person in your new relationship interacts with the role you offer. If it is in an Entitled's nature to take advantage of a Support, if they know the other person is a full Support from the beginning, the signs of their irresponsible Entitlement will be easier to spot without the Support's defenses in place. That is because the true Selfish Entitled will pass through the "best behavior" or "honeymoon" stage quicker and show their abusive behavior. If it is in someone's nature to be too needy a Support, if as an Entitled, you act as you naturally do, you will see these signs much quicker than otherwise.

I once heard that if you put a frog on a frying pan that is hot, it would immediately jump out. But if you put that same frog on a cold pan and heated it up, it will stay on the pan until the heat fried it to death. This is the same in battered or abusive relationships. If the abuse given at the end of a relationship were given in the beginning, the person would immediately exit the relationship, whether it is work, intimate or any other situation. However, if abuse is increased little by little over time, it is too often accepted. The Support enables this to occur. In either case, anyone masquerading is usually doing so because of insecurity of obtaining their desires or goals and fear of people abandoning them. Despite externally perceived happiness, they are hiding strong feelings of a lack of fulfillment. Masquerading is often where different cultures need to be considered as well. Latin, Asian, Middle Eastern and other cultures often promote women publicly following Support characteristics and men Entitled, but many times this is not the case within the couple's home environment.

When you are operating from your true category, you feel content at the level of your soul. It feels as though you are fulfilling your purpose. This contentment is more than the short-lived happiness you feel when you receive something pleasurable to your ego, such as a piece of jewelry. When you've helped someone or inspired them to do good with their life the feeling settles differently and will last longer; it is the same with your true category. Discovering where you naturally support or provide care for others can help find the contentment you have been looking for. I have worked with many people in extremes (Selfish Entitled or Blind Support) that have discovered many things they don't like about themselves; knowing their category gives them awareness of what they are capable of, allowing them to create a different result.

The upcoming chapter provides a series of questions to help you find which category you fall in as well as what percentage.

CHAPTER 8

THE PROFILE

The questions below can be used as a guideline to suggest as to what percentage you are either Entitled or Support. I would suggest taking this once for intimate relationships specifically, and again for work relationships. A person can be Support in their working relationships and an Entitled in their intimate relationship or vice versa. It is also a good idea after taking the survey to have a trusted friend or loved one take it for you to get an outside opinion. Generally people can be either too self indulgent or too critical of themselves, so the results will often surprise you based on the perception you have of yourself versus how others see you.

The Profile

The Profile is a series of questions that will help you to break down the qualities in each category you tend to favor. Choose just one number on the scale below each question that you feel represents what is typical of you. The plus and minus signs in the scale in no way represents good or bad value judgments, but are used for calculation purposes. Explanations of the questions and answers follow the Profile.

1. Do you prefer to be the center of attention, or would you rather someone else provide the entertainment, information, conversation, or action?

(Prefer to go Unnoticed)   **(Center of Attention)**

Almost never me	Rarely	Unusually	Neutral	Sometimes	Often	Almost always me
-5	-4 -3	-2 -1	0	+1 +2	+3 +4	+5

2. Do you feel that unless you are leading, nothing is being done properly?

I prefer to trust following the lead of another	Often I prefer others to lead	It is not typical for me to lead but happens infrequently	Neutral	Sometimes I lead	Often I am leading because no one else can get it right	I am almost always leading
-5	-4 -3	-2 -1	0	+1 +2	+3 +4	+5

3. In life, in most situations are you a "guest," or a "host?" Hosts go after what they want and guests wait for someone to bring it to them. Hosts initiate conversations and new relationships. Hosts execute ideas. Guests are often shy and tentative, while hosts move forward despite risk or discomfort. Guests might tend to hesitate when they want something, feeling that possibly someone else deserves it more.

(Guest)   **(Host)**

Almost always a Guest	Often a guest	More so a guest	Neutral	More so a Host	Often a Host	Almost always a Host
-5	-4 -3	-2 -1	0	+1 +2	+3 +4	+5

134

4. When you are given the "rules" of an organization, do you think, "That doesn't really apply to me"? Or do you follow the rules as strict guidelines, even changing the plans you had before knowing them?

(Follow the rules)   **(Alter the rules)**

I strictly follow rules	I mostly follow rules	I lean towards following the rules	Neutral	I lean towards breaking rules	I mostly alter the rules	I almost always alter the rules to fit my vision
-5	-4 -3	-2 -1	0	+1 +2	+3 +4	+5

5. How often do you find yourself excusing people for inappropriate behavior against you?

(I ignore rudeness allowing people to get away with it)   **(Never let people get away with rudeness)**

I almost always excuse people's rude behavior against me	I often excuse people's rude behavior	I do sometimes excuse people's rude behavior	Neutral	I sometimes stand up to other's rudeness	I often stand against rudeness against me	I almost always stop any rude behavior against me
-5	-4 -3	-2 -1	0	+1 +2	+3 +4	+5

6. Do you emotionally take on the problems or stresses of others when they confide in you?

(I never take on others emotions)

(I often take on the emotional pain of others as if it were mine)

Almost never me	Rarely	Unusually	Neutral	Sometimes	Often	Almost always me
+5	+4 +3	+2 +1	0	-1 -2	-3 -4	-5

7. Do you either create, enjoy, or instigate drama, chaos, problems, or other negative situations for yourself or others?

(I avoid upsetting people in every way I can)

(I usually create drama)

Almost never me	Rarely	Unusually	Neutral	Sometimes	Often	Almost always me
-5	-4 -3	-2 -1	0	+1 +2	+3 +4	+5

8. When a person is upset, or feeling bad emotionally, do you want to help them in every way you can or does it mostly feel as though they are sabotaging your energy and they are bringing you down?

I feel they will take my energy and I try to avoid them	I rarely get involved in another's crisis and sometimes avoid them when I know they are upset	I would listen but most times realize I can't do much to really help		Neutral	Sometimes I will console and help them with what I can	I often feel inspired to do everything I can to console and help others		I almost always console and help, with all my resources, despite other plans
+5	+4	+3	+2 +1	0	-1 -2	-3	-4	-5

9. How eager and open are you to hearing the other side of an argument and move off your point to help the other person feel expressed?

(I'm more concerned about making my point)   **(I feel compassion for my partner when in disagreement and want to help satisfy them)**

Almost never me	Rarely	Unusually		Neutral	Sometimes	Often		Almost always me
+5	+4	+3	+2 +1	0	-1 -2	-3	-4	-5

10. When you are feeling negative energy, such as being upset or frustrated, how much are other people forced to deal with your mood? This could be verbally or with non-verbal gestures you make to try to force others to feel as upset as you are.

(Never, I keep negative emotions to myself) **(I can't help when I'm upset but to force it on others)**

Almost never	Rarely	Unusually	Neutral	Sometimes	Often	Almost always
-5	-4 -3	-2 -1	0	+1 +2	+3 +4	+5

11. If you had to pick either yourself or your partner, who is the "star" in your relationship?

(My partner is the star) **(I am the star)**

Almost never me	Rarely	Unusually	Neutral	Sometimes	Often	Almost always me
-5	-4 -3	-2 -1	0	+1 +2	+3 +4	+5

12. Who has initiated your current or last few relationships?

(My partners have initiated them) **(I always initiate relationships)**

Almost never me	Rarely I initiate	Unusually	Neutral	Sometimes	Often I initiate	Almost always me
-5	-4 -3	-2 -1	0	+1 +2	+3 +4	+5

13. Who usually gives in to the other during an argument?

(My partner usually gives in)   **(I usually give in)**

Almost never me	Rarely	Unusually	Neutral	Sometimes	Often	Almost always me
+5	+4 +3	+2 +1	0	-1 -2	-3 -4	-5

14. In order to get what you want, under what circumstances are you willing to lie, despite any recourse outside of yourself? (This could include anything that gets you what you want exclusively from an employer, business partner, investor, spouse, girlfriend, parents, friends, etc.)

(I never lie under any circumstance even if it benefits me)   **(I will lie to get what I need small or large)**

Almost never me	Rarely	Unusually	Neutral	Sometimes	Often	Almost always me
-5	-4 -3	-2 -1	0	+1 +2	+3 +4	+5

15. Everyone likes approval and recognition but how often do you go out of your way or try to impress others or seek recognition?

(I prefer to recognize others)   **(I seek recognition often)**

Never me	Rarely	Unusually	Neutral	Sometimes	Often	Almost always me
-5	-4 -3	-2 -1	0	+1 +2	+3 +4	+5

16. How important is it that you have influence over other people's decisions?

(Not important)   **(Very important)**

I don't feel comfortable to risk giving a strong opinion in case I am wrong	I rarely need to have influence over others	I prefer others to decide on their own and I support that	Neutral	I like to have an influence over other people's decisions	I often have an influence over people's decisions	I give advice when I'm sure I'm right and expect people to listen
-5	-4 -3	-2 -1	0	+1 +2	+3 +4	+5

17. Do you often have the feeling you are missing out on something? That there is something better going on outside of where you are, or that you could do better in relationships, situations, work, fun, entertainment, etc.

(I feel content with where I am)   **(I often feel I am missing something better)**

Almost never me	Rarely	Unusually	Neutral	Sometimes	Often	Almost always me
-5	-4 -3	-2 -1	0	+1 +2	+3 +4	+5

18. Do you find yourself criticizing many things or other people? Often thinking how you would have done it better.

(Never criticize)   **(Criticize often)**

Almost never me	Rarely	Unusually	Neutral	Sometimes	Often	Almost always me
-5	-4 -3	-2 -1	0	+1 +2	+3 +4	+5

19. Most of the time, do you truly listen to what others are saying, or are you just waiting to make your point?

(I really listen to others)   **(Mostly waiting to make my next point)**

I always listen with full interest	I mostly am content to listen	I enjoy listening	Neutral	Sometimes I am just waiting to make my point	Often I am just waiting to make my point	Almost always I just want to get my point across
-5	-4 -3	-2 -1	0	+1 +2	+3 +4	+5

20. Have you tolerated abusive behavior in a relationship?

(Have been abused in many relationships)   **(Have never accepted abuse)**

In more than one relationship I have accepted physical and psychological abuse	I have accepted physical or psychological abuse at least once.	I have overlooked psychological abuse.	Neutral	At any sign of verbal abuse I make it clear to my partner I will not accept it.	I have ended relationships immediately at any sign of abuse.	I *have been* psychologically or physically abusive *to others* in my past relationships
-5	-4 -3	-2 -1	0	+1 +2	+3 +4	+5

141

Paying close attention to the pluses and minuses (because they switch sides with questions 6, 8, 9, and 13 to avoid a pattern) tally up your score. If the result is in the positive, you are an Entitled; if it is in the negative, then you are a Support. Next take simply that number, without the plus or minus, and divide it in half, and add 50 to it. This is the percentage which represents how often you show up as the Entitled or the Support. So if your result is +18, then you are Entitled 59% of the time (18 /2 = 9 +50 =59). This means that in about 6 out of 10 circumstances you will act Entitled: and about 4 out of 10 times you will support someone else. Therefore, your most complementary match is someone who will act as a Support in 6 out of 10 circumstances, following your lead. If your partner is not within about 10 percentage points of the your opposite type, (in this case, approximately 59% Support), and a high percentage of couples are not; then take advantage of the communication exercises, as well as the other guidelines for creating harmony, in chapter eleven, Getting Along. That is because your personalities interacting together may naturally conflict so a higher level of awareness is required to harmonize with one another.

Keep in mind, the results may be biased based on your emotional state at the time you completed the Profile, so it is best to take this under a normal emotional state and not after a fight, a break up, or in the lust or "honeymoon" phase of a new relationship.

Profile Explanations:

1. Do you prefer to be the center of attention, or would you rather someone else to provide the entertainment, information, conversation, or action?

In most cases if you like, and especially if you *need* to be the center of attention, you are Entitled. This is behavior typical of thinking of yourself before others. Thinking of others first often would include taking the attention away from yourself to let them lead, which would be categorized as Support. If two people are competing for attention, this is an indication of two Entitleds together. (Chapters 3, 10, 12)

2. Do you feel that unless you are leading, nothing is being done properly?

Entitleds have a difficult time letting go while someone else is leading. They often think of where things could be done better, or where something could go wrong when others are leading. Supports often can easily wait for direction from a leader and will take comfort in that process far more than an Entitled. (Chapters 1, 3, 11-14)

3. In life, in most situations are you a "guest," or a "host?" Hosts go after what they want, and guests wait for someone to bring it to them. Hosts initiate conversations and new relationships. Hosts execute ideas. Guests are often shy and tentative, while hosts move forward despite risk or discomfort. Guests might tend to hesitate when they want something, feeling that possibly someone else deserves it more.

Entitleds move through life with a certain ownership of the space they occupy more than Supports. Supports seem to wait for the Entitled to make a move and then follow through once the lead has been set. That is what being a guest or a host means. This goes for introductions, pursuing work, career, relationships and other desires.

Examples include how Entitleds more typically go after what they want, while Supports hesitate. Entitleds typically initiate new relationships and conversations. Entitleds execute ideas more than Supports do. Supports typically come up with ideas they want to do with others. Supports are typically more timid, while Entitleds place more importance on working through their shyness and fears.

How deserving do you feel for the things you want? Blind Supports often have ideas that others are more deserving than themselves, while Selfish Entitleds overcompensate for this, pushing to get more than they feel they deserve; which is part of why they are often difficult to please. (Chapters 1-4, 7, 16)

4. When you are given the "rules" of an organization, do you think, "That doesn't really apply to me"? Or do you follow the rules as strict guidelines, even changing the plans you had before knowing them?

Entitleds often bend rules at will, to satisfy their needs. Selfish Entitleds act on behalf of their own rules, even overcompensating to prove they don't have to do what they are told. (See also explanation of question number 16.) Supports will often change plans if told by another person they can't do something. (Chapters 3, 5)

5. How often do you find yourself excusing people for inappropriate behavior against you?

It takes a lot for Supports to speak up because they tend to avoid confrontation. The important part of this question is not just noticing bad behavior but either excusing it or confronting it. Supports often excuse it, allowing it to occur again, even though they would like it to stop. Entitleds, especially Selfish Entitleds, will usually confront someone when they are rude. (Chapters 2, 4, 6, 16)

6. Do you emotionally take on the problems or stress of others when they confide in you?

This is more typical of Supports. A Support will often jump right in the boat with others who are feeling bad. This is why Entitleds often call Supports in times of sadness as opposed to calling other Entitleds. It is important for Supports to remember to consciously take on people's successes rather than their failures. Nothing good comes out of giving someone such extreme empathy that you feel terrible yourself. (Chapters 2, 6, 15, 16)

7. Do you either create, enjoy, or instigate drama, chaos, problems, or other negative situations for yourself or others?

Usually the more drama someone has in their life the more Entitled they are. It could be just dramatizing your own stress to others. All of the Selfish Entitleds I have worked with have a high amount of drama surrounding them. Drama surrounds SE's because they do not believe in themselves, in who they are, that they are loved, or feel insecure in the position they are in, so they always have to prove themselves. Drama is often the easy way to try and do so, or at least create a distraction, so that people may not notice their insecurities. Drama is easy to produce and, in their mind, justifies their existence, the "love" they receive, or their importance to people. Drama produces a result. Selfish Entitleds often think if they make drama, and people help them, they are in control. It makes them feel that they are "leading," they are "loved," they are the source of attention, but it is all false. This is unjustified entitlement. (Chapters 3, 5, 14, 16)

8. When a person is upset, or feeling bad emotionally, do you want to help them in every way you can or does it mostly feel as though they are sabotaging your energy and they are bringing you down?

Supports often will take as much time as a person needs in order to help them feel better. Blind Supports will put too much of their energy towards this often feeling drained afterwards, while Selfish Entitleds will become annoyed when someone wants help from them unless something is in it for them.

Supports typically notice others' emotional feelings better as well. They often can spot it from across the room, while Entitleds especially SE's can live in their own little bubble unless they turn those sensors on to avoid someone, or get something they want. (Chapters 2, 7, 14-17)

9. How eager and open are you to hearing the other side of an argument and move off your point to help the other person feel expressed?

This is obviously more typical of Supports as well. Entitleds want to make their point, be acknowledged and then possibly hear the other's point. Entitleds often assume they understand the other person's point and see it as wrong, so in their mind, they have to get their own point heard.

Supports too often do not say anything about inappropriate or abusive behavior against them because they are thinking of the other person's side. The communication exercises in the chapter on getting along will help to avoid this. Couples who get along great are always open to their loved one's point or communication, and encourage them to express themselves. (Chapters 14-17)

10. When you are feeling negative energy, such as being upset or frustrated, how much are other people forced to deal with your mood? This could be verbally or with non-verbal gestures you make to try to force others to feel as upset as you are.

Projecting your energy on others is a sign of being Entitled. When Entitleds are unhappy, especially Selfish Entitleds, they fall into the trap of wanting everyone else to be unhappy. They may use guilt or subtle hints of anger. The problem with this is that once they are happy again, which often comes after they have made everyone else unhappy, then they want everyone to be happy again with them. Often passive aggressive, this is highly abusive behavior. Any action to make others feel bad because they feel bad, is abuse. This is clearly an attempt to put everyone around them in sacrifice. It is part of a control issue Entitleds need to be mindful of. It comes from wanting to know they can control everything including other people's emotions and the mood of the environment they are in. (Chapters 3, 7, 14-16)

11. If you had to pick either yourself or your partner, who is the "star" in your relationship?

The person who is the star is Entitled. This person has to be the center of attention and get what they want, when they want it. If you are both fighting to be the star that's a good indication of two Entitleds together. (Chapters 1-4, 11, 12)

12. Who has initiated your current or last few relationships?

The Entitled usually makes the introduction, carries the conversation, initiates the first kiss, sex for the first time etc. This also includes a person who is covertly manipulating a situation to get the other to take more initiative. (Chapters 1, 2, 7, 16)

13. Who usually gives in to the other during an argument?

This is usually the Support. It is important to note that, when someone gives into an argument, it very often is in support of the relationship, not in loss of the argument. Self-righteousness is a quality of a Selfish Entitled and is suffocating to a relationship. One of the many important lessons learned in a loving relationship is the value of moving off your position for the greater good of those involved. (Chapters 11, 12, 16, 17)

14. In order to get what you want, under what circumstances are you willing to lie, despite any recourse outside of yourself? (This could include anything that gets you what you want exclusively from an employer, business partner, investor, spouse, girlfriend, parents, friends, etc.)

Of course almost every person tells small lies on a daily basis. This is more aimed at lies that give a person an advantage over another and could disadvantage the other in some way. This is not a lie designed to protect yourself or someone else. When it comes to getting what they want, Entitleds are better liars and more apt to lie to get the result they need. It is a simple matter of thinking of oneself over another. Supports are not usually good liars unless they are lying for someone else. (Chapters 3, 5, 9, 15)

15. Everyone likes approval and recognition but how often do you go out of your way or try to impress others or seek recognition?

As part of being in the spotlight, Entitleds often think of ways in which they can win the approval or get recognition from others. This does have positive qualities to it and promotes success in every field. It becomes unhealthy when a person bases their happiness on recognition or does this outside of their primary relationship. For example, that would be a situation where a man is more interested in impressing someone more than his own wife. It is also unhealthy when someone grows tired of impressing people who they feel are already impressed with them and just move from one to the next desperately looking for more approval. This is often the case with cheaters. Supports often enjoy recognizing others equally or more than themselves. (Chapters 3, 5, 16)

16. How important is it that you have influence over other people's decisions?

Entitleds are more interested in having influence over other people and often get mad when their advice is not heeded. This surpasses influence and enters control. Selfish Entitleds are often controlling. Needing to be in control differs from offering an opinion or idea, which can be a healthy standpoint of either type. Blind Supports will often avoid giving an opinion out of fear of being wrong where as Entitleds will often give an opinion even when it is not invited.

These are not always questions you can honestly answer, so checking with trusted people around you for their unbiased honesty can be the best way to find out. Think of and ask about different situations. For example, with sex, do you sometimes tell your partner no to sex, just because you won't be in control of when it happens? After you tell them no and they accept, then do you want to have sex? This is typical behavior of someone who doesn't want to be controlled, and who wants to have control. Do you have to be in charge of what your loved one is doing while you are not there?

Another way to know how you feel about control is how easily you accept what is told to you about the way things have to be. Entitleds are challengers, especially to authority figures. Do you disregard what people say and think the rules don't apply to you?

This is what makes Entitleds move forward on their path, have follow through and vision. It is also why they behave argumentatively, get in trouble or disliked. Thinking of yourself makes you challenge others, not support them. When someone says something that is perceived as taking control away, Entitleds do not like it. When someone tells you that you cannot do something, what is your instinct about what they are saying? If your instinct is to prove them otherwise, you're most probably an Entitled. (Chapters 3, 11, 12, 14)

17. Do you often have the feeling you are missing out on something? That there is something better going on outside of where you are, or that you could do better in relationships, situations, work, fun, entertainment, etc.

Entitleds can often feel as if there is a better place for them to be. In relationships thinking that there is something better out there is abusive. This is the opposite of the support or care that a relationship requires. That is, unless thinking of a better place encourages one to exit an *abusive* relationship or work environment. Outside of that, a conscious practice of being in the moment will help you achieve happiness individually as well as in a relationship. (Chapters 5, 14, 16)

18. Do you find yourself criticizing many things or other people? Often thinking how you would have done it better.

This is Entitled. Supports see wrong and want to help or advise; they sincerely advise to benefit other people, not to make themselves look smart. Often when Entitleds are advising how they would have done things better, they are doing it to show how smart they are. There are clear differences between advice and criticism as well as when advice is welcomed versus inappropriate. These can be assessed through insight as to whether or not a person is ready, open or even interested in input from others. Advice is often encouraging while criticism is more often the opposite. (Chapters 3, 5, 11, 14)

19. Most of the time, do you truly listen to what others are saying, or are you just waiting to make your point?

Of course this will vary in different conversations, but the question is aimed at what you do under normal circumstances. Entitleds often just want to be heard or make a point; they are typically not very good listeners. People who are "know it alls," or experts at everything are in most cases Selfishly Entitled, or Support masquerading as Entitled. They are looking for recognition and will do anything to get it, in order to overcome their feelings of insecurity. Most of their actions are based on what they think people will think of them. One of the many problems with being around a person like this is they often have to make themselves appear to be smart by putting others down. If someone has deep-rooted insecurities about needing to prove their own intelligence, making others look dumb can be a main weapon in their arsenal. Any time you feel you need to prove yourself you are entering into Entitled behavior.

When in conversation, Supports are physically more animated. They want to make it clear that they are "with" you, showing you they are listening and supporting you. Supports are also highly intuitive about what other people are feeling without them having to say anything. Often they can feel people's emotions from across the room. Entitleds (especially Selfishly Entitled) are more likely to just wait to express the point they want to make without noticing the other person's body language. If you are upset, and yet tell an Entitled you are happy, he might just believe you. Selfish Entitleds often do not relate very well when you are having a difficult situation, but they want everyone to completely relate to them when they have one. (Chapters 1-4, 11, 16)

20. Have you tolerated abusive behavior in a relationship?

You must be careful as a Support about the type of relationships you attract because it is easier for your type to be bullied. Blind Supports are the people that are often receiving abuse. They usually will support anyone and everyone at any time; which is why they are so often taken advantage of. These are the people that go from one abusive relationship to another. Much of this is caused by an abusive childhood, which they are unknowingly trying to recreate because that is an environment in which they understand love. If you've even been a supporter of someone's negative pathologies or accept abuse, that usually indicates that you are a Support, and most probably in the subcategory of Blind Support. (Chapters 3-6, 11, 16)

Other Clues to a Person's Type

In figuring out what category you are, it is not so much what you do; it is the motivation behind the action. You could say someone who steals is totally Entitled and selfish. But then if you hear it is a woman who is broke, and has a husband in the hospital and has to feed him and her children, you can realize how something terrible such as stealing could be a supportive act. To put that into a more practical example, think about what motivates you in your day-to-day actions. Let's look at your motivations to get people to like you. Is it so that they will listen to you, or so that you can call on more people to do things with/for you? (Typically Entitled) Or is it because you feel you have protection knowing more people? (Typically Support) Is it so that when you are fighting with other people you then have more people to call upon to prove how well liked you are? (Typically Entitled) Is a desire to be popular designed to hide what a bad person you think you are? (Typically Entitled) Is it because without somehow helping people in your life you won't feel much contentment? (Typically Support)

It is difficult to say a particular action is either Entitled or Support until you know the real motivation behind it. That's why it is more important to know your strong and limiting attributes rather than exactly which type you are. This allows you to look for someone who complements you. Becoming more aware of your motivations rather than focusing on what you are doing is important in discovering your personality type.

Even simpler, do you generate change or do you generate supporting another's idea for change. Obviously, to live in this world you have to do both, so take it on a smaller level: In your intimate relationship, do you generate movement most of the time, or do you support the movement happening? Do you get in the way of movement? (That's two Entitleds together.) Do you want to generate movement but are too insecure to do that? (Entitled masquerading as a Support.) To answer these questions is one thing, but in real life, do you prefer to have someone else do something, but then you think, nobody else can do this right so I have to do it myself? (Entitled.)

Even simpler than this, with whoever you are partnered with, in relationship or at work, is it easier for you to guide or to be guided?

CHAPTER 9

ENTITLED MASQUERADING AS A SUPPORT

Why would an Entitled masquerade as a Support? There could be many reasons, but at the heart of them all is insecurity. Insecurity often dampens the drive in Entitleds, and could bring them to masquerade as a Support. Their drive evidences itself in small areas, for short periods of time, until the idea that they are undeserving of what they want to create prevails. This happens because they don't quite have the confidence to pursue their vision, or they may find themselves with someone who has a much stronger vision than theirs.

A person may also masquerade because they feel they need to submit to another Entitled to which they feel indebted. For example, if a woman feels she should serve her husband because he is paying all their bills, she may put her own needs aside.

Their insecurity may also lie in an area in which they have previously tried and failed. An Entitled I worked with named Jason tried to start a financial company on several occasions but failed. He later found employment in a high position for a company similar to the one he tried to start, with an abusive boss whom he disliked. He was given a good salary, but he carried a lot of resentment. This was partially due to the way his boss treated him and partly because his ideas were never being implemented. Jason kept up appearances because of the fear of losing his salary and the insecurity stemming from his past failures.

It would have been okay to work there if he liked his employer and had been giving the opportunity to follow through on his visions and create what he wanted with someone he respected. That would have been an environment where he had a creative outlet, less risk and could see his ideas to fruition. Instead, in this situation, he crossed the line from Entitled and masqueraded as a Support, building further resentment every day for his boss as well as his situation.

Of course, Jason's resentment affected his marriage as well. Because his ideas were not being implemented, my suggestion for Jason was to begin looking for a similar position with another company where he thought he could implement his ideas. If not, he would ruin his marriage and lead a very unsatisfying life. It took him over a year to find the position he wanted, but the search made him feel better because it provided hope that he was not trapped.

If an Entitled constantly finds that another person wants to change his vision, he should realize this is a common way in which their insecurity will find a scapegoat. An Entitled who doesn't believe in himself or his vision will have a pattern of this. Look back to see if you have a history of scapegoats. These are people or situations that always seem to get in the way of your vision. What did you do after your plan was not accomplished? Did you submit to another's vision, abandoning your own? Or did you alter your vision too greatly, to the point that it became something you didn't want? After that occurred, did you then masquerade as a Support, or did you jump to another vision, seek another scapegoat and repeat the offending pattern? A healthy Entitled would exit himself from a situation where a person is getting in the way of their vision. However, if they did not believe they could accomplish the vision or goal, that person or situation (the scapegoat) could be used as a perfect excuse why success was not obtained.

The struggling actor I mentioned earlier who was taking risks and following his vision, is an Entitled, but he had a strong belief that he could not make it as an actor. His wife, also Entitled, had a finance company and constantly took him off his path because she needed so much help and support. Leaving him little time for anything else, she provided a perfect excuse as to why he could not make it as an actor. He was always quick to say how successful he would have been if not for having to be a good husband. We found out this had been a pattern for him: to date women who got in the way of what he wanted to accomplish, while he masqueraded as a Support to them. To remedy this, we worked out clear times where his wife was not permitted to ask him for anything so that he could no longer use her as an excuse not to follow his vision and find success.

Masquerading could also occur because the Entitled has been around stronger Entitleds for a prolonged period of time. For example, a person who grew up with an older sibling could have been kept from pursuing his or her own visions. This could also be the effect of an overbearing parent. How many people do things just because their parents want them to? These Supports also typically end up with Selfish Entitleds later in life as friends, intimate partners, or employers, because they are accustomed to giving in to stronger personalities. As much as they might not like certain aspects of the Selfishly Entitled, they are also inspired by their follow through, drive, risk taking and their lack of concern for people not liking them.

The insecurity could show up in any way. For example, people find excuses as to why they can't be married, can't start a business on their own, can't raise a family, can't write a book, etc. This could all lead to getting on board with another Entitled's vision and supporting it when what they really want to pursue their own vision. This isn't to say that everyone who has had the idea to pursue something and didn't is masquerading as a Support. That said, insecurity could cause excuses to take hold and a masquerade to happen. If you are fulfilled in Support even though you feel that you really are an Entitled, then no change is necessary. The contentment you feel can override the category, because the point is to find that feeling. However, you want to avoid becoming unduly resentful towards someone.

Most people give many signs of who they are and what you can expect from them. Entitleds often project the idea that others will be doing things their way. Supports advertise that they want leadership. Entitleds masquerading as a Support actually look to give a different feeling for themselves than what is naturally there for them. So instead of giving the impression others will be doing things their way or from their leadership, they actually put out a feeling that they are looking for leadership. This eventually makes a turnaround if they build enough resentment, realize a lack of contentment or get in touch with their own leadership.

There is a big difference between an Entitled jumping the line to *give* support and an Entitled *masquerading* as a Support. Support is given out of love, generosity or appreciation. Masquerading is fueled by pathology, fear, insecurity, or worry that without giving that support they will lose something. They appear to be graciously offering help, but they are in reality covering up deeper feelings of unworthiness. Entitleds who give support make no mistake about who they are. The masqueraders actually want to be perceived as always being supportive. Instead of saying what they feel or acting for self, they act like something they are not.

This is different from an Entitled that has a lesser vision for the same goal with a partner they are supporting. This person will still act Entitled, speaking their mind, expressing disagreements, showing leadership and pursuing their vision while realizing his partner's more clear or experienced vision and leadership. This Entitled with the lesser vision will however be expecting respect as another Entitled with a vision. Supports often do not say what is on their mind because of a fear of confrontation or abandonment, especially Blind Supports; masqueraders often mimic this fear. If the masquerader would show his true self as an Entitled, they fear they might lose their job, financial protection or whatever they have gained by masquerading to begin with.

If this is confusing and you are still having trouble identifying what a masquerader is and why, think back to your teen years or early twenties. Many people in their teens to early twenties are often masquerading, though it may not be from being an Entitled to a Support. They often have strong desires to get things their ego wants or strong insecurity based on fear of never getting what they want. At this age, people are also concerned with what their peers think, instigating more insecurity. Allowing the masquerade often creates situations that you would not find yourself in otherwise. That is why during this age, people find themselves in situations they do not repeat at any other age.

We've all heard of stories where a successful CEO of a large corporation worked as a gas station attendant for a month in his twenties before he got his life in order. Or how someone was strung up from drugs before they had an "awakening." Neither was fulfilling their vision because of insecurities. These years often are times to experiment and gather information on what you want, based on what you do *not* want. Often a self-realization of a masquerade is identified with such strong negative emotions that the person never returns to the masquerade later in life.

Entitleds could also find themselves in temporary Support positions, chasing their vision while supporting others until they are able to do what they want exclusively. For example, a waiter whose vision is to one day be an artist could be supporting something that he feels is more important than his ultimate goal. Financial support for his children or support for a spouse's project he believes in at the present, more so than his own could delay his desires. People in circumstances such as this could be putting their vision off to a later date when they feel they would be more equipped to fulfill it. This is not truly a masquerader because they are still pursuing the visions and goals important to them. They are also choosing to cross the line with purpose and are not particularly those who need to learn not to masquerade. They are justified in crossing the line.

Masqueraders can be risk takers who like to protect themselves with another Entitled that they feel will save them if their risk goes bad. For example, if a person wants to take a financial risk where he puts all his money into a business that may or may not be successful, it will be easier for him if he is in a relationship with someone who has financial security in case success is not achieved. His true Entitlement will often be revealed, often as resentment, if his success is not achieved. On the other hand, if he does have success, he might leave the person that backed him.

As an Entitled, jumping the line is often manipulative with an expectation of something in return. If you are interested in reforming, you need to realize your responsibilities as an Entitled.

What exactly are you trying to gain in the manipulation? If you are looking to attract another Entitled by jumping the line to a Support, once you start to act like your natural self, the relationship is doomed. If it is a Support you are pursuing, they would rather see your leadership and vision as an Entitled; and a Reformed Support would never fall for the routine. Setting the right tone for a relationship prevents problems in the future. If someone is acting Supportive when he is really an Entitled and choosing Entitled partners, the mask may start to crack if they have a time limit on their goals. For example, a woman who wants to get married by age thirty and is with a guy for three years who has no interest in marriage will break out of her Supportive shell. She will become more interested in thinking of herself, feeling she has wasted too much time with him.

Almost all of the Entitleds I have met that are masquerading as Supports have a strong desire for everyone to like them. They are very concerned with what people think of them. They are very charming when they meet people, and they know how to get people to like them. They often suppress their anger and can be subtly manipulative. Their type of manipulation goes unnoticed mostly because they do not appear to be connected to an outcome. (It should be mentioned, however, that their manipulation doesn't necessarily carry bad intentions or ill will, even if it may turn out that way in the end.) Their anger suppression causes outbursts when they get mad enough, but this is a surprise to the people around them because it happens so infrequently. They are experts at keeping their public appearances looking good.

When an Entitled gets angry, they don't try to hide it, but for Entitleds masquerading as a Support the bad temper can go unnoticed. The masquerade will often be noticed when the masquerader is in an argument or fight. Once evoked or emotionally engaged, they have a difficult time keeping up the masquerade. They lose the desire to be liked by the person they are arguing with. When the disagreement is over, however, they will usually have regrets and want to be back in the good graces of the person they were fighting with, especially if that person can ruin the offender's reputation. This goes back to them needing everyone to like them. Their utmost concern is what people think of them. They even want people they dislike to like them.

Further examples of how Masquerading such as this could occur can easily be found within a person's childhood. Often as children, we are taught to absorb our anger. We are not allowed to express ourselves and even have to apologize for our emotional outbursts. Many times, the result of this is turning the anger inward. We start believing that anger is a "bad" emotion. We tell ourselves we are bad, unworthy, a terrible person. We can move towards self-loathing because of these judgments. This could force a person to have an unnecessary need to prove to everyone that they are not bad, unworthy, and most of all, that they are not angry. Deep down, they suffer from what they wish to keep a secret, an unshakable conviction that there is something wrong with them that they should be ashamed of.

They could become compliant, submissive, and will generally do what they are told. In the meantime, they build anger and resentment, continuing with the habit of turning their frustration inward and creating more self-loathing. This sets up the potential for abuse. That is, until one day there is the eruption of the volcano. The resentment held from childhood is included in the explosion. The years of mounting abuse will be turned on anyone in this person's path and that person is then the abuser, until the guilt sets in, which then allows this person to accept more abuse. This cycle runs its course mostly in primary intimate relationships.

Children who are not permitted to express themselves often learn that expression of emotions is needy and unattractive, damaging their self-worth. This can translate into adult life as a person who avoids painful decisions or encounters, i.e., not taking risks, avoiding confrontation, not asking for what they deserve and not walking away from abusive relationships.

The process could look something similar to this: *I want/need to be liked. I have to be nice to be liked. I cannot be angry if I want people to like/accept me. Nice people are not angry and do not have hate in them.* The idea is to be supportive enough and liked enough to get their parent to love them as a child, and that responsibility is seamlessly carried over into their adult relationships, especially with their lover, but the process can be inclusive of everyone they meet. Remedying this requires self-approval. This is called Repetition Compulsion, further defined in chapter sixteen.

Other typical behavior could be that they need to do everything and excel at everything that the person they are with can do. This is part of wanting people to like them. If the person they are with is good at a certain sport, then they need to be good at that sport. When they exit that relationship, then the next person they are with may be good at music or any other hobby, or even just watching football, so they will become an expert at that. They will surprise people with how easily they are able to become knowledgeable or skilled in a new area. Their true Entitled personality carries a lot of drive and talent and once they have a vision to follow someone in a specific area, they will prosper.

A woman I worked with named Nicole, who was an Entitled masquerading as a Support, dated a professional motocross rider. In just one year, Nicole became a competing motocross rider herself. After they split, she then dated a musician and learned to play the guitar very well. Once they split, she started to realize she had many visions of her own, but she kept getting caught up in other people's visions. She had successes but didn't get the satisfaction she wanted out of them.

If you recognize yourself as an Entitled masquerading as a Support, the first step to making choices for yourself and your happiness is to stop worrying about what everyone thinks of you. How much work do you put into trying to get people to like you? What is your motivation? You do not need to include everyone in your life, especially people you do not particularly like. When you are taking actions to portray a certain image, it drains time and energy from what you really want to do in your life.

Entitleds masquerading as Support are afraid to be alone. I recommend that these masqueraders, as well as the Supports who can't make decisions on their own, take a weekend trip alone, in order to get in touch with their Entitlement. It is a good practice to let go of your addictions to needing people to like you. You can learn to be comfortable being alone. Take some time to analyze what relationships you currently have which are abusive, potentially abusive or do not bring positive energy to your life. Then ask yourself, are they that important for me to have, or do I keep them based on some insecurity, fear or pathology?

When in this situation, you also have to be aware of the negative things you tell yourself that fuel the insecurity. The conversation going on in your mind needs to be changed for a more positive outcome. For example:

1. Instead of telling yourself that you cannot make it on your own, look for evidence of successes you have had and stop dismissing them. This will allow you to change the way you speak to yourself and have the confidence to know you can obtain your goals.

2. Instead of dismissing your talents and skills, appreciate your proclivities in even the smallest of areas, even

if they don't interest you anymore. Know yourself and what you are capable of, instead of just focusing on your shortcomings. Accept compliments to heart instead of just the criticism.

3.   Instead of pointing out why you do not deserve what you want, realize the ways in which you deserve it more than many people who already have what you want. Be aware of how responsible you are with the good things you have acquired in your life. Know that it is human nature to receive as well as it is to give and you cannot give anything unless you receive. You must practice the balance. All of this includes gratitude and appreciation of what you have accomplished, even though you may not think of it as anything special.

4.   Instead of thinking that you can't do something without a certain, impossible resource outside of yourself, know that if you need to, you can do it on your own. Also know that if you do need something outside of yourself, then that resource will be presented to you. That may be a person, a teacher, a book, an employee, or money. Know that when you are ready, the lack of resources cannot stop you unless you allow it to. You have all the evidence of this that you need; you just need to stop ignoring it and dismissing your successes as isolated coincidences.

If you are masquerading either as an Entitled to Support or vice versa, look at the deeper question of why you feel you need to do this. What is your fear? Why don't you love yourself for who you are? How long will you keep this up? How much more destruction are you going to cause in another person's life? How can someone fall in love with you, when they don't know the real you?

Look to see other places where you are manipulating others. Every time you alter a story to make yourself sound better by making someone else a little less, who are you hurting? Why is it so important to hurt them in order to bring yourself up? Is the person you are trying to impress really that important? How many more artificial relationships are you interested in creating? Is the damage you are doing to others so beneficial that it is worth hurting them? At what point will you realize that maturity will benefit you more than the artificial relationships you have been creating? Being responsible enough to see yourself in this masquerade is a huge step in the right direction. Even though it may take time to get to where you are happier, knowing this, you are already halfway there. Let time take its course. Be patient and content with your process of realizing your self-worth.

Qualities of Entitleds who masquerade as a Support:

- Insecurity in obtaining goals.
- Unfulfilled in pursuing another's vision.
- Fear of confrontation.
- Fear of abandonment.
- Fear of unworthiness.
- Need for people to like them.
- Fear of having enemies.
- Repressed anger.
- Conflict avoiders.

CHAPTER 10

SUPPORT MASQUERADING AS AN ENTITLED

Just like in the case of Entitleds masquerading as Supports, shame, insecurity, and fear are strong factors contributing to why someone would masquerade as an Entitled. But often this false façade happens from Support to Entitled when someone feels a need for self-protection. Many of the people in this category could easily be described as arrogant, but all the while they are in reality covering up an insecurity that has led them to adopt this unnatural masquerade. Supports masquerading as Entitleds have the feeling that they are alone in the world. In relationships, they are worried they are going to be hurt again, so they use Entitlement as a defense not to let people in.

Entitleds masquerading as Supports, detailed in the previous chapter, may go unnoticed because of their desire to be liked by people and a seemingly subtle nature. Supports masquerading as Entitleds, on the other hand, can be easily noticed as trying to be something they are not. There are various reasons someone would masquerade like this. They could be naturally supportive, but come from such an abusive environment, that in order to protect themselves, they act Entitled. When two Supports are together, one may feel the need to take the lead, but the unnatural leadership position is very stressful to them. This person might lead with anger or frustration, instead of from a place of support, where they are most comfortable. Sometimes, when Supports cannot find an Entitled who has the vision they believe in, or if someone is rejected by the Entitled they wish to support, they create their own false Entitlement. In this case, it often looks like resentment, or someone trying to prove him or herself.

Supports could find themselves masquerading as Entitled when they are young (thirty and under), because they have not yet found, or are too immature to find, the right mate or career. When a person is unfulfilled by not finding contentment in their path, they may find pathologies such as anger, rage, and frustration easier to lead with. This phase is okay for a person to go through, as long as they recognize they are not acting as their true self. From this position they will have a harder time finding their true self, or any fulfillment under the masquerade. Resentment can build here too, like a great dancer who cannot find the right partner to dance with.

Fear of Loss

Many times Supports who masquerade as Entitleds believe people would think less of them if they lost something, and they become insecure about losing that thing, whether it is respect, money, a position, fame, etc. Anytime someone is masquerading, they are concerned with what people think of them. In this case, it is as if they have a secret that they are afraid people are going to discover. They feel that they are not as smart, well trained, wealthy, successful, knowledgeable, or powerful as people think they are. They are worried about losing the thing that makes them accepted. People like this worry they are going to be discovered a fraud at any moment, so they have to be on the defensive to prove they are what they pretend to be. They play a role in order to live up to perceived expectations of others. Spoiled, not on a fulfilling path, and angry at the world, they often take their frustrations out on others. People who get a lot of cosmetic surgeries often fall into this category because they are trying to keep up with the image they think others have attributed to them.

If you find yourself in this position, instead of worrying that you could lose something, look at what it took to get to that point. In general, the people who do not acknowledge the work they did, or do not respect what they did to get something are the ones worried about losing what they have. They think they got lucky, or could not re-create the path again. It is also very rare to have to start from zero if you did lose your safety net. If you feel this way, ask yourself, *If the people in my life would not respect or love me without it, why do I want them in my life?*

There are a lot of unpleasant results that come from masquerading. I worked with a woman named Alisha who was masquerading as Entitled because she was insecure about who she was and thought she was too plain to be accepted as herself. She felt acting Entitled added drama and excitement to her life. She caused drama in order to feel like she was important to people, to show that she mattered, and to prove she was "someone" to them. She was protecting herself from a fear of not mattering to anyone and using drama to prove she did. The drama took up so much time and energy in her life, she had not had a successful relationship in some time and couldn't hold a job long enough to feel secure in business either. This had to do with pathologies she learned very young through the emotional abandonment of her parents. Similar to a Selfish Entitled, she was good at making friends, but not good at holding on to them or developing real relationships.

It is very important to know when and if you are masquerading. In the beginning of a relationship, people often get caught up in obtaining a specific result, such as keeping the relationship going. Because they want it to work so much they do not realize they are in survival mode and are not acting like themselves. They might be playing the opposite role that is natural for them, just to make the other person happy.

Often a person is attracted to an Entitled, but after they are together as a couple, they try to change them to act as a Support. After they have changed them, many times they no longer feel the attraction they once did. This happens when a person is chasing a childhood pathology rather than a genuine relationship. It is also important to realize if you are a person who does this know that in the end, it only creates more problems. On the other hand, if someone is trying to change a Support to an Entitled, the new role will cause the Support a lot of anxiety and undue pressure trying to live up to the demands placed on them. As explained in chapter 17, they can work to take on some of the positive qualities of the category not typical to them but to change completely will often cause a lack in fulfillment.

Masquerading is very different than a Support jumping the line to offer genuine leadership. Most Supports offer Entitlement in at least some areas. I even like to call some of the people I've consulted on this, "Entitled in their Support." They are so confident in their support of their boss or spouse that they feel no one aside from them, is better suited to support that person. The difference between them and those masquerading is that they don't try to overcompensate with rudeness or other insecure actions in order to prove themselves. A masquerader of Entitlement feels as

169

if they cannot show any side of themselves that is not a leader (or what they perceive of as a leader). They often create confrontation to prove they are not afraid of confrontation.

Qualities of Support Masquerading as Entitled:

- A need for self-protection.

- A feeling others would not believe in them, or would think they are "weak," if they acted like themselves.

- A position of having to pretend that they have it all under control at all times. (Leaders don't mind asking for help or admitting that they are out of their league. The Support masquerading as Entitled is too insecure to admit that.)

- A need for people to think they are abundant in something – power, money, knowledge, respect, etc.

- A fear that others will discover their insecurity, so they overcompensate. This could manifest itself in the need to always be right.

- A tendency to exaggerate about themselves. Their attitude is the opposite of modesty.

- A general lack of contentment in who they have become.

- An issue with unworthiness or abandonment.

What Do You Do if You Have the Qualities of a Masquerader?

To start, appreciate and respect the people around you that help you and offer support to get what you want. Masqueraders often show a lack of appreciation because they think they might lose something if they tell these people how valuable they are to them. They think if they show appreciation to the people around them, others might think they do not have to do as good a job because they are doing enough to get their gratitude. This has been proven to be false in almost all cases. People respond better to positive affirmation.

If you trusted everyone around you, would you be happier? Instead of constantly needing support, how will giving support make you feel better about yourself? Can you still achieve your objectives? Is there someone trustworthy around you that has a vision for you in which you could support? Be careful to choose someone worthy of your trust because you are allowing them to have a vision for you greater than your own and following the steps they think would achieve that. The misconception a masquerader has about trust is that they think people will not respect them, or will take advantage of them if they offer support. This self-protection occurs from supporting the wrong person in the past and not wanting to repeat the same mistake.

Appropriate Times to Jump the Line

When a Support is being abused, and doesn't separate, the reason it is difficult for them to get out of the relationship is because they are too deeply rooted in the Support mind-set. They are unnecessarily supporting the abuser or the relationship. The fear of something, such as abandonment or unworthiness, is acting as a psychosis to keep them in a bad situation or to provide support to whoever wants it. They could also be supporting society's idea that this is the "right thing to do." It would be more appropriate in this situation to jump the line and become more in touch with their Entitled side, to gain a clearer vision of what is better for them, even temporarily. Sometimes it is important to think more of yourself and the happiness you desire rather than the reasons to support a relationship, especially if the person you are supporting is irresponsible. Supports often suffer more during a break-up especially if they make their life about the relationship and no longer themselves. A trusted and compassionate Entitled will keep his Support partner from moving into codependence.

I've heard that when Eddie Murphy got turned down by *Saturday Night Live* after his first audition, instead of being upset or depressed, he thought, "Wow, these idiots don't have any idea what they're doing." He was completely Entitled in his confidence. He had a vision that couldn't be broken. The next year he got on the show. It is obvious, however, if he hadn't, he would still have been successful because of his unwavering vision. His Entitlement protected him from failure and extreme upset. This is the type of Entitlement that is okay to get in touch with instead of supporting something unfavorable to you, like an abusive relationship. If Eddie Murphy was depressed over not making his first audition, he may have diverted from his path and left acting. It is the same with exiting an unfavorable relationship. It is better to get in touch with your Entitlement, instead of supporting a relationship that no longer serves both parties.

Another appropriate time for a Support to jump the line is when that person is not in a relationship with an Entitled but is seeking to follow through on some goal. If a single Support is looking to create a business, get in a relationship, or has a desire to aggressively pursue something, they need to get in touch with their Entitled side. Most relationships have started because of an Entitled aggressively pursuing their vision, whether it is in business, an intimate relationship or a personal goal. Without that self-interest there would be nothing. When a Support is alone, they need to assume the role of Entitled as well. Without both, they run the risk of not following through and losing opportunities presented to them. The bottom line is: when you want something, get in touch with your vision of it, your desire, your deserving of it, and your self-interest in receiving it. Then pursue it with all your Entitlement available.

CHAPTER 11

GETTING ALONG TOGETHER - ENTITLED AND SUPPORT

PART I - Introduction to Getting Along

The following chapter is designed as a road map for getting along. Broken into three parts, it will be helpful to reference it whenever you feel lost and want to positively change the dynamic of your relationship. It should be read by both partners, and referenced when needed, even if both don't read the entire book. It will be helpful in finding harmony when both partners are committed to using it. (More on this and other ideas for finding harmony are discussed at *www.TheArtOfUnity.com*).

There are certain traits that are typically more prominent in one category than another. Not understanding these traits can limit a relationship, but they can especially hold back personal growth. The traits I'm speaking of are the negative ones that come up when a person is engaged in an argument or fearful over something. An important part of knowing who you are, is being aware of your negative traits and when they surface. This can also help you find a partner who can complement you in your growth, whether an intimate relationship, friends, employees, etc.

Communicating from Support better promotes compassion and harmony in an argument or negotiation. To fight from pure Entitlement constricts things to yourself and not the shared relationship. Communicating from Entitlement normally involves thinking about what is best for you or your ego over anyone else. It includes reacting, defending, yelling, belittling, insulting, manipulating, pointing out you are right, and not seeing any other side or having compassion for others. It disassociates any partnership agreement and enforces only the self. The more reactive you are in an argument, the more ego-driven you are, and the less chance you have of a satisfying resolution. Unfortunately, the first place people often go when put on the defensive is this reactionary place, and it brings people the furthest apart from resolution. It is where many people fight from when they don't communicate well.

When a disagreement comes up, ask yourself if you are being Reactive or Proactive? *Am I leading, or am I just fighting?* When you fight, it is better to speak with your focus on the commitments you have for harmony rather than typical reactive behavior. Ask yourself, based on the way you are speaking, *is this the man/woman I want to be?*

Also speak to your partner's commitments rather than their behavior. If you know they are committed to the relationship, you can respond rationally without worrying that your differing opinion will drive them away. When you know you are acting responsibly and are grounded in your position, as well as have the best interests of both of you in mind, there is no need for aggression.

Is conflict part of a loving relationship? Of course! The only people who never have conflict are afraid of it and avoid it unnaturally. If we were able to split ourselves in two, we would have conflict with ourselves. In fact, we don't even have to split ourselves; almost every person I've ever met has tons of conflict within themselves. The conflicts within ourselves come out in all negative emotions: anger, fear, anxiety, guilt, unhappiness— and anything other than absolute love.

If you add another person to this, of course there is going to be conflict, so don't fear it. You can try to run from it, but it will just be there in the next relationship. The only thing you can plan for is how to respect and care for one another despite the conflict. If you learn one thing from this book, it should be that we are absolutely different from each other, yet absolutely need one another, and thus the source of the conflict. Our brains are wired differently, but we require connection. The good news is, when you operate in your conflicts through love and respect of one another, it creates more intimacy, more connection, more understanding and more oneness. This requires respect for your partner shown simply by listening, but what often gets in the way of this is the tone of voice in which each person responds to the other, making it worse. Conflict, if handled properly, is good! It creates solutions; unresolved conflict is what causes escalating problems.

Blind Supports are anxious about conflict and think of it as the enemy. Selfish Entitleds overcompensate by conflicting with everyone around them to prove they don't mind conflict and won't be controlled. Neither is healthy. Someone who explodes has a fear of conflict, because they let their anxiety build up so much that it is only recognized when they erupt.

Love, trust and respect must be ever-present in any argument, fight or conflict between intimate partners. Think of the typical actions of an average couple in a fight. They deflect, avoid, change subjects, lie, attack, manipulate, blame, accuse, overpower, yell, insult and more. On the other hand, they almost never admit wrong, show vulnerability, listen, try to understand and have compassion, or investigate how they are wrong or could help the other person. What are the results? A lack of intimacy, emotional abandonment, poor or no communication, anger, rage, frustration, fear and insecurity; The rate of separation and discontent amongst people who were once devoted to one another is still souring! This is a pretty good indication that it is time to try something new, including the opposite of what your fight or flight instincts tell you.

The first thing is to realize that you have reflexes and finding harmony means learning to control them.

- Tolerate your partner's emotions without involving your own.

- Find compassion. Anger usually comes from hurt, hurt comes from sensitivity, and sensitivity comes from love. So anger is a form and expression of love. That is, if the relationship is healthy. This requires trust and responsibility of both partners.

PART - II - How Is All This Done?

Of course this isn't easy even when your intention is to follow these guidelines. Lets break down a bigger path as to how it can all be done.

Care in Crossing the Line

During an argument, fight, or negotiation, Supports should be aware of inappropriately jumping the line to their Entitled side; and Entitleds should make an effort to jump to Support. If Entitleds are not in support, then they should be providing care in order to further expand the relationship. If you question your motivations, this will create awareness of where your commitment lies.

- Does your commitment lie in yourself, or the relationship?

- Are you committed to being right, or being understanding and compassionate?

- Is your creativity committed to understanding the other, or is it being used for manipulation? (Desire to manipulate occurs when you are not interested in what someone is requesting of you but only getting what you want. It is also bad for both parties: neither is getting what they want in the way they want it.)

- Are you committed to being heard, or to both you and your partner expressing your ideas? Do you just want to speak, or is it important that even if you can't agree on a point you listen and respect one another's point of view?

For those who have identified themselves as potentially accepting of abuse:

- Are you committed to your self-respect and what you deserve? Or to avoiding confrontation at the cost of your happiness.

- Are you committed to optimistically finding the partners you want, or are you stuck in a belief that you cannot change anything for the better?

When a Support is crossing the line to Entitled to fight, their head is not in a place to make any important decisions and they may say something they regret later. This is not to say that anger should not be expressed, especially in the case of Supports, but abuse of the other person should be avoided. Often when you go from a natural Support and jump the line to Entitled, it is a reactionary defense mechanism. If this happens or you are easily frustrated, it is likely you are unhappy with the situation you are in, rather than the incident you are reacting to. You might want to look at why you are being defensive and how often that happens. For example, if it is an intimate relationship, is there a lack of trust or a feeling of uneven exchange? Do you feel that you give more than you get in return? Do you feel as though you deserve more? Getting in touch with what your expectations are and communicating them to your partner is suggested before resentment builds.

Supports looking to evolve towards reform and create great relationships discuss these things with their Entitled partners. Reformed Supports realize they have the potential for accepting abuse and that the abuse only becomes more intense if not stopped along the path. Jumping the line to fight from an unnatural place of Entitlement is a good indicator something is wrong. More possibilities for this could include unexpressed anger, anxiety, rage, or a need for protection or manipulation. Crossing the line to Entitled in an intimate relationship too quickly could also mean that the person is putting the responsibility of the issues with their parents onto their partner. "Too quickly" means at the first notice of something wrong, without any warning the Support suddenly reacts with rage or anger. You can tell this based on how personally they take things, or how angry small things make them. Awareness as to why a person would react this way should be explored.

Importance of Who to Choose as Your Partner

Open and proper communication with trust in one another's intentions is the key to respectful disagreements. If there is something happening, or not happening, that the person doesn't like, they need to know they can address it. A pattern of anger and abuse will continue to repeat itself from one relationship to the next if unchecked. Supports need to learn to fight from a Support standpoint because they are most comfortable there. Unless it is warranted by a *need* for self-protection from abuse, not just an unreal fear, Supports will be more effective in their natural role of Support during an argument, and that requires trust in a responsible partner.

It is important to choose a trustworthy partner to foster your own personal growth. You want a partner who is moving towards reform. Your trust should only be placed in this type of person, and all this work is based on them being trustworthy. Reformed Supports only have people in their lives they know not to be abusive. Knowing this, they are confident enough to be vulnerable, not feeling a need to defend themselves. Instead, they can fight for the relationship. The Reformed Support will also surrender when they feel defensive and communicate that. They can speak of how they feel about the situation rather than counterattack.

If the other person (Entitled) continues the attack, the Reformed Support recognizes this as abuse and exits themselves from the situation and possibly the relationship. If the Entitled is not protecting the Support, then the Support has to protect him- or herself, diminishing their ability to support. Entitleds should recognize how difficult a time they have continuing to care for someone when they are emotionally engaged. Evolution means getting over the fears and insecurities you were taught by your parents, who were in turn taught by their parents. Entitleds trying to control or manipulate a person or an argument instead of allowing open expression is the opposite of evolution. This is part of the care or protection Reformed Entitleds offer. Entitleds need to accept responsibility. When a Reformed Entitled has people around him who are unhappy or unexpressed, they are open to their communication. As an Entitled, you can be prone to want attention, drama, chaos, conspiracy, and more. None of this is transformative, evolved or reformed. This neediness should be dismantled. Supports should be aware of this and not give in to it.

Consideration with Your Emotional Energy

In the same way two people rowing a boat can feel any subtle change in the other's energy level, people in an intimate relationship can feel one another's change in energy or love towards one another. Supports can be prone to take on Entitled's problems, desires, and frustrations, as well as their happiness. If the Entitled is upset, the Support becomes upset; if he is happy, they are happy. This occurs to Supports not just in intimate relationships but also with friends, employers, and family. Reformed Entitleds have a keen sense for this and are responsible to not complain or create unnecessary negative emotions that can bring Supports down. Being responsible to the sensitivity of your partner includes being upfront about why your energy is down, so your partner does not take it to mean they did something wrong. Reformed Entitleds know that Supports are eager to know when they are happy, so that they can enjoy the same positive mood. This is a way to show appreciation for them.

For the Support, the negative sensitivity and acceptance can be dangerous because it creates a certain outer dependency and victimization. It also is associated with looking for constant approval instead of getting that from within. Like children who feel they have done something wrong, Blind Supports and some Constructive Supports wonder what they have done when their moody partners are upset. Often it is just the Entitled's own issues. If the Entitled is taking advantage and manipulating the

Support as a way of non-verbal communication, the Support needs to recognize it.

If you identify yourself as a Support, and are unhappy, look at the people around you. Are they happy? How much of your unhappiness have you absorbed from them? This acceptance of energy can be from your parents, siblings, business or intimate partners, or friends. If you are not the source of your own unhappiness, then you need to identify where your unhappiness is being absorbed from and change the connection, or eliminate those people from your life. Let go of the people or even places that are unsatisfying, and stop supporting them to pursue your own happiness. Reformed Supports use unhappiness as a trigger to identify discontentment in others around them. They know as a Support it is challenging to be happy with unhappy people around them.

Offer Appreciation

For both Entitleds and Supports, if you are *not* offering appreciation to your partner or someone around you, ask yourself:

- Is it because they actually don't deserve it? This being the case, then figure out why you are with them. If you don't come up with a satisfactory answer, request changes in the relationship to have what you desire, or exit the relationship.

- Is it because you are afraid they will have some sort of control over you? If you acknowledge a favor they did for you, will you now owe them one? If this is the case, then that fear of it being thrown back at you somehow should be expressed to them.

- Is it because you are afraid they will expect something of you? This should also be expressed. If it is true, then they should be told you will not accept any undue expectations.

- Is it that you are afraid they are doing more for the relationship? Do you think showing appreciation will reveal this to them? If this is the case, then surely showing them appreciation is recommended—because not showing it will actually be what tips them off to your feelings, not the other way around.

- Is it because you are just being lazy? In this case, you are probably taking your partner for granted. The idea is that they will be there no matter what, so why should you put forth the effort of appreciation? This is the fastest way to make others and yourself unhappy and should be recognized and changed as quickly as possible.

If you don't actually have any appreciation for your partner or people around you, then exiting those relationships is recommended, or find a reason to appreciate them. You can bet they already know you don't appreciate them, and the relationship is already becoming abusive in some way. Appreciation should be expressed, no matter what the cost to your own pride and ego. It is the glue that binds good relationships and always will be. Recognizing this can save a bad relationship and create more good ones.

As a matter of appreciation and preventing disagreements a Support can ask their partner, "What can I do or what have I done that has made you feel I am supporting you?" An Entitled can ask, "How can I make you feel more protected or cared for?" This can also be used to start a conversation to get what you want while avoiding unsolicited advice of how they should be treating you. Also note that the answer can change with evolution, time, day, mood, so be open to changing your acceptance of the answer.

Play Your Role in the Relationship

When a Support asks an Entitled, "What do you want to do?" they are opening the door for you to give your opinion, so they can grab on to something. They are pleased to do what you want, so giving them a clear vision, even at the simplest level, will allow them to offer their ideas.

Entitleds can request, "I want to have dinner here, then drinks here, and wake up at eight am and go to breakfast here, etc." After being specific, an Entitled should be open to their Support's input in order to share ideas so that the experience will be an enjoyable time for both parties. Create the vision and let them fill in the spaces. Then share your happiness with them, for they will absorb that from you. This is a way of taking care of them and letting them know they are supporting someone who cares for them. Supports often wait before giving ideas until they know what their Entitleds' intentions are, so they are not supporting something different.

With two Entitleds together, instead of asking what the other wants to do, one of them should offer an idea important to them with openness to doing something else. If the other Entitled does not agree, figure out whose vision seems more important. They will have to take turns realizing their visions, or else the neglected party gets burned out, and then resentful. As stated, this will be challenging, but if they have respect for one another, it can be done happily.

Intimacy within Conversation

Genuine intimacy requires complete honesty and absolute trust. Trust is needed so that neither person is hiding anything from the other. If a person has the feeling that something they want to tell the other will be taken offensively, then it won't be said. People who lead with trust have the ability to laugh at themselves and are able to create a high level of intimacy. When you can be honest with someone at the deepest level, then nothing needs to be said, that is trust.

You may have experienced a level of intimacy with someone you love where nothing needed to be said, yet the intimacy is felt by both. Language is needed so that our egos can express themselves. Silence is the highest level of intimacy, but it requires absolute trust as well as absence from fears and insecurities. When you have this level of trust, every word matters. If you want this level of trust in an intimate relationship, be mindful as to what you say. Sarcasm and jokes designed to playfully instigate your partner do not work because security in relationships is always unpredictable, and sarcasm can be taken to heart and undermine the trust you're trying to create.

If you don't have exactly what you want now, then different actions from what you have been doing to get you here need to be taken. As part of the first step in attracting what you want, be as clear and specific as possible with yourself about what you want. If you don't know exactly what you want, then that is a good sign as to why you are not getting it. If you want a great relationship, think about the actions or things you are about to do or say to your partner and first ask yourself, "Does this statement or action promote the healthy, creative relationship that I want?" This makes you responsible for allowing the great things you want to come to you. People who expect to have great health don't eat everything they want to eat and people in great relationships don't say everything that comes into their mind. There is a balance and you need to judge between feeling 100 percent expressed and what is not as important for you to say to a person you know loves you. If you feel tension in a relationship and you are not fighting at all, that means one or both of you are not expressing yourselves; if you are always fighting, it means one or both of you are not listening. When you are confused about what to say, the communication exercises coming up will give you insight as to how to say it.

There are many important reasons to have open communication, some obvious and some not. If you do not express your fears or insecurities the other person is left to interpret what is behind your communication. For example, if someone is protecting you, and they ask you to walk on a different street than you normally walk, you could accept this in many different ways. It could make you feel wonderful that they care enough to tell you, or it could make you feel that they think you are an idiot, or that they want to control you. Expressing where and why you are vulnerable increases the intimacy in any relationship.

Telling others how you feel will get you more of what you want and less of what you don't. If you tell a person what makes you feel special, this indicates to them what you want. If you tell them what makes you feel like an idiot, they can either explain why they said the offensive remark, speak differently to you, or no longer offer you something you do not require from them. Not communicating your appreciation can also stop inspiring people from telling you things you want to hear. Appreciation is also something to ask for if you are not getting it, as opposed to complaining about it. The quickest way to inspire people to give you what you want is to give it back to them.

Why We Blame Others

When arguing, instead of listening and looking to reach an agreement, learning from the experience or evolving in any way, people often look for anything they can find to satisfy their need to be right. The objective in a fight is often to imply that the other person is wrong and responsible for the problem. This takes away personal responsibility.

Too often when a person feels they are not going to "win" an argument, they try to get out of the conversation. They get frustrated, angry, become abusive, yell, walk out, or say things like, "We aren't meant to be," or "We're too different to work this out," and they break up. If they make it past that step, most will then justify why they had to do that. But make no mistake, not only does this not fool anyone, but it also moves the relationship backwards.

In either case, Support or Entitled, you either have blame or growth. When you feel someone else has gotten in the way of the plans you have made, you have one of two things to do. You can sit in blame and declare that it is the other person's fault or you can learn from the experience and overcome it together. Moving on to a new plan, without resentment, anger, judgment or any other negative emotions that keep you in the past is advisable. Blame and reacting prevents growth and keeps a person in the past. Forgiveness leads to growth in the present moment and also improves the relationship for the future. This, however, does not mean continued acceptance of a bad situation.

Blame can often act as a convenient excuse to keep you in the past without needing to pursue your future goals. The ego's objective often seems to be "Seek, and do not find." The mistake to avoid here is not looking within to see where the actual problem resides. Not taking responsibility halts growth. It keeps a person in their comfort zone, instead of finding success or improvement, and in turn, they continue to repeat the same mistakes. This is often a reason why people in abusive relationships, who blame everything on how bad their partners are, continue to find the same bad relationships over and over again. Their partner becomes the perfect excuse for them not to succeed.

Not blaming others anymore gets us away from being a victim, or a victim of circumstance, and gives us responsibility and therefore control. In order to no longer be a victim, it is necessary to release blame from your life. Waiting for another person to change something in order for you to get over something takes any kind of control you have away from you. Accepting the responsibility allows you to realize you are the one in control and allows change to happen. Anytime you find yourself in blame, a trigger should go off to know you are preventing your own growth. Blame is a way to conveniently prevent you from pursuing what you really want. Blame is an escape and an excuse. It would be like skiing down a mountain and stopping in front of a tree and blaming it for not allowing your progression. When you are progressing forward, there is no time for blame.

When blaming others, ask yourself, "Am I actually blaming this person (or situation), for things I don't want to take responsibility for myself?" "Have I assigned the same type of blame to other people in previous relationships?" This could be an indication that you are either choosing to be a victim and finding the appropriate person to help you correspond with that role, or that you are putting your responsibility on other people.

Entitleds also have a harder time letting go of a point in an argument. They sometimes feel that they must hold on to a point in order to gain respect from the other, or else it will come up again. It seems the amount of a person's entitlement versus their evolvement can be based on how easy a time they have letting go of an argument. The ability for a relationship to survive is based on compromise, but specifically letting go of the need to be right. This could also be part of a control pathology, where a person needs to make the other prove their love. Or it could be part of a manipulation because of your own sensitivity.

In relationships one can either be sensitive, thinking their partner is trying to hurt them, or they can pursue and receive the things that they want. The people who choose to be sensitive in a certain area never get what they want. If a businessman wanted to be sensitive every time he had an issue with someone, he would have a difficult time obtaining any success.

If you find yourself acting overly sensitive, you either need to work on your own neediness, and figure out why you need to have the attention all the time, reassess the other person's intentions, or you need to eliminate the people in your life you feel are constantly abusing you. If you cannot eliminate them, then empower yourself, and choose to get what you want instead of being sensitive. A question to ask when blaming, being sensitive, manipulating, insulting, arguing, fighting or making any other decision to change the harmony negatively in a relationship is: *Is this going to expand the relationship or constrict it?* It is easy for anyone to realize that insults are constrictive and not constructive to any type of relationship, yet people still use them when engaged in an argument. When necessary, there is a way to speak to someone with tough love that is supportive and expands the relationship. This can open doors for more expansion and make things better in the future, something insulting never does. Expansion includes changing complaints into requests, fear into passion, and contribution or shame into love, intimacy and connection.

There are six things that will take your energy and destroy a relationship unless you eliminate them:

1. Blame

2. Judgment

3. Need to be right or win

4. Lack of compassion

5. Pride or stubbornness

6. Need to have control

These should be replaced with:

1. Understanding

2. Compassion

3. Forgiveness with recognition

4. Empathy

5. Appreciation

6. Unconditional love

Look at your past relationships. Which did you have more of? How was the result? Now look at your current relationship and decide if you need to make a change.

Self-righteousness and Forgiveness

For those of you that have questions and cannot find the answers, the first thing you have to ask is, do you really want an answer to your question, or are you just asking to further prove your point? A Selfish Entitled I worked with named Howard asked, "How do you forgive someone, or apologize without putting yourself in a position of weakness?" His point was that if the other person sees you forgiving or apologizing, they immediately feel they are right in the situation, and in the future they will continue the destructive behavior because by apologizing you have admitted to being wrong.

First, it is easier just to avoid dealing with people like this. If it is an intimate partner, they need to learn that the stronger person supporting the relationship gives in to disagreements. Second, if you have really forgiven them, the question wouldn't arise because it would concern the past and have no bearing on the future. Admitting wrongdoing or apologizing doesn't mean you have to give anything up. You don't give up your power when you admit others are right; you give up your torment and let them give up theirs. If you feel you are giving up power, then what you are seeking is for the other person to stay in torment. Howard thought forgiveness was a position of weakness because he would be giving the other person strength in saying they were right. In reality, when you forgive, you empower both parties, especially yourself. Forgiveness and apology puts the situation in your past instead of bringing it forward.

Not releasing your self-righteousness is similar to what the Buddha says about anger: "Holding on to anger is like grasping a hot coal with the intent of throwing it at someone else; you are the one who gets burned." Without the release of forgiveness, you have a whole range of negative emotions that will cause you to suffer. You also release the person you are arguing with; if they do not accept it, and they wish to continue to abuse themselves, that is their business. Let them hold the hot coal. If they continue with this abuse, it will overflow to you, and this is why it is not recommended to have dealings with people like this. The stronger person, the supporter of the relationship, recognizes wrongdoing, forgives, apologizes, and does not wish to hold onto self-righteousness. The weaker person needs to hold on to the negative feeling. Those who choose to hold on to self-righteousness can never hold on to good relationships. Investigate to see where you have a *need* to be right. Statements like, "I don't want to fight *but…*" are usually starting a fight because this person just wants to be right about something without hearing the other side. The ability of both parties to give up their self-righteousness defines a relationship.

This was not acceptable to Howard. He asked the question, not because he wanted an answer, but to confuse others to come to his side. His justification meant that he never needed to apologize or forgive. If he accepted this explanation, that meant he had to forgive, apologize, and in his mind, admit that he was wrong, something he never wanted to do. So he asked the question to try and justify his actions. He tried to think of more difficult situations where his case was true. For me to spend any more time on the solution to his problem was a waste of our time and energy. He asked the question because he wanted to prove his point and instigate others to do the same, not because he wanted to be free. Because he was not free, he wanted others to be imprisoned as well. It is important to remember you either have self-righteousness or good relationships with others. The same can be said with self-righteousness and compassion; they do not exist together.

This is not to say that everything should always be forgiven. Sometimes, in the case of continued abuse, the relationship needs to be severed. There are conditions to forgiveness in a continued relationship. This is to prevent wrongs from being forgiven without consequence, or having the negative behavior repeat itself, in this relationship or others. The problem is often more for Supports than Entitleds. Too often Supports don't acknowledge abuse but instead rationalize it away; while Entitleds often don't forgive it. Both are very important pieces of the puzzle of evolution and finding harmony within relationships.

For the Behavior More Typical of Supports

If you don't acknowledge or recognize abuse, you will accept more of it. If you make excuses for the abuse against you, or justify, rationalize, or over-forgive it, you deem it okay to happen again. That also includes future relationships and especially applies to adult relationships with parents as well as intimate relationships. With extreme personality types, Blind Supports often forgive others and crucify themselves and Selfish Entitleds are prone to crucify others and forgive themselves. The irony is neither realizes this, and both think they are doing just the opposite. We rationalize when we go against our better judgment because of fear. One fear that allows Supports to rationalize abuse could be that they will lose this person, or something they are providing. Forgiveness without recognition is just the hope that the person is going to magically morph into the loving person they are hoping for, due to a realization of their love and care.

A person is not suddenly going to wake up and say to their partner, "I have been so unloving to you for so long, and I want you to know it's all going to stop now." If you forgive too much, you are actually being selfish. You are only considering the person's effect on you, not on others, and not on themselves. For example, let's say for extremes, that a friend of yours has a temper and frequently reacts by punching you. If you are physically able to accommodate it, perhaps you could forgive it. Forgiving it, in that person's mind, gives them the okay to continue the behavior. So what happens when that person punches the wrong guy? They are then in serious danger. A more practical example is parents that give in to their children's temper tantrums. It is laziness on their part to reward their children for poor behavior instead of putting a stop to it. It is the same with any form of abuse. When I forgive abuse without considering any consequence, because it's inconsequential to me, I'm teaching that person to only consider the results, not the behavior.

Often abuse is such an ingrained part of people's lives they don't even realize it is happening because they are so accustomed to it.

Conditions to forgiveness should include:
1. Acknowledgement (without justification) by the one who was hurt of what occurred. Without understanding that you are being abused, you don't know to stop it from happening further, thus keeping yourself

in harm's way. Don't run away or turn your back on the problem, allowing it to come back. The pain and hurt needs to be expressed, even if it is just you writing it down. (When unsure about abuse, ask yourself, would you treat/talk to a person like that? If the answer is no, then you are acknowledging it is, at minimum, inconsiderate and possibly abusive.)

2. Honest communication to the abuser why it is unacceptable behavior and their acknowledgment. If you fear this communication, then you are allowing it to go on further and often escalate.

3. No longer ignoring the abuse now or in the future. This goes for all other relationships as well.

This can restart a past situation and keeps you and the relationships you are involved in focused on the moment. This gives both parties an understanding of what the other person is capable of, what to expect and what not to expect, and not tolerating any more poor behavior. These are conditions in which exercising forgiveness and carrying on a relationship in the now (not the past) will work. If not, putting the abuser out of your life is recommended. These conditions of forgiveness should ensure you are no longer a victim. You will recognize and not accept that abuse any longer, becoming stronger for the experience and recognizing that new strength for yourself. It is not real forgiveness unless you are out of a position of weakness. Weakness would be feeling that you have to forgive in order to avoid some other personal fear. For example, you forgive the person because you feel that he will fire you, or break up with you, or cut you off financially if you don't. That's not truly speaking your mind, but giving in to fear, which will build further resentment.

The actual definition of abuse is to speak or treat someone in a harmful, unjust, harsh, injurious, or offensive way; any behavior that is designed to control and subjugate another through the use of fear, humiliation and verbal or physical assaults. If you feel scared, helpless, controlled, or unexpressed, this is abuse.

When someone says, "At least he doesn't hit me," they need to realize that the results are the same only the weapon is different. If you are not sure if you are being abused, you can ask these questions: (To know if you are abusing someone, you can turn them on yourself and see what your answer would be.)

- "Could I be any safer than I am in this person's presence?"

- "Do they have my best interest in mind?" (If you are not sure, the unbiased opinion of a friend or family member should help.)

- "Regardless of their intention, am I at all in harms way?"

- "Is it possible I can go wrong submitting to this person?" (This one could be tougher to answer, but you have to think about what are the risks in submitting to them.)

- "How do I feel about the actions committed against me?" Do they feel unjust, harsh, injurious or offensive? If simple communication does not put a stop to them, then further acceptance of this relationship should be in question. The next question with this one can be, "Has this occurred before?" If so, then it will again, unless the abuser pursues professional help.

For Behavior More Typical of Entitleds

If you don't forgive, or let go of abuse (often along with the abusive person), you will never move past it. Forgiveness is more for yourself than the other person. It is a release of energy that can hold you back, but this doesn't mean accepting it further. There is a difference between unconditional love and unconditional acceptance. You can still love someone and not have them in your life. If you are holding on to resentment because you feel someone has not acknowledged abuse against you, and changing your point of view on their intentions is not satisfying, then it is recommended to exit the relationship until your perspective is able to change.

Adam, a 37-year-old man, was at the intersection of not forgiving his parents or taking actions to remove them from his life. Much of what he felt and talked about was the abuse, inconsiderate behavior and lack of protection that occurred to him as a child. His parents had no acceptance for him or his lifestyle. In an effort to "change" their beliefs, he continued to attempt to gain their acceptance, which led to further fights and more abusive communication from both him and them. As it is when you are in a car, the intersection is where a lot of the danger occurs. Adam's lack of forgiveness caused his anger to rule his communication and his parents' defensiveness ruled theirs, creating no constructive result. Adam was under the impression this constant fighting with them was better than not speaking to them at all.

His parents were not ready to recognize any wrongdoing on their part. They felt they were still doing what would be best for him. In this type of stalemate, the only solution is to change your point of view on the other person's opinion, and move past it and often away from the relationship. Neither party would have any effect in changing the other, based on the way they were choosing to communicate, so the change has to occur inside themselves. This is where knowing the other person and what they are capable of is helpful. Nonetheless, forgiveness could still occur for Adam solely for his own benefit.

Let's examine his process. He recognized the abuse and lack of acceptance, so it is unlikely it would occur to him again. He could also be aware of a possible pathology to relive this in any future relationships, especially intimate ones. Although they were not accepting of it, he made many honest communications to his parents regarding the situation, so it should not be built up inside of him. He could even find agreement within himself that nothing from his parents occurred with malicious intent. And most importantly, he was aware that he would not accept that abuse any longer in his life.

Obviously, these steps will often require the help of a professional, depending on the severity of the wound. However, the steps had to be met on Adam's part so he could have the foundation for forgiveness and healing. Releasing the energy through forgiveness could then help him to contribute in some way from the negative experience. Something else to consider is that those who don't forgive certain behaviors have a tendency to perpetrate the same abuse themselves. They are often not able to forgive others for qualities they don't like in themselves.

To explore compassion for those who do not wish to apologize, we need to understand why they make that choice. Entitleds have a difficult time apologizing because they feel that if they apologize, they are admitting they are not taking care of the other person or that they are admitting wrongdoing that may not have been their intention. They feel that this will cost them something in the future, when the opposite is true. An Entitled will actually gain trust from a Support by admitting wrongdoing.

As a manipulation, Entitleds also can have a tendency to put up many fronts to avoid admitting they are wrong. They may bring up others who would agree with them, point out past problems they feel they were right about, and often try to use guilt. They will even say how they have been the one who was hurt in the whole situation, explaining that no one was taking into account their sensitivity. This can all be avoided by just allowing the Support partners to express themselves and by acknowledging their feelings.

Supports are not immune to this behavior, but usually would only resort to it when they are at the bitter end of not feeling as though they are being heard. Often, being able to express themselves is all Supports want in a communication, and *not* hearing them could turn a small issue into a big one. Entitleds should take the leadership role and apologize when someone doesn't feel taken care of, even if that was not their intention. Once the Support is heard, then the misconstrued actions can be explained to them. People almost always judge others based on their actions, but they judge themselves based on their intentions. Reforms do the opposite with compassion for others. Everyone would be much happier in their own lives if they exercised that compassion. If you have to judge, base the judgment on someone's intentions. This will alleviate almost all feelings that people are trying to hurt you. Everyone would also create a better space for themselves if they judged or performed actions that reflect better their intentions.

The most important quality for a person looking to forgive, drop resentment and especially reform their family problems and issues is compassion. Finding compassion is the key element in gaining acceptance and freeing yourself of resentment and hate. Compassion, as well as putting yourself in someone else's shoes, at their age, with their experience, education and upbringing, can give you the answers. Develop an under-standing of their fears and their insecurities, as well as their expression of love and their comfort in it. This does not mean accepting more abuse or inconsideration from any relationship. It means not letting the past continue to plague your future.

Keys to Letting Go:

1. Find compassion and look in other areas to find grati-tude for the people who have hurt you.

2. Accept that it is a part of your past and determine how you can move on from this and how it can possi-bly contribute to yourself or others because of it. Realize that it is not going to happen again unless you continue to give it attention with a self-fulfilling prophecy.

3. Find out how those experiences made you a better person, and how even the worst of experiences have benefitted you in some way.

4. Discover ways in which to contribute to yourself or others from the negative experiences, or how you already are contributing from them.

If forgiveness is not within the realm of possibility for you, consider at least letting go; this can be done by asking the right questions. You can find your own specifically, but some exam-ples are:

- What purpose does the negative things I hold on to serve?

- Do they help me to get what I want in life?

- Do they work in my favor or add to my success or happiness in any way?

- How am I benefiting by choosing to remain a victim? (To take this a step further: Do you think you benefit from people feeling bad for you? Is it giving you payback?)

Suffering is almost always the only purpose for us to hold on to the negative past experiences we have. Knowing this makes it easier to let go. Once the first steps have been completed, ask yourself as part of the release, what would your life look like if you did not take offense to the other person's actions? What would your life look like if you let go completely? How would you be moving on and having success, obtaining goals and finding happiness?

If you are finding it hard to forgive, you are choosing to hang on to some emotion. It could be regret, sadness, hurt, fear, guilt, blame, anger, resentment, revenge, or others. If you find out which one specifically you are holding on to, you can further discover the process to release it. Another step to help you release the energy is acknowledging any and all good things the person has brought to your life. In order to remove hate, find gratitude. Finding the will to let go is important for you to move forward and have success and happiness in your life, whether the people you want to forgive are with you or not; even those who have died you may need to forgive. Equally important is to ensure you are not repeating the pattern yourself. This is part of your evolution.

Communication

It should not go without saying that listening is the most important part of communication. Many of the problems in a relationship stem from poor listening, and listening involves much more than just hearing. It's about understanding your partner's feelings and addressing their concerns. This can be more challenging for Entitleds or any Support crossing the line in anger during an argument. The key when listening is to exercise empathy. That is, put yourself in the other person's position and think how you would feel. If you do not react the same when in a similar situation, then have compassion for their struggles, different fears, and sensitivity. You may not always agree with another's attitudes or fears, but having empathy brings compassion. Getting along in harmony involves concern for, and sensitivity to one another's needs as well as appreciation of the things that make another person special. Communication is not about agreement; it is about being respectfully acknowledged.

Proactive versus Reactive

Establishing lines of communication is important and often not as easily done for Supports. That is because Entitleds are more accustomed to speaking their mind when they do not receive what they want. The key to this is feeling that your partner will accept what is said. When your partner communicates something to you, are you proactive or reactive? Awareness of when you are reactive will automatically help you to stop reacting. Even within conflict, it is possible for both parties to remain connected until one or both partners react.

When your partner is upset with you and communicating, do you feel:

Group 1:

- Concerned for them?
- Interested in why they are upset and how you can help them feel better?
- A need to listen to see where you can help make things smoother for your future together?

OR do you feel the need to:

Group 2:

- Immediately go on the defensive?

- Intimidate or submit them?

- Criticize or insult them?

- Blame them for feeling that way?

- Cut them off or stop them from speaking?

- Create a distraction, sidetrack, rewrite history, or lie?

- Not allow them to speak so they don't try this behavior again?

- Start telling them why *you* are upset before listening to their feelings?

If you answer yes to any of the questions in Group 2, there is some work for you to do. People who react in these ways are not in a trusting relationship, are Selfishly Entitled or abusive, and have difficulty with honest communication with their current partner and future relationships. They must make a change to allow other people to have expression of their feelings. If your feelings fall into Group 1, and you have concern for the other person and want to help, the communication exercises in this chapter will work well. To go a step further, it is not just important how you feel, but how you act. I have heard many people say they feel concerned when their partner is upset, but then they still react in a way similar to Group 2, regarding what they are saying. To avoid reacting, it will be helpful to identify the emotions you are feeling and what you feel you need to defend yourself against specifically.

After they communicate, do you try to make them feel:

Group 1:
- Acknowledged and heard?
- Cared for even though you might not agree with what they said?
- As if their request will be taken seriously?
- Understood or respected?

OR

Group 2:
- "Wrong" for feeling that way?
- Insignificant and small?
- Humiliated or stupid?
- Crazy?
- Needy or helpless?

Once again, if you fall into Group 2, you are promoting an unhealthy relationship and are acting Selfishly Entitled or abusive and should make a change in order to care for your partner and yourself. Now, if your partner makes you feel this way (Group 2) when you communicate your unhappiness to them, then you should identify you are in an abusive, or at the least unhealthy, relationship, and it is recommended to either exit it or seek the help of a professional.

On a side note, there are many people (especially SE's) who believe that when they experience something unwanted from another person, if they can control their behavior through rules, manipulation, or threat of punishment, then they will find harmony. That is not the truth. Let's face it, as living beings we want attention. We respond better with positive reinforcement.

Let's think about the reverse. Typically when people want an action from their child and the child gives it to them, they don't really make a big deal out of it. However, when the child does something they don't want, such as misbehavior, bad grades, not cleaning up, etc., often parents make a really big deal of it, giving them lots of attention. We are teaching our children to create negative situations in order to receive the attention they crave. If you get more attention from bad behavior than good, what are you going to do more of? The point is to reward the good behavior you want more of. Praising a child for putting his toys away rather than criticizing him when he does not will have better results.

An important way to show you are listening is by not interrupting. Listening also doesn't include thinking about what you are going to say next, in order to win the argument. That means the person speaking should give the other time when they finish to think about their response, or allow them questions if they do not understand. Giving someone time to speak shows that you are not just seeking to be right, but would like their feedback. If you disagree with something your partner is saying, then wait to understand why they feel that way; they will be telling you where your actions have not corresponded with your intentions, so it is important to know.

As a side note, it would be easy to make a case that the leading cause of cheating is a lack of appreciation. There are so many ways people begin to feel unappreciated. Cutting off someone from speaking, or not listening to them, are certainly big ones. It is okay to interrupt under two circumstances: asking for clarification of what has been said, or to repeat what has been said so far. Ask and be open to either of these, because between two people in an argument or discussion, many things can be misinterpreted. This also shows that you are listening.

Only Selfish Entitleds feel they must win every argument they have. Using justification and reasoning only builds resentment. If your partner is upset with something that has occurred, despite your reasons, unless you are abusing them, you want them to feel resolution. So listening and acknowledging will cause both of you to be happier. When you have to "win" every time, you are stubborn and closed-minded and are not showing any respect for other person's feelings.

Good communication often requires guidelines, because so many emotions can be involved. These exercises are designed to ensure both parties have the opportunity to express themselves, are heard, and feel respected and appreciated in the process.

Communication Exercise #1 - "The Repeat Exercise"

An important exercise during any disagreement is to repeat what your partner has just said. This is so there is no misinterpretation, but also to let them know you are listening and understanding them. Not listening, or anticipating the other not listening, is what causes much of the tension and conflict in arguments; this exercise immediately eliminates both possibilities.

When your partner speaks, after a few sentences or they have made their point, before responding, you repeat what they said or at least the point of what was said. Then you respond and they repeat what you said. The point here is not to "win," but to give both parties the feeling of being expressed and heard. This is especially good for Entitleds to do and is also especially challenging for them. This also helps to avoid being defensive because it stops quick defensive responses, and puts both parties at ease with one another.

It seems much of what people argue about is regarding the other understanding exactly what they are saying. If that is accomplished, the argument usually will not escalate, and the time of disagreement is cut to a minimum. Think of what is being said as not right or wrong, just a different interpretation. In almost all cases, no one is 100 percent at fault or "right."

Communication Exercise #2 – "The I-Feel exercise"

Avoid at all cost starting sentences with "You..." This is the start of an accusation and puts people on the defensive immediately. This prevents them from listening. If you rephrase everything you say with "I *feel* (hurt, upset, anxious, unloved, frustrated)..." or "That makes me *feel* (bad, lonely, unimportant)..." you will be heard and understood much better. This is more vulnerable and requests compassion, protection, sympathy, and understanding as opposed to defensiveness. For example, "You never listen to me when you watch TV," becomes, "I feel unimportant to you when I'm speaking and the TV is on." "You never kiss me when I come in the door," becomes, "I feel so loved when you kiss me when I come home." Instead of, "You are so selfish," say, "I feel as if I don't matter to you when you do that."

This will require a person to look deeper into why they are hurt and express that, so the other person can understand better what not to do. Other ways to start a sentence without an accusation are, "I have this perception...," "I interpreted that...," "I believe that...," "I perceive you to be...." These are all designed so that you can talk about what it is like for you in the first person without accusing them of anything.

Communication Exercise #3 – "The Write it Out exercise"

If either party feels that they are *not* being heard, then writing the communications down and reading them out loud in their entirety can help. No interruptions can be made until each party has finished. This might seem silly, but it can save your communication and make both parties feel heard. Be courageous with your discomfort in these exercises. The love and relationship is more important than the way these exercises make you feel.

Communication Exercise #4 – "The I Appreciate You Because... exercise"

When you notice yourself or your partner complaining a lot, go back to why you are together in the first place. List the positives, in your mind or, even better, on paper. Concentrate on those, and it will bring you back to where you want to be together. If the list of what you do not like (in your mind) is far greater or more passionate than what you do like, then possibly you are not the best match. Spending time apart to bring the positives back to your passion or going to a professional is recommended. Be sure not to make a decision to leave the relationship during a time of anger or high negative emotions. You can also take time to understand the other person's stresses in life and in the relationship to bring further awareness, compassion, respect, admiration, and love for one another. Take the former complaints and turn them into the request you have not made from one another.

Communication Exercise #5 – "The Here is What I Heard exercise"

After making a statement or a point, the other person repeats what was said, *then says what they heard (their interpretation)*. This differs from #1 in that the other person's interpretation of what was said is included. Often people hear communications completely differently than what is actually being said. The misinterpretation comes from fear, insecurity, desire, or past experience.

Example – A person might hear, "I don't want to go to dinner with you," as, "You don't love me." "I want to go out with my friends," could be interpreted as, "You're saying you don't want to be with me?" This exercise is very effective for people who often say to their partner, "No, that's not what I said." This requires care and empathy for the person you are asking to repeat what they heard you say. You need to genuinely care for what they are telling you they are hearing without dismissing what they tell you. This should make you more careful and aware of what you say and also how you are saying it. Your partner is giving you a direct explanation of how what you say is being interpreted. This is often the most enlightening and easiest of all the exercises. It immediately solves communications that are misinterpreted. This exercise often points out areas where a person's own shame, self-criticism, ego, or self-fulfilling prophecy causes them to hear something completely different that what is being said and can destroy their own happiness.

Communication Exercise #6 – "Overcoming Stubbornness"

This exercise can be the most challenging for the ego, but also the most effective for change. After an argument couples may be waiting for the other to do a certain something such as clear the air, make the relationship feel whole again, or reconnect together. *During* the argument either partner might be waiting for the other to do something, such as start one of these communication exercises.

You may find yourself asking, "Why is he not apologizing to me?" "Why is she not talking to me?" How long will he keep this up?" "Why doesn't she appreciate me?" "Why isn't he telling me he loves me?" "Why doesn't she come and hold me?" This often can be a moment that defines a relationship. This exercise consists of making a mental list of what you want your partner to do: That might mean apologizing, acknowledging your side, telling you why you are valued, holding you, etc. The next step is to break the chain of self-righteousness and initiate what you want by offering it to your partner.

Although this may be challenging for your ego, pushing against someone's stubbornness only makes it worse; the way out is by moving in the opposite direction. Acknowledging your partner's point and giving them what *you* want, including suddenly telling them why you appreciate them can break this pattern.

Two stubborn people need to learn the art of compromise. Without this, they will either part ways or spend a lot of unhappy time together. Acknowledge their side of the story; agree to disagree, compromise for your own happiness. Ask what you can do to help your partner overcome this terrible feeling they have inside of them causing their stubbornness.

Note that this can be a slippery slope for a Blind Support. This is not an invitation for more abuse nor is it an opportunity for an Entitled partner to not give up their own self-righteousness in the future. The other partner should recognize and respect the selflessness being offered in breaking the stubborn pattern and do the same moving forward.

Communication Exercise #7 – "Time-Out"

Sometimes arguments become so heated with emotions running so wild they run out of control. This is when people start saying things they really don't mean in an effort to bring the other person to their same state of hurt or upset. It could also be done to intimidate or control the other person. At this point, there needs to be a realization that nothing constructive is going to be accomplished, and that they are only hurting one another further. Couples can make an advanced agreement to take a break at this point to avoid hurting one another. When one or both of the people arguing feel it has gotten to this point, they will stop talking, and return when their emotions aren't so out of control.

Many times there is something that each person does that seriously hurts the other. It is often something they have had unpleasant experiences with in the past, either in other relationships or with parents. It could be yelling, cursing, pointing a finger, walking out, hanging up the phone, etc. These actions should be communicated to the other with a request not to employ them during an argument. They can act as the trigger that the argument has escalated to the point that it needs to be returned to at a later time. Emotional intelligence, as well as the ability to reason are lessoned when under serious stress. This is why coming back to the argument or debate at another time is important. This exercise is dependent on letting go of pride and putting a "time-out" on the fight. Realization of the love and connection between each other is more important than any disagreement.

Because arguments can often become so heated either partner can lose themselves, it may be a good idea to create a list of guidelines for when to stop fighting and return to discuss the issue at another time. It may include that you will stop in the following situations:

- When one partner communicates that they have to stop, the other should recognize this and agree. Often one partner is so mad they will want to keep going even though the other partner can't hear them any longer because they are overwhelmed. (This should not be overused, though, because respect for this rule will go away.)

- When insults or threats become part of the argument.

- When the argument keeps going in circles and the same issues are being addressed with no resolution.

- When one partner feels they are in danger, or the relationship is in danger.

- When certain phrases or actions either partner has serious issues with become part of the argument, such as: loud yelling, finger pointing or breaking things.

It is difficult to start and continue communication exercises, especially at first, because it is not something you have ever done. Because of this, do all that you can to encourage honest and open communication such as showing your vulnerability and complimenting your partner for taking these steps. This creates a safe environment for dialog and will prevent drama and explosions.

An example of a healthy dialog would be: "I understand how hard these exercises can be, and I often want to just blurt out what I'm feeling, but that has never worked with success for me. I appreciate you doing them and I understand how hard they can be. You are so good at restraint and an amazing person to be with."

You might not like the support you are receiving and your partner might not like the care/protection they are receiving, but it is still present at some agreed upon level. The respect could be shown in the mere fact that, even though you are mad at your partner, you won't let them get hurt or be in a dangerous situation. Even in the midst of the worst fights the unspoken rules are still in place. This can be a point of appreciation that can be stated to bring one another back to calm and loving care. So despite how mad you are at someone, you can still let them know you are happy they have not crossed the line to abuse despite them being upset. Loving couples still care, protect, and support one another, even during the most emotional times.

"I don't like to fight; I just want to be sure my point is clear." This was a statement one of my clients made in one of her sessions. This is exactly what a fight is made of; two people, feeling unheard, who want their different points to be clear. As funny as it sounded to me at first, I realized it is an idea most people share. These exercises will handle the issue of your point being made clear. When you feel you are trying to make your point clear or not getting someone else's, a trigger should go off reminding you of these exercises.

Being a good listener requires effort from both parties. Men usually want to hear the bottom line, and women want to give details. If women want men to listen better, they have to tone down the details and tone up the point. Men, however, knowing women like more details, have to have more patience in this area. Also, what is important to one person might seem silly to the other. This is another case in which both parties must respect one another and be open to make considerations for the other's needs.

Something else to consider is, in order to expect your partner to be a great listener, you need to be less selfish and more of an interesting speaker. If one person is always talking, complaining, and causing constant arguments, it is of course going to be challenging for the other to listen. This is more typical of Entitleds. It pulls the other person from support into sacrifice and creates tension.

Working to be an interesting speaker means having a sense of care for the other while you are speaking. Watching body language and facial expressions, taking cues of disinterest, and not wearing out your listener's energy are good things to learn. If a good listener is giving their attention and energy, then that should not be taken for granted. Noticing when someone is not listening is a good time to change the way you are saying something to make it more interesting to him or her.

Ask, "How are you feeling? Has my desire to talk overcome your interest in what I want to share with you?" Great conversationalists make adjustments even in difficult conversations or arguments to keep their listeners interested and feeling respected, as opposed to blaming their disinterest on them. They get the attention they feel they deserve by respecting what the other wants.

Indirect Communications

When people are not good communicators (especially typical of, Selfish Entitleds and Blind Supports) they communicate non-verbally and expect people to read their mind when they are mad, upset or want something. This is a poor communicator's solution to avoid expressing how they feel. Their strong emotions usually lead their verbal communicating to a fight, so they try non-verbal communication to avoid that. It typically makes the situation worse.

Look at where you are using indirect communication with your partner regarding a change you would like. Are you cold or shutdown? Do you make fun of them excessively? Do you put them down in ways that you know will hurt them? Do you withhold sex? What are you really looking to express? What are you not saying that you would like to change because you don't think your direct words will be effective? Your unhappiness should be expressed, or the relationship will only get worse until clear communication occurs. If it is not attempted, the relationship will continue to get worse until it is no longer a valuable and healthy endeavor.

Something else to consider is the reason why you are not making those communications? Do you feel unexpressed when

213

you have tried to speak to your partner? Are you not being heard? Do you feel overpowered? Do you feel that nothing you say is accepted and s/he fights you on everything? Do you feel guilty for bringing something up that is uncomfortable? Do you feel as though the uncomfortable communication makes no difference? If you feel overwhelmed or hopeless, that nothing you do will make a difference, then seeking professional help is advised before exiting the relationship; if you are this poor in your communication, your next relationship will no doubt mirror many of the same negative qualities of this one.

Importance of Same-Sex Friendships

We've all experienced situations where we just need to relate to people of the same sex and take a break from our spouses or loved ones. Research has shown that men and women have different neural pathways and general ways of thinking, especially when communicating. Women are generally more emotional, empathetic, and verbal, as well as typically better listeners. Men are generally more to the point and logical thinkers. When people spend time with same-sex friends, their communication methods and ideas are validated, which helps them lose the sense of doubt that can arise in their differences with the opposite sex. It is a way to recharge batteries and come back fresh and happy to your partner.

Preventing the Cycle of Abuse

Honest communication and compassion is important in every relationship because without it, a cycle of abuse and misunderstanding is possible. For example, if one partner does not initiate sex because they are afraid of rejection, that could lead to the other partner thinking they are unattractive or unloved, or worse, that their partner is cheating with someone else. Simple communication of the fear of rejection will stop this cycle. We have all been in situations where our thoughts have brought us to places that we later found out were a simple misunderstanding due to a lack of communication. These thoughts put us in a self-induced emotional prison because there was no communication.

Importance should be placed on completely open communication, with respect to the other's feelings of course. There are things that people want to say, but they are afraid of hurting the other person, or they fear that saying them will lead to worse problems. For example, people often hold back thoughts that will hurt their partner's feelings until it's too late.

"I think the way you eat is unattractive."

"You have been gaining weight, which makes me want to eat more as well, so I would like to come to an agreement with you that we should both be dieting."

"Your not bathing (or cleaning up after yourself) is becoming bothersome to me, and I don't want to lose my attraction towards you."

Any one of these statements could disrupt or even end a relationship, but without making them, they will surely lead to the end of attraction if not the relationship. Trust and allowance for statements like these will lead to growth and continued attraction. There are also considerations that should be made depending on which personality type you are dealing with.

How to Get What You Want From Each Category

Manipulation never has a positive end result for either party and is not recommended. It takes the joy out of supporting others and forces people to do things they don't want to do, often out of fear. However, there are ways you can increase your persuasiveness and have others actually feel respected and interested in doing something, rather than agreeing out of guilt, obligation, or fear. In order for that to happen, it is necessary for you to speak their language. People in the different categories process information differently; often what feels inclusive to a Support can feel threatening to an Entitled. Typically Entitleds want to know what is in it for them, while Supports want to know what is in it for the harmony in their relationships. If you speak to a Support in terms of supporting, he will be more apt to help you. If you speak to an Entitled about how it will benefit him, then he will be more apt to help you. This includes even the smallest of requests.

So instead of saying to an Entitled, "Please stop chewing your food so loud. It bothers me," you can tell them how unattractive they look to people when chewing their food so loud. Whereas when addressing a Support, you can just tell him it bothers you. It is a matter of breaking it down in terms of what motivates the person.

If you feel you are not getting through to your partner, change the way you have been speaking to them. Whatever their leading quality is give them appreciation for it; if you are with an Entitled who is a protector or an initiator, let them know how comfortable that makes you feel. The same goes for the Support qualities. If you have a Support who is an adaptor, let them know you appreciate how they adapt to your changing needs. If you are with a creative thinker, encourage their ideas.

Part of this book is to become aware of what to expect from people and what they would like from you. As a Support knowing Entitleds like recognition, you can start with that. A Support might tell her Entitled partner that he is the best she's ever known at taking care of, protecting, or making her feel safe in their relationship. This inspires an Entitled to continue doing that, even if he hadn't been. At that point she might add something she wants, such as, "I feel that most of all when you are cleaning up after yourself because I know you don't like to do that." Or, " That's why I know you will be mature and responsible with your finances." Ordering an Entitled such as, "You better stop spending your money on crap we don't need," probably won't work but will create resentment. Entitleds do not like to be told what to do. A better plan is to tell them, "You're the only one who will decide to spend your money responsibly, but I know that's the man you want to be." This is what is meant by speaking to their commitment to who they want to be, rather than their issue. During an argument a Support might say, "You have a better ability to work with me on the communication exercises suggested in this book, than anyone else I know, so I know we can work through this to have the relationship we've always dreamed of."

Typically it will be easier with Supports, because they will accept being told/asked what to do if they believe in the vision. Many times the Entitled can just let them know they want them to work together on building their relationship stronger and the Support will follow the lead the Entitled presents. That means the Entitled must actually do what they are suggesting first, and then they will follow. If they are not following your lead, they either don't respect you or don't believe you will be committed to the new behavior. If it is beneficial to the relationship, continuing the action will gain their respect and get them on board, if not, consideration should be put on exiting the relationship.

PART III - Is It Really Possible for Us to Do All This?

After reading Part II of this chapter it might seem impossible for you or your partner to accomplish what is explained. Lets take a closer look at your possibilities and what needs to be present in the relationship in order to overcome the challenges.

The Rules

It may sound ridiculous to plan how you are going to fight in the future, especially since most fights happen spontaneously and are attached to high emotions. However, if you do not change your actions, you are going to have the same results; which is probably the same results from past relationships as well. Yes, it's challenging to make a playbook for fighting, but you can play by certain rules agreed on by both parties no matter how emotional you are. This establishes trust in heated situations and lets each partner know that no matter how angry or upset they get, they are still a team, and can work anything out together. Setting boundaries allows you not to accept too much and then carry resentment for it later. The rules also maintain respect and dignity with people who argue or want changes made in their relationship. The rules could look something like the examples below and you can always add more or tweak these to include things that are important to both parties.

1. If one person starts *the repeat* communication exercise (#1), or any other conversational exercise in an effort to create unity, the other has to follow as well.

2. Even though you are arguing, which is okay, verbal attacks should be avoided as much as physical ones. This includes passive aggressive behavior. Recognize when you are doing this, then resist and apologize for it. It is okay to express anger as long as it is not abusive.

3. Recognize that arguing or fighting does not make you enemies. This happens between even the best of couples. Disagreements are expected and are healthy, as long as they do not become abusive, or result in

more importance being placed on being right than the well-being of the relationship.

4. It is acceptable and safe to disagree. You and your partner do not have to agree with one another on every issue in order to stay together. This is part of the unpredictability, attraction, and admiration that you have for one another.

5. It is not acceptable to use something that has been told to you in prior confidence as a weapon against the other person. This breaks trust and encourages keeping secrets. This includes making any attempts to evaluate your partner such as, "You are only saying that because your last boyfriend cheated on you!" Or, "You are acting this way because of the way your mother treated you!" This dismisses any feelings your partner has and contains accusations that will further the argument. When past issues or situations are used against someone it cuts off the availability to be vulnerable and intimate in the future and puts trust in danger. Without trust, the relationship can never go to a deeper level. The same goes for your own past such as, "My ex-boyfriend would never do that to me."

6. Never make important decisions with your negative emotions while in the argument. This includes leaving the relationship. Often we think when we are emotionally engaged that it is the perfect time to make important decisions because we are motivated by the negative emotion. Know when it is time to take some space or a break and return to the conversation. Remember if the person you are talking to loves you, then they are sensitive to what you are saying to

them. This should not be taken lightly. Too often in relationships, break-ups occur as a threat, manipulation, or from fear that the other might be headed in that direction. In serious relationships where love is involved, a break-up should occur only after times of serious thought on the subject with strong reasoning or professional intervention. This gives both parties the idea that there is commitment and trust that each party can express what they feel with confidence, and no one is wasting any time together. (Some exceptions to this are any abusive relationships, especially physical abuse.)

7. Never walk out of the room or hang up the phone without saying you want to take a break from or end the argument.

8. Never make any threats as to what you are going to do physically or pulling away power you feel you have over the needs of the other. That means taking away money or security or safety the other has in you. That also means subtle threats such as, "You better not do that," or, "You better not talk to me like that." Phrasing like that implies, "or I will…"

9. Avoid being sarcastic. This might be fun with friends, but in a relationship, every word counts and is accepted in your heart and your partner's. There is never room for sarcasm in intimacy.

10. Agree to acknowledge the other person's feelings of why they are upset, whether you agree they are right or wrong, as long as they are genuine and not part of a manipulation. If you feel that the fight is a manipulation, then that should be stated as well.

11. Agree *not* to assume your partner is just out to hurt you, but has some desire within the argument to bring the relationship closer to harmony. This also carries a responsibility to not have any interest in hurting your partner, but to understand you are arguing to achieve some understanding of future harmony.

12. Don't go in circles rehashing the same points over and over. Request what you want that will make you happier. Rehashing is usually a result of one or both partners not feeling as if they are being heard. It could also be that one person is expecting the other to absolutely agree with them, and this is not always necessary or possible. Work to find a solution to the unhappiness or problem that you can agree on. Not bringing up the past and staying in the present argument can accomplish this.

13. There is no such thing as mind reading. Each party has a responsibility and a right to express themselves. Using phrases like, "You should have known..." Or "I shouldn't have to tell you," do not expand the relationship. Demands for mind reading could also be combined with guilt, shame, or manipulation. "A real man would just know..." This should also be avoided. A person may need to be told the same thing over and over because they are purposefully doing the thing you object to in order to avoid something else. It is often more a problem of communication that is *not* being made, rather than ignoring the other's needs. In other words, they are unhappy about something, so they do what they know will get a reaction out of their partner. At this point, instead of accusing and going deeper into the argument, be clear about what you

want and put an end to it. State your intention. Ask, "By continuing to do [the thing you don't like], what communication are you trying to make?" Otherwise, when someone expects the other to read their mind, typically they are not good communicators or do not know how to express themselves and want to blame their partner in their frustration. Being patient while they try and request what they want will be helpful.

14. Be specific about what you are upset about. Don't say things like, "You are the worst boyfriend!" This is not a good communication, but if absolutely necessary, you can say, "I don't feel you are living up to your responsibility as a boyfriend because..." or "I don't like the way you treat me when..." A better way to express your discontent is, "I feel hurt because..."

15. Establish times to talk and not to talk. When a person is tired, hungry or about to run out to do something or in the middle of work, it is not the time for a heavy discussion. This is also not an excuse to avoid talking. If you are always busy, then setting up a time to talk to strengthen your relationship is advisable.

16. Be courageous with vulnerability. Have trust and go to that place of insecurity and admit that. Talk about why you are hurt or upset and what you would like changed to make you feel more loved. This establishes more trust instead of accusations.

17. Finally, have patience for your partner's progress. Keep in mind most relationships, unless you had your eyes closed when you met, have started with something physical. They are not based on good communication during difficult times. Communication is not

something we are taught very well growing up, and we did not always have the best examples. If someone is trying to become a better communicator, then be patient with their progress.

These rules or exercises, as well as other exercises, will not work in abusive or untrusting relationships. When a person wants something done their way, wants to be right, or wants to "win," they will not play by these rules because these rules include the input and valued expression of both parties. Abusers such as Selfish Entitleds hear expressions of what other people want as a threat or an attack on them, which means they will counterattack. If you are in an abusive relationship, attempts to bring these rules or exercises to a Selfishly Entitled or substance-abusing partner will prove futile, until they first agree to make serious changes.

Repairing damaged relationships will require more than one or all of the above recommendations. It also requires some self-discovery and disclosure and possibly a professional to help in the process. This will include a lot of communication and readiness to do so. It's like an overweight person needing to go to the gym frequently, establish new habits and hobbies and even make new friends. If you want different results you have to take action very different from those that initially got you there.

Separation: "I want a great relationship, but there is too much to work on."

I've often seen people who are unhealthy or in poor shape say they want to get into shape or even run a marathon, only to quit soon after they start exercising. This happens because they are not prepared to do what it takes to be in shape. They just want to have it, or wish for it without wanting to put in the time, commitment, or do any of the work. It is the same with relationships. People say they want to be married or to be in a great relationship, but the minute things don't go their way, they decide to quit. They don't want to put in the work it takes to maintain passion and stay together because it's easier to quit. In their fantasy of marriage, their partner disagreeing or arguing with them doesn't exist. If that were the case, there would be no growth. As with getting in shape, the fantasy that building a great relationship is going to be easy is ridiculous. That is why there needs to be love and passion. Also give yourself permission to have a relationship that sometimes looks ugly or just imperfect; that is not a bad thing, it's a part of life and growth and although the ugliness can be used to destroy it can also bring those who work together even closer together.

Despite all this, if you are still considering divorce or separating, to feel comfortable that you won't repeat the same pattern in your next relationship, explore all the potentially negative reasons why you were originally attracted to your partner. Once you have worked on consciously moving away from these formerly attractive qualities, then you can feel confident you won't repeat the pattern by being attracted to the same attributes you no longer want in your life. At this point, after working with a professional to explore why you are not feeling harmony together, and the relationship is still not working, then separation could be the correct decision. That includes exploring the causes of why you are experiencing high-level emotions such as anger, neediness, blame, abuse, and jealousy. Without working on making the changes necessary to break your typical patterns, you take extra baggage into your next relationship and are at high risk of repeating the pattern.

If your relationship contains any of the qualities listed below, it is recommended to work on them prior to exiting the relationship, because you will probably create a similar situation in your next one:

- Blaming your partner for your unhappiness and feel the problems are mostly because of your partner and not you. This is not taking responsibility for your own life and emotions. If you are honest, you made negative contributions to their actions as well as your own.

- If you have lost your attraction for the same reasons you were originally attracted to that person. This could be anything such as their adventurous lifestyle, risk taking, promiscuity, them lying, or being abusive, etc. (This applies to anything unacceptable to you now that was attractive to you when you met.)

- If you are impulsive and have not worked on controlling this, ask yourself which is more typical of you, emotional reactions or true self-awareness? Don't make a snap decision to get a separation or divorce just because it's a phone call away and you think you will hurt your partner into realizing you were "right" about your disagreements. That's using separation as a manipulation. The decision to separate should be made when you are in a more positive and less emotional state of mind, and not an attempt to teach your partner a lesson.

- If you have a low tolerance and are rigid in relationships. You will be better served finding compassion for others and their actions as opposed to always thinking they meant the worst towards you.

- If you look for others to fulfill you. You need to love what you do in life and if you don't, don't expect someone else to fill that gap. Your life should feel complete without someone else, and that allows them to add wonderful things to it instead of providing it. Depending on someone else to make you happy leads to resentment from false expectations.

- If you have come into your current relationship with unreasonable demands or expectations that led to your own resentment. Working with a therapist to learn from where you do this, decreases the chances of you to doing it again.

Even though the passion and intimacy may be gone from the relationship, if the couple still cares for and loves one another and each are willing to learn about their own contribution to the failing relationship, much can be learned and worked out from the experience. This often causes the relationship to heal or leads to a better experience in a future relationship. When these qualities are not worked on during the relationship and the couple divorces or separates because of them, they are often unhappy soon after they left. Being honest about these qualities can tell you whether or not separation is right for you.

Compatibility

Couples often ask, "Is it possible for us to get along?" If you're wondering if your relationship can work, ask yourself what is important to you in a relationship, and break that down into categories. You could discover a new relevance to the question that can help you make the decision if it can work. To give you an example, the categories below are basic to most relationships. Complete the list with what is important to you specifically.

Categories for knowing who you may be compatible with:

- **Love** – Do you love your partner? Are you in love with him or her? Are you both compatible in your expression of love?

- **Intimacy** – Are you inspired to be intimate with your partner conversationally, physically and creatively? Do you feel freedom of expression in this area, and do you feel he or she feels free with you in this area?

- **Sex** – Are you compatible? Do you feel connected during sex? How attracted are you to your partner? How attracted could you be if you overcame the challenges?

- **Fun** – Hobbies, interest, travel, athletics, social events – What do you do together for fun?

- **Work** – Do you agree with or can you support the other person's current work or future plans/dreams? Do you feel you are taking second place to their work, vision or goals? (If so, do you still feel respected, and are you okay with that?) Are you a part of those, or are you separate? Are you okay with that? Do you want your partner to be a part of your work, vision or goals?

- **Responsibility** – Who is responsible for what in the relationship? Can you both agree on these responsibilities?

- **Financially** – How important are the finances to you? Are you happy with the situation you have together now, or with the potential situation you foresee for the future?

- **Children** – Do you both want kids? Can you agree on how to raise children?

- **Family** – Do you get along with one another's extended family? Parents, siblings, and other close family? Is that important?

- **Friends and Social** – Can you get along with one another's friends? Is that important, or do you need or want to look for new ones? What social groups do you both like or dislike being in?

- **Trust** – This is in all obvious areas, including money, love, and sex, and also the not so obvious ones, such as how comfortable you are making a request and knowing you will receive it.

- **Emotional** – Do you feel enough trust to express yourself emotionally regarding fears and insecurities? Can you admit when you are emotional, fearful, or insecure, or do you try and hide it? Do you use your emotions as a manipulation?

- **Communication** – Do you feel your ideas are expressed? Do you feel heard by your partner?

- **Spirituality/Religion** – How important is this to you and your partner? How important is it that you agree? If you don't agree, can one partner change or can you agree to practice different religions? What about raising future children?

- **Humanity/Ethics/Morality** – Are you in agreement with how your partner treats others?

- **Political** – Do you agree with your partner's political views? If not, how serious is the disagreement, and how important is this to you?

- **Desire and pursuit of goals** (This could also be described as a person's drive) – Do you feel freedom in this area, or does your partner get in the way of this? Do you feel they are working hard enough for their future (or your future together) or are they willing to seek help to increase drive or motivation here? Are you in complete disagreement here, or do you both share the same level of intensity here and this is not an issue?

- **Cleanliness and living standards** – This might go unnoticed at first, or before a couple lives together, but it is often important enough to make someone feel respected or not.

Out of these categories, which works and which does not? Are you in agreement in more than 60 percent of the categories? Some of these categories might mean more to you than others, so that should be taken into account as well. For example, spirituality might not matter much to a couple, but trust does. There are also categories that are mandatory to a person. If trust is so important to you that you think it matters more than all others combined, then if you have no trust you know you are selling yourself short of what you deserve.

Of course there are many X-factors such as, how you feel when you are with and without this person? To mention a couple of things I look for in healthy couples: First, do they accept one another's "gifts"? Each person has something to offer. It could be anything from a beautiful smile to expertise in health or law advice, stellar dance techniques, or good cooking, etc. The point is, if a person has something wonderful to offer their partner, but it is not accepted, often there is a compatibility issue. So if one partner is an expert in health and nutrition and the other is constantly sick and won't accept any advice, then there is a major disconnect between them.

The second thing I look for in healthy couples is their ability to ease each other's pain. Can a person listen, advise, or somehow make the other feel better when they are upset. That might even mean just laying down next to them for comfort. If this desire from your partner is missing, then often there is some level of respect or trust not shared.

Compatibility does not mean finding someone who is just like you. Your partner could be the kind of person you are looking for, but that doesn't mean they need to be like you, but it should mean committing at the same level. The questions below might help if you are having problems and want to know, "Is it love, or are we wasting our time?"

- Is what he or she is able to offer enough? - Take away all the problems. Is what you are offering one another enough to enjoy and sustain the relationship? If not, then there is no need to fix this problem because there are deeper problems.

- Are you together because he or she is just better than your other options? - Then he or she is probably *not* enough, and working on this will not be a good test because you will probably just go from one issue to another, never getting along.

- Are your expectations of what the other person can deliver too much? - Often we expect too much from our partner and they can't possibly live up to what is unfairly expected of them, and neither can almost anyone else you will find.

- Do you expect your partner to be just like you? - In relationships many times we have an expectation that our partner should be just like us but in most great relationships, that is not the case. What can/should you reasonably expect from your partner? Once you know what category your partner falls into, you can have a better idea of what to expect and what to ask for.

To take this to a further level, you can repeat all of the questions from the inside out. Starting with your last question, you can flip it to: "What can my partner expect from me?" In general, that's what someone should always be doing: seeing whether the efforts match.

- If your partner is not matching your effort with what they have to offer, then you know they are not as committed as you.

- Likewise, if you are not matching their effort, then you know that you are not as committed to them.

Related to our theme of which category you fall under:

- If you are not bothered by your partner committing more than you are, then you are Entitled and are probably putting your partner in sacrifice.

- If you are not bothered by committing more than they are, then you may be in sacrifice.

Eventually, one has to determine why they are in the relationship. For instance...

- If both partners are *not* providing 100 percent, they might be together for practical reasons such as an unsaid arrangement; this could include love but is usually less than love.

- If you know you are providing less than 100 percent, this often means you're in it because you are lazy and probably selfish.

- If you know that you are providing 100 percent or more, and your partner is not, then it is likely you are operating out of desperation or sacrifice.

Mirror and Complementary Relationships

Of course, there are many different categories of relationships, and the benefits you gain from them should also be taken into account when asking the questions above. In a "mirror" relationship, the people involved have similar energies, but provide considerably less growth. These are relationships of people who are very similar to one another. They tend to have a lot of rapport and understanding for one another quickly based on trust from familiarity. Often people in this type of relationship can relate to one another well, both with qualities they like in each other and qualities they dislike. The qualities that they do not like can often be found prominently in themselves. That is, if you are in a mirror relationship and hate certain qualities in your partner, you can bet you possess them yourself.

These are opportunities to look in the mirror to see what we can keep in ourselves and what we can refocus. At best, people are brought together in these relationships for soothing, but not for growth. They are usually lacking in complexity to provide much expansion. They do not have the push that expansion requires. There is great value in these relationships to find what you want, and do not want in future relationships. You enjoy each other's company, feel safe and can relate on many levels, but do not help one another to grow very much. This is okay if that is not important to those involved.

"Complementary" relationships are those of two people quite different than one another that fit together like a puzzle. When they intermix well, although they are not the same, they work better together. In these relationships, people realize that it's not a 50/50 split. One person excels in areas the other does not, and both partners appreciate and accept this. Despite the bigger compromises, often the relationships with much growth and accomplishment are based on this type.

As an exercise, think which relationships you had that were mirrors, and which have been complementary? What was your experience in both? If you continue to pick the same type, have you been evolving at a satisfactory pace, or are you not evolving? What lesson do you keep missing and need to repeat? What problems is your ego trying to re-create just so that they can be overcome? Is it possible to alleviate this problem in the intimate relationships you choose? (Often, it is an unfixable problem based on choosing the same type of person you originally had the problem with, or something that needs to be changed within you.) Are you seeking to change what is inside of you by searching on the outside?

If you are worried your current relationship is more mirror than complementary and neither of you are evolving or growing together, then go out of your way to learn new things and share with one another what you are learning. What separates the two categories is growth as a couple, but lack of growth is often just laziness. Ask yourself, what are some things that you have recently learned that you can share together? If you are not coming up with anything then your relationship may be in danger or getting stale. Find a class or hobby that will be interesting to both of you and encourage growth as a couple, even if it's just dancing.

With regard to the mirror/complementary model there is the third type of relationship called an "uncomplementary" relationship. That can be based on either being similar or different. It is uncomplementary because neither partner will accept or appreciate the good qualities of the other. This is a relationship where there is a very low level of respect and appreciation for one another so that even good advice is ignored, just because it came from the other person. They are just unable to accept one another's strengths. They also don't care enough about one another, and often themselves, to want to know any other way to operate to enhance the other. They are usually only together because of fear; it could be fear of being alone, unsafe, abandoned, unworthiness, or jealousy. With awareness and work from both partners, especially on communication, an uncomplementary relationship can become complementary by following the guidelines mapped out in this chapter.

Of course there are additional "human" factors outside of the science of relationship types. A lot of what comes up in couples counseling is what each person wants from the relationship and whether or not their partner wants to provide it. A typical question I like to ask is, "What exciting or fun things have you done lately?" The couple is often surprised by this question, which surprises me, considering that is what a lot of attraction is based on. Most people come together for mutual interest and fun. So why does that stop after a certain time? What surprises and spontaneity have you created for one another? What have you done to excite or turn on your partner, to remind them you are still the fun person they met years ago? Or what are you doing to be the fun person now, even if you were not then? There are many people that still like one another, but decide to separate, and often this is the reason. I can see people are sometimes set on not taking the initiative to do something fun for their partner, because the same is not being done for them. To that I say, do it for selfish reasons. Do it for yourself. You want to have fun in your life too, so take the first step and they may get on board and do the same.

Having fun is an art, and just like other arts, it often requires creativity. If you are bored or not having fun, then you are not being creative enough. If you are willing to put your ego aside and learn something new there are unlimited resources available to you to have fun. People often avoid doing something new because they fear they won't be good at it, they will look foolish, or that they will get hurt. Put your vanity aside and stop choosing that over having a great relationship. This means going out and finding a dance class, music lessons, exercise, martial arts or yoga class, having a picnic finding free events in your city, bowling or other games and sports, etc. You could body paint each other in chocolate if one of you like that, just try and step out of your comfort zone. Let go of inhibitions and learn to consistently challenge yourself mentally or physically and your relationship will prosper. This also means being committed to fun. That requires trying something new and *never* saying no to your partner when they take initiative to try something new.

CHAPTER 12

CAN TWO ENTITLEDS MAKE IT TOGETHER IN A RELATIONSHIP?

When Bill came to me after only one year of marriage, one of the things he said about Samantha was, "Why can't she ever see things my way?" After talking to him a bit more, I told him, "She probably never could. You were seeing things her way." This is because they were both Entitled and in the honeymoon stage of a new relationship, so he was doing what he thought a "good" husband should. She simply had her own vision, as did he. The question was, could their two visions correspond with one another? It is easy for two Entitleds to come together initially because of mutual thoughts, ideas, feelings, and attractions. There is a general feeling of "this person is just like me," but there can be many challenges.

It is the same as with two leaders working together, a lot can be accomplished together but without certain agreements, there is potential for serious conflicts. A relationship like this can work if the two people have the same vision. However, problems arise when they deviate in the path necessary to complete that vision. The one who gives in has the lesser vision, or the lesser investment in the survival of the vision. That person might be less Entitled (or more of a Support), or just more evolved. Typically, the partner who can move from their position faster is more open-minded, happier, and more compassionate. For example, both partners agree they want children and a stable family. If that is an important enough vision to both Entitleds, having two or three, which religion, what schools they attend, how they dress, etc., can be worked out as long as they focus on the importance of the overall vision at hand. On the other hand, when one Entitled has a vision of a family, and the other has a vision of traveling the world, the one who does not get what he or she wants can become resentful.

It is very difficult for someone to maintain a position they do not naturally fit into. If an Entitled person is not being recognized for their vision and is put in a position of supporting another's, it cannot last for too long without resentment building. When two Entitleds are together, they both have to recognize one another's visions and how they can interact. At least one needs to believe in the other's goals and fit them into their own. The one Entitled leading also has to keep updating their vision, and being specific about moving it forward; otherwise, the other partner will either take the lead, build resentment or leave.

Two Entitleds usually come together, and more importantly stay together, because they feel comfortable with the protection they each provide for one another. Inevitably, each person in this type of relationship excels at something that the other doesn't. One might be better at social situations while the other is financially more independent. One might be better in operations and the other marketing. There are many possibilities, but the two have combined to complement one another in that area. The trap people in this type of relationship fall into is to use that skill or protection to control or manipulate the other. So if one has an attitude toward the other of, *I'll do for you if you do for me*, that is dangerous, even though that is the underlying understanding. That may sound confusing, but the point is to be generous with your protection/care of your Entitled partner to avoid confrontations. When you withhold protection against another Entitled to get them to do what you want, they will do the same to you. This creates a vicious cycle of neither party protecting the other.

Needing to have control in the relationship and jockeying for this position can terminate the relationship. Because the two Entitleds will often offer protection and care in different areas, sometimes obvious and sometimes not, these areas should be recognized by both and respected. If one wants to learn the other's skill, that should be stated and respected, but it should not become a source of competition. This will cause the type of power struggle two Entitleds specifically need to avoid. There are many examples of two or more great leaders working together in harmony, it just has to be done with respect.

Upon meeting Bill's wife Samantha, an executive with a lot of confidence and creative ideas she had been working on, it was confirmed to me that she also was an Entitled type. Because they were both very stubborn, it took a lot to work through the exercises in the communication section of chapter eleven. This helped them develop the mutual respect they needed in order for them to get along. Luckily their visions didn't conflict, so they didn't have the major conflicts two Entitleds together sometimes do, that eventually leads to separation, they just needed to feel the respect from one another.

During a disagreement, it is often the more evolved person that gives in. It's not that one person "lost"; they are just more interested in fighting for the relationship than they are the matter at hand. This is an important realization in any relationship combination. With two Entitleds, a conscious effort to work at this must be in place. Until this realization is made, a lot of fights will either go on for far too long, or be pushed under the rug, creating a window for the issue to be opened again or resentment to build.

Without a Support, one person will have to consciously get in touch with their supportive side to support the relationship. Two Entitleds can easily get caught up in their "principles" if they don't make a conscious effort to have more commitment to the other person and the relationship rather than whatever they are fighting about, or their own self-righteousness. This commitment starts with communication.

First, allow the other person to express themselves. Second, make sure the other person knows they have been heard. This allows them to also cross the line in support of the relationship over the disagreement. They need to be aware of what type of arguments they are engaging in and recognize how their pathologies have a hand in them. Controls, fears, and attachments need to be dismantled quickly in order for two people of the same type to exist in a harmonious relationship. So if the underlying issue in a disagreement is jealousy, fear of abandonment, or any other fear or insecurity, this has to be admitted in the conversation and not hidden. This can be very difficult but will strengthen the bond of any relationship especially two Entitleds together. Without revealing this vulnerability to your partner it will remain a source of unresolved conflict.

Because Bill and Samantha were disagreeing on everything, it seemed as though each always wanted the other to do something different than what they were doing. This caused them both to feel like they were being controlled. Neither really wanted to control the other, but they were losing trust because they both were in fear of being controlled and therefore lashing out. Both were defensive about their specific goals and were not admitting any of this to one another.

They each needed to state their vision and what part of it could not be compromised. When they felt their goal was being compromised, this had to be expressed. Often two Entitleds together will wait for the other person to give them what they want, without asking for it, feeling the other person should just know. When it doesn't come, it is natural for them to build resentment and not give the other person what they want. They think that if they relinquish control, then they will once again experience a relationship they were unhappy with in the past.

When there is real trust it overrides everything. When this trust exists, jealousy and insecurity are eliminated. Disagreements are cut to a minimum because you trust the other person has the best interest of both parties in mind. Often, people have a *knowledge* that the other person won't hurt them based on past experience. But this knowledge can be easily shaken when unexpected circumstances and fears arise.

Real trust is also based on full communication. If a person feels comfortable telling their partner how they feel, or where they are insecure, then there is a foundation of trust. Without full communication, each partner has to guess what the other person wants, often missing the mark and causing resentment. For two Entitleds to make it, they must both be willing to give up control and have total trust, not just knowledge. This is imperative so that whenever disagreements begin, the trust in one another can override any conflict. With this foundation they can stay together happily.

The other thing to be aware of with two Entitleds is that they often emotionally abandon one another naturally because they both do what they want to do. They often have their life first, and then think about the life of their partner, not operating as a unit. This applies to many aspects of their life and can especially be true in their disagreements. In conflict, either one can walk away and ignore the other for days or longer. In life, they could be in their own world, working, without regard for what is happening with the other. This is fine if both are happy with that, but this could spiral out of control until they are both leading completely separate lives. For the long-term success, they need to know if they are wanting, capable, or even able to give their partner what they want, as well as how and where their visions meet.

Agreement versus Submission

You cannot get in the way of a strong Entitled's vision. You can alter it with agreement, but be careful the agreement is not submission. There is a distinct difference between agreement and submission. If the desired result is not achieved after an Entitled submits, the Entitled will be resentful and blame the one they submitted to. The vision of an Entitled is their life force. It drives them. Other visions or desires can work in conjunction with it, as long as they do not get in the way.

Suppose an Entitled has a vision to set up a business, and an intimate partner wants him to spend more time on their relationship together. If the businessperson submits to her only because of an implication that she will otherwise leave him, there can be a lot of resentment in the end if the business does not succeed. On the other hand, a Support partner usually won't change the vision of an Entitled. They will see how they can combine what they want with what their partner wants. They will, under the right circumstance, accept the vision and explore where theirs could complement it, so both can be achieved. If the businessperson does not give in at all then this promotes an unhealthy relationship.

I worked with a successful female actress who was Selfishly Entitled and only attracted to "strong" men, as she called them. What she liked were not *strong* men, but *Entitled* men. But her vision and will was usually stronger than the men she dated. She was interested in having a family and continuing her work. This would leave the man in the position of working less to raise the family while she made money. Every time the man submitted to support her on this, suddenly her attraction level was diminished. This was because they became too predictable to her and she found no attraction in security.

The problem did not reside in the men she chose—it was hers, specifically her unhealthy attraction to unpredictability. The men were simply complying with what they perceived as a healthy relationship by doing what their more Entitled partner requested. Be careful here because when you are asking someone to submit, you might not feel the same for them if they actually do. Her problem was in part because of a pathology that she carried from her parents of never getting the approval she wanted from them, so she tried to resolve that in her intimate relationships as an adult. Once she got the approval, she no longer needed it and would move on. This was not only abusive to the men involved, but it also contributed to her constant lack of contentment.

As an Entitled, be careful if you are picking other Entitleds just to gain approval from a person whom it is more difficult to get it from. This is another case where not knowing the roles and not accepting your complementary relationship can eventually lead to unhappiness. It is important never to get in the way of a strong Entitled's vision, find a way to work with it, not against it. Unless it is enhanced in their mind, changing it will never happen without some resentment.

Like two Alpha males from different clans, two Entitleds need to respect one another in order to prevent war. The respect needs to be felt or expressed otherwise resentment is likely to build. A good way to show that respect is through constant appreciation. Everyone wants love from and co-creation with others, but that starts with recognition and respect of who they are and what they can contribute. Also when two Entitleds argue, a Support should not get involved or accept the energy of their tension. Arguing, negotiating, bickering, etc., is often how unreformed Entitleds operate in their world comfortably. They take satisfaction in negotiating disagreements that Supports cannot understand; in the same way, many Entitleds don't understand how Supports would accept abuse or do things for the other person just for their own pleasure.

If you are Entitled and keep ending up with other Entitleds, be aware of why. Reasons might be:

- You are purposefully looking for the wrong type of person.

- Taking time away from someone with a vision makes you feel acknowledged or important. Is there some dissatisfaction or lack of attraction to someone who is absolutely crazy about you? Why is the approval of wholehearted Support not enough?

- You are charged by the chaos of fighting about crossed paths because that is familiar to you. Do you use your winning battles over others as confirmation that your vision is the right path?

- You do not have confidence in your vision and want a scapegoat.

- You do not quite believe in yourself and want someone else's plan as a backup. Perhaps you feel unworthy to achieve your goal.

Looking into this could give you awareness to pathologies you have, allowing you to have more ease in future relationships. For example, you might feel unsafe in a certain area and want to seek outside protection. If you don't feel that you can create your own stability in life, particularly finances, you may pick someone you feel has stability even though they are also Entitled and you know will be in constant conflict with you. Knowing this you can work on getting in touch with why you feel unsafe, alone, abandoned, or need someone outside of yourself to protect you.

Often picking the wrong person replicates a familial challenge. For example, picking someone who doesn't give you their full attention recreates a problem familiar for someone whose mother or father pulled their love from them as punishment. There is strange comfort here but also the false hope to overcome a childhood battle. Usually, neither party gets what they want in this circumstance, and only pathologies are chased and supported. When the more Entitled partner is ready to take the relationship to a higher level of intimacy, often the other loses attraction because they no longer need to overcome the lack of attention.

It is quite possible for two Entitleds to co-create together harmoniously, even though there is a lot of potential for unhealthy interaction. To avoid this, they need to follow the rules of respecting one another as Entitleds. It also helps to be aware of any pathology underlying in why they might be together.

CHAPTER 13

CAN TWO SUPPORTS MAKE IT TOGETHER IN A RELATIONSHIP?

Ryan came to me with an unusual amount of anxiety over seemingly small decisions he was being forced to make in his relationship. He knew he loved his fiancée, but he felt overwhelmed with all the responsibility he had, mostly because he had not had to make all the decisions in his past relationships. When he would ask for her help, his fiancée kept telling him, "I don't know. The man is supposed to make those decisions." This applied to everything including where to go to dinner, how to spend their money, where they would live, go away on vacations, etc. As a Support, he was used to following the lead of a more Entitled partner. Now, engaged to another Support, and recently cohabitating, he felt as though he had taken on more than he could handle.

Of course, many factors are involved in attraction, but after a roller coaster ride from an abusive Entitled, a Support seeking an easier ride could find him or herself attracted to another Support. They may find themselves more easily relating to another Support at first, but they are frustrated soon after because that person does not take charge as someone they are more suited for would. Two followers staying together will eventually force one of them to lead.

How can two Supports work together? It is not as common as two Entitleds together, but two Supports can find commonality in helping others together and having a laid-back view therefore easily relating to one another. They need to perceive where their partner is more supportive than they are and take the unnatural leadership position in that area, and create details and vision not natural to their personality. The combination of two Supports can have challenges getting things done that will be fulfilling to both parties. For example, a Support might have a strong desire on his own to have a flourishing career, but his partner wishes to travel the world. They should then concentrate on how his vision to make money can support her desired travel ideas. For Ryan, we needed to start small and have him get comfortable with the household decisions and develop strength for leadership, without so much anxiety.

Two Supports together will have a lot of ideas, but they could face challenges with follow through. When two Supports are together, one or both are forced to be in the unnatural position of having to make all the decisions. This could be even as minor as deciding where to go for dinner. Supports often put too much on making the "right" decisions or the decision that will make everybody happy. When something goes wrong and they have to reconfigure and make another quick decision, they can become very anxious, frustrated, and uncomfortable.

Seeking shelter from having to make any decisions is part of the reason why they find themselves in abusive relationships with Selfish Entitleds. They feel less pressure under abuse than dealing with the pressure of possibly making the "wrong" decision. Supports need to realize that it is better to put minor, self-inflicted pressure on themselves and make small decisions, so they can realize it is not a big deal to others if it doesn't work out perfectly.

With two Supports, the Support who is not making the decisions will have to outwardly show support and appreciation for all decisions made. Supports need to realize, when they take the lead, they don't lose their credibility when they are wrong because they are not claiming expertise. So in the example above, if one Support says to another, "What do you want to do for dinner?" If they legitimately want to know what the other person wants to do, then they are offering dominance to them. That being the case, if the restaurant is terrible that night, neither loses any "credibility."

Ryan wanted me to make many simple decisions for him, which would have been easy for me to do because I knew they didn't have much consequence, but that was the lesson I preferred him to learn for himself. He had to learn that most of the decisions could be made in an instant, with no stress or anxiety, because the result was not important. There was no life or death decision, when it came to which car to lease, or tacos versus chicken for dinner. He had to stop worrying he would be "wrong" about a particular decision. His fiancée Emma had to understand that it is not the "man"who often decides this, but rather an Entitled. She needed to acknowledge that making decisions was unnatural for Ryan, and support him in this and avoid complaining when something didn't go as expected. Ryan would take complaints to mean he was not good enough for her or become very stressed out about her unhappiness, thus hurting his ability to make future decisions.

Two Supports together have the potential to hold a lot of resentment against one another. This is because if both are unreformed, they are not typically good at fully expressing themselves. They are not usually good at asking for what they want, or stating what is bothering them. Another reason resentment could build is because the other is not doing something they are used to their previous partners doing, like taking charge. The relationship could seem like a lot of work because both parties will typically prefer their partner to take a strong stance, and neither partner in this case is used to initiating one.

How to Strengthen and Bond a Relationship Between Two Supports

This relationship will require leadership and initiative, which can be shared but is necessary in all areas. First, figure out who has a stronger vision in which areas. Together, you can break down the important categories. For example, home (and the many aspects of it, including how it will be run, where it will be, etc.), family (immediate and interaction with extended), social, business/career/work, communication (who will initiate it – including even talking about this), sex, spirituality/religion, and anything else important to either party. This may seem strange to bring up these topics with your partner because they usually either come up naturally or cause arguments in many relationships.

With two Supports, however, it is often not clear who has the stronger vision, so this needs to be explored. It also might seem like a lot of work, but know that in this type of relationship, more work will be necessary to create inner harmony. The decisions can be made based on who is more versed, experienced, educated, or concerned about a subject. This person should make the decision and follow through in that area. However, it is not the person who is most worried about the outcome, that would be leading with fear; although this can have results, it will create more tension overall.

For example, if someone has a fear of running out of money, in an otherwise comfortable situation, he will choose to run the household based on a lack of money, thus creating tension and unrest. This person should have input, but the person not in fear should make the final decisions, as long as they are not on the opposite end of the spectrum (i.e. careless). The same is true of the relationship itself: if one party is always worried the relationship will end at some point, they should not be entrusted with important decisions concerning its future. Leading with fear is a default mechanism and not truly leading. The person in fear should express their concerns, but they should not be the one to make the decisions. When in a relationship together, Supports have to remember to continue challenging themselves in order to keep things fresh and moving forward. Without a lot of vision and follow through, actions, activities, new developments, excitement, and unpredictability could be lacking in this relationship.

In addition to making decisions, another thing Ryan needed to work on was receiving support from his fiancée. It was hard for him to accept that she would be okay doing what he decided. He kept looking for additional feedback after he made a decision. He needed to realize no feedback was not a silent complaint, as was often the case in his prior relationships. Supports are often uncomfortable receiving support from others but they should acknowledge their partner's effort. The Support initiating should also ask for appreciation when they are not getting it. This will avoid any resentment.

Other Things Two Supports Together
Should be Aware of:

- Get used to fully expressing how you feel and what you want, so the other person can give it to you.

- When two Supports argue, they should seek results instead of just complaining. Ask for what you want instead of just pointing out what you are not happy with. Turn complaints into requests.

- Make a commitment to bring fears and insecurities forward to have awareness of them and deal with them sooner than later in order to achieve harmony in the relationship. Many times Supports are afraid to follow through because of fear or insecurity. If the relationship is to maintain itself, those insecurities have to be overcome. Sharing insecurities most often will save a relationship, but it is dependent on the love shared between the two Supports.

- Be sure to find a vision for yourself, as well as one for the relationship, which is satisfying for the both of you, then work to follow through on that.

A two-Support couple I consulted was not satisfied with the path their life together was taking. They had been together for just under two years and loved one another very much. Talking with them, I soon learned a therapist they had been seeing was making all their decisions for them. Essentially, their therapist had become the Entitled in their relationship. They both had problems making any decisions or requests from the other unless their therapist intervened and gave them direction. They had developed an addiction to his vision for them, yet they were not finding contentment in that, and were unaware as to why. Supports need to be careful that the person's vision they are following is exactly what they want. This could occur with an overbearing parent of one of the two Supports together. When discontentment arises between two Supports, exploring whether or not they have a vision and if others are trying to create one for them is beneficial. Although often born from good intentions, the vision of someone outside the relationship does not prove to be the most satisfying.

A metaphor to describe an Entitled and Support together is a teeter-totter. When one person is a Support, they are on the bottom of the teeter-totter, and the Entitled is on the top. That can easily switch with agreement between the two. Sometimes it switches naturally, with harmony of the two, and sometimes not. Two Entitleds together is like a v-shape teeter-totter with both people on top. It is more difficult to balance but possible with work and agreement, depending on their level of Entitlement. When one side goes down, it may come crashing down and then aggressively switch, hence the power struggles possible with these two types. Two Supports together are like an upside-down v-shape teeter-totter. It may be easier to balance but not much is happening, and there is not much excitement or play. It takes a lot of effort to get one to the top, and without working at it they never are fully on the top.

If you identify yourself as a Support and you are in a relationship with another Support, as long as you are content or can make a few adjustments to be happier, all is well. If not, ask yourself these questions:

- Why are you not taking risks to challenge yourself, or to be with someone who challenges you?
- What are you afraid of? Is your self-protection realistic, or just a function of your last abusive relationship?

- Have you given up on the idea of a relationship that challenges you and are content with being stagnant?

- What other places are you lacking passion in your life? Are you escaping by watching TV, drinking alcohol or using drugs, playing video games, etc., so that you don't have to face not going after what you truly want for your life?

- Are you allowing past relationships with poor choices of partners (who you now know to be Selfish Entitled) dictate current partner choices? Learn the difference between a Benevolent Entitled, a Selfish Entitled and a Reformed Entitled. Knowing the characteristics of each will give you the ability to know which you will have a better and more fulfilling experience with.

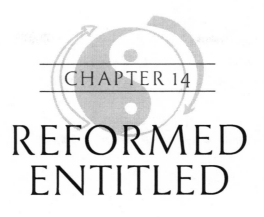

CHAPTER 14

REFORMED ENTITLED

Both Reformed Entitleds and Supports are transformed to a place outside the box that the rest of the categories operate in. At their level of evolvement and compassion for others, you could make a case as to why these Entitleds are Supports and vice versa. These Entitleds use their successes, talents, and creativity to help care for and support others. They use their ability to follow through and visualize supporting both Supports and other Entitleds.

A martial arts instructor I was lucky enough to train with was Reformed Entitled and he would be the first to say that he could not have gotten to the level of emotional intelligence he had attained without many years of training in many different healing arts. I met him just as he was graduating from acupuncture school at the age of sixty. I began to practice martial arts with him in a very unusual class with people from all walks of life. There were CEO's, older women, teenagers and fighters in their early twenties. All the people learning from him practiced together in harmony, despite their different skill levels.

After class, he would have a question and answer with the class for hours, and it seemed like only ten minutes. The questions would range from running a large corporation to avoiding bullies in school, from meditating to improving a failing marriage. The people in the class were determined to find a flaw in Sensei Hofler, but he lived his life the way he coached. He cared for and protected everyone he came in contact with, and you had that feeling from him immediately. He pursued excellence in everything he did, and he focused on caring for others.

This is what I consider a Reformed Entitled (RE). I have witnessed many acts that seem to indicate a Reformed Entitled, but these may just be fleeting moments of inspiration. I would bet that anyone reading this book has had moments of this type of selflessness that have even surprised themselves. We all have moments where we truly desire to protect and care for others wanting nothing in return; aspiring oneself to this level whether it is achieved continuously or not is a goal that will improve the quality of any life or relationship.

I should mention that I don't love the word "Reformed" in this category because it implies that a person is somehow not whole or needs to alter themselves, as opposed to making adjustments to become happier within themselves. Yet, I choose the word reform because no matter how evolved a person is, they may continually find themselves removing faults and improving their conduct.

The Vision of an RE

When Reformed Entitleds do not believe in their vision, they may act in a few ways. They may first go to someone who is accomplished in the area for help or advice. Unreformed Entitleds are typically too proud to ask for help. The Reformed Entitled may divide the vision that seems unobtainable into more obtainable parts. A truly Reformed Entitled will only have a vision that can be accomplished by his or her means. In other words, they don't think so far outside their means that they just talk about their lofty, unobtainable ideal and never follow through on it.

Entitleds all have visions, goals, and strong desires to succeed. Without being able to execute them, they will be anxious, frustrated, angry, and unhappy. It could be that your goals are set higher than what you believe you can accomplish. If so, breaking them down into smaller tasks could be helpful. If not, determine what thoughts or beliefs are holding you back. You could be telling yourself that you are not smart enough, that you need more money to start, that you need to be in a better position, that you need better contacts, etc. Once you have identified the limiting belief, then imagine the unhappiness you will experience in your future, six months, five years, or even ten years from now if you do not eliminate these thoughts. Is it more important to hold on to them, or to creatively find another way? An Entitled's emotional health depends on a positive outlook.

The Care of an RE

Reformed Entitleds do not accept abusers in their Support's life. Selfish Entitleds often suck people dry of their energy while Reformed Entitleds care for and give back energy for serving them. Those supporting them feel appreciated and inspired to provide continued support. Reformed Entitleds do not take advantage of others even when they are willing to put themselves in sacrifice.

Reformed Entitleds take care of their Supports in many ways. They offer things the Support desires but may not ask for. They also use their knowledge and skills to support and teach others. They have usually done some spiritual or psychological work on their pathologies and use them to contribute and create. When they do things for others, they don't attach conditions to it. They are not expecting anything in return, unlike Selfish

Entitleds. They offer their services with no obligations for something in return, and they are not afraid to ask for anything they need. They accept responsibility for their wrongdoings and move on and associate with people who do the same. They are of the mindset that the more evolved person can admit to being wrong, in a commitment to their relationship, rather than needing to be right.

Reformed Entitleds think of the other person's point of view and work to have compassion for others in an argument or negotiation. This does not come naturally to an Entitled, but it will make them feel better than taking things personally. Reforms only associate themselves with more evolved people who know of the RE's leadership and evolvement and are respectful of that. They often give up on their idea of being right and let others "win." They look for the lesson in the problem, rather than staying inside the box, wanting to be right. Reformed Entitleds know that you cannot be a victim and be powerful at the same time. They do not waste time telling stories of all the wrongdoings forced upon them in life, business, or relationships; they know it is just part of the process. They are okay with the idea that not everything comes easy, and they enjoy challenges as part of the game. The Entitleds that have to "win" all the time are constantly making themselves the victim whenever they don't.

Keeping Your Relationship Fresh

Part of what gets old or stale in a long-time relationship is the fact that people take others for granted. Making efforts to be aware of when you are taking others for granted will always make relationships better. When we do things for others with obligations attached, it diminishes the relationship. If you are expecting too much of others, you often feel they are expecting too much of you. However, good relationships do have stated and unstated agreements in which the people involved know their roles. Obligations are anything you expect of someone that is not agreed upon or they do not feel comfortable with, and yet you still expect it from them. Obligations or expectations usually come with no appreciation. Appreciation starts with both parties in a relationship coming from a perspective of "What can I offer?" instead of "What am I getting?" The transformation occurs from a desire to receive and is replaced with a desire to share.

An easy way to show appreciation for your partner is simply letting them know you are listening. This starts the process of good communication. That includes body language, facial expressions, moods and clear signs showing a person is interested. It also includes noticing when a person is unhappy. The first communication exercise about repeating what your partner is saying, in the chapter eleven, on *Getting Along Together*, is very useful for all Entitleds. This often points out to people how little they have been listening and just trying to make their own point. The exercises let the people they are with know that they are actually listening.

Reformed Entitleds take responsibility for the fact that that their energy often determines the mood of the relationship, so if they are upset, they do not impose that on others. If an Unreformed Entitled is upset, they make others upset; if they want tension, they create it. When Entitleds are unhappy, they need to make a conscious effort not to make others feel that way.

List of Things for Entitleds to Do to Evolve to a Reformed Entitled:

- Be aware of when you are justifying your actions. This is not always an easy task because Entitleds often confuse their own logic with justification. Being reformed is being open to the possibility that your logic may be a justification. For example, your fears are not everyone's fears. If you are worried about money and it feels like a "fact," instead of just your fear, that can easily be turned into a justification for actions taken, such as being dishonest with financial dealings. This goes for all justification of your actions.

- Practice compassion and see the other person's point of view. Listen and relate to their situation. Release selfishness, and find meaning in what is important to others, such as when someone wants to do something that is in conflict with what you want to do.

- Acknowledge others. This could be as small as telling someone they did a good job. As an Entitled and a leader, it is a good exercise to be aware of how often you do this.

- Don't put obligations or expectations on anyone unless it is necessary and has been discussed in advance. For example, one partner expecting the other to want a family without prior discussion, adding additional expectations on an employee/partner, or even just taking a friend for dinner and obligating them to do something for you.

- Release fears of letting other people be right and you "wrong."

- Release the fear of losing control in areas where control feels important. If you have a fear of losing something you have achieved, often it is because you have forgotten how hard you worked to obtain it in the first place. If you remember to account for the hard work, connections, and good fortune you've had in acquiring something, then you won't worry about losing it. When you are familiar with that concept, then you know even if you do lose something, you deserve it enough that you can get it back.

- Make a conscious effort to care and protect the people around you in a way that is important to them.

- Let go of what you think you deserve from others, causing you to take them for granted. This promotes humility in relationships, keeping the appreciation present. This could require a trusted partner in the relationship to tell you what you deserve.

Other Qualities of Reformed Entitleds:

- Possess strong personal ethics, especially in leadership.

- Take responsibility for their leadership. They know people look to them for inspiration, and they are not abusive with that, nor do they ignore it. They inspire others to succeed and set an example for people to follow to find themselves in a happier, healthier place.

- Do not use guilt or criticism on people around them; instead they choose gratitude and appreciation. They motivate with positive reinforcement giving compliments and acknowledgment often.

- Act – They take action on their vision instead of just having it. They calculate the risk but don't run from it. If their vision is too big, they find the way to start it in a smaller place, or get in touch with the people who can make it possible.

- Lead without domination. Everyone around them has free will, and the freedom to give their input. The Supports with them always feel that they have choices and can do as they wish.

- Don't hold on to anger the way Entitleds, especially Selfish Entitleds do.

- Have a positive message and a path, and pursue it with integrity.

- Receive trust from people of all walks of life who look to them for leadership.

- Are not afraid to express themselves, especially to help people, even if it is hard for the other person to hear.

- Have full expression in relationships, and have partners that trust their integrity and are open to hearing what they have to say.

- Allow their partners to be heard and acknowledge what they say even if they don't agree with it. They let people in their lives know their opinion is valued.

- Stand up for people, always.

- See solutions before others know there is a problem.

- Accept people as they are and decide whether or not to have them as part of their lives. They don't try to control or manipulate people into being what they want them to be.

- Do not assume the worst in people. When they are wrong and get burned, they move on from it with the lesson learned.

- Apologize easily and genuinely without holding on to a need to be right.

- Prefer to be respected over a need for people to admire or like them. This is because they have a healthy admiration of themselves and what they have been through and strong self-esteem. They don't want to be disliked or hated, but they also don't mind or dispute it. Their success often causes jealousy, but is not their concern, knowing that is other people's issue. (Success means getting what they want out of life and leading and inspiring others to do the same.)

There are many seemingly successful yet unhappy people. I was working with a very wealthy Entitled who was on the verge of being bitter at the world. Everyone looked at him and said, "How is he so angry all the time? He is so rich, he could have anything in the world he wants!" With all his perceived power in the outside world, he felt powerless on the inside. No matter what he did, he realized that because he had no control over himself or his feelings or emotions, he was absolutely powerless. We found that he was not on his path, but was running from fears, so he had nothing significant in his life he was striving for.

In order to break out of the facade of having the perfect life with everything in place, Reforms are willing to face their fear. This is, for example, the well-to-do person who has always worked so hard out of fear of being destitute, yet everyone around him knows being destitute for him is an impossibility. An Entitled seeking happiness will let go of their ego in order to have a more fulfilling life instead of one built by insecurity and running from fears. To do this, the first step is awareness. Despite overwhelming discontent and depression accompanied by some form of escape, Entitleds usually don't have any awareness of the problem being their own imagined fear. This is because there are so many layers of justification built up in every aspect of their lives as to why they are right about the path they have chosen. There are a few reasons that will cause this person to change:

1. They hit rock bottom of some kind causing them to feel great pain or loss. (Financial, drugs, major

depression, spouse or other loved one leaves them, or the realization of pain they are causing others, etc.) This is why the most dangerous Selfish Entitled is a successful one because without any perceived failure, they never experience a catalyst to change.

2. Their unhappiness becomes so obvious to them that they want something better. (This is a more evolved option than #1.)

Once this realization is made, the steps to changing their life can come next:

1. Becoming aware of their fears and realize the actions they have been taking to avoid them is justification, not logic. So in the prior example, a wealthy, greedy man needs to realize being cheap with his employees is not being smart with his money, but is actually abuse of others. He might even justify it by thinking he is protecting his family, but he is hurting the people responsible for his business. Because Entitleds think their fears are logical, they will create multiple layers of justification to avoid any guilt.

2. Breakdown of the justification – they must realize how these beliefs are untrue and are responsible for their unhappiness.

3. Realization that constant comment on themselves and others leads to criticism and then recognizing it as abuse. (It is not necessary, but it may be helpful to realize the childhood source of this. Your parents, teachers, older siblings, or friends may have been the people who taught you so much criticism. Seeing them for who they are and how unhappy they were,

as opposed to the person you admired so much, can be helpful.)

4. Creating a new story that is in direct opposition to the one you have been creating up until this point. If you tell yourself nobody will respect you unless you know all the answers, then try vulnerability and see how people respond.

5. Being aware of the stories you tell yourself when feeling negative emotions such as anger or frustration over why you think people take advantage of you. These stories enforce the negative belief system that you need to protect yourself from people that are out to harm you. Try focusing on people's intentions rather than their actions, and being aware of your own fears. These negative emotions towards others are based on having too high expectations of people, creating disappointment or hurt. Even forgiving others is acting as though they "did" something to you, and at the highest level of evolvement, you will realize no one can do anything to you if you have no expectations or obligations on them. In order to transcend any negative emotion, it is necessary to take full responsibility for having them. Release the false idea that it is someone else's fault for "making" you feel this way. If you think someone else is making you feel a certain way, then you have to wait for an action from them in order for you to move beyond the negative emotion. Taking ownership for your emotions puts you in control of them.

6. Realizing that your own self-righteousness is present even in fears. The idea behind self-righteousness

is that a person will not admit being wrong about anything. Unreformed Entitleds have to get over the fact that they are wrong sometimes and do not know it all. They do not lose any power when they do so. Their self-righteousness is the source of their unhappiness.

7. Committing to your partner's happiness and having compassion for others.

8. Working towards having the life or career that gives you contentment.

9. Contributing with what once were your most limiting qualities that now, with new awareness, will be among your biggest strengths. This includes helping others of lesser means than yourself.

At some point in this process, logic begins to show people how their limiting beliefs have *not* been protecting them but rather, making them so unhappy. The pathology that was in place for so many years loses the fight to logic and your internal desire to find the evidence to constrain your ego driven fears. Often this is why a maximum amount of unhappiness is needed in order to want to fight that pathology and create change. A person doesn't become an RE without a lot of self-discovery and emotional, spiritual, or psychological work.

Attempting to live as a Reformed Entitled does not mean trying to live a life of perfection. That is not realistic and thinking this would lead to more judgment of yourself and others. I suggest to look for ways you can be just a little better each day and see how your life and relationships improve. People often find the most happiness and contentment on a path such as this.

CHAPTER 15

REFORMED SUPPORT

Reformed Supports operate at such a high level of creative ideas they can more easily envision a path to follow a plan to its end. However, they have an almost spiritual awareness that they are here to co-create with others and look for partners with which to do so. They have the ultimate appreciation for those evolved and evolving, and you have a feeling for that at all times when you are around them. Similar to Reformed Entitleds, I have only had the pleasure of knowing a handful of Reformed Supports. They are harder to spot than a Reformed Entitled because unlike Entitleds, they are not interested in outwardly teaching others, but more in helping a select few they admire and trust. All of them lead extraordinary lives in full service to others.

A Reformed Support I have the pleasure to know, Craig, has computer patents for design ideas he came up with in the Eighties. Highly creative, he helped design many aspects of software we still use today. His background is in psychology, and he understands very well what makes people's lives easier, and his designs are based on that. Now in his late fifties, he enjoys most of his time in support of a small group of friends, who because of his tutelage, all live extraordinary lives themselves. Each of them would tell you that they would not have the success they have had in their personal and professional lives without the help and support of Craig. That support includes his advice, connections, knowledge, and any of the access he has in their lives. All of which I can tell you, any intelligent person would hope to have.

He offers his support only to people who can and will accept it. Reformed Supports operate without judgment and have a keen sense of who appreciates and can accept their support. They choose to support *only* those who display integrity, ethics and forthrightness, as well as their own ability to support them. If Craig doesn't feel useful—that is if the person he is supporting doesn't or can't take his help or advice—he will not continue to provide it; this includes follow through. A master chef does not cook for people who only eat hamburgers. It's not that you have to be a Reformed Entitled to get his support, but you have to be working hard at becoming evolved. This avoids dramatic or unhealthy situations. When you work to become your best, these are the type of people that will magnetically come into your life. The biggest thing Craig asks of his friends, in return for his support, is that they live their life pursuing the things they want; that is part of accepting his support.

Craig has an almost immediate sense of who is going to deplete his energy, and he will not spend his time with them. He notices a big difference between someone seeking more knowledge to understand him and someone arguing that they are right and he is wrong. That's not to say that he's always right, but he would not offer support on a subject that he is not well versed in. Reformed Supports do not allow their ego to continue to hold on to negative feelings or arguments; nor do they have the need to "win" arguments, because the people they surround themselves with do not either.

Craig, typical of a Reformed Support, is 100 percent support-ive, but when a relationship shows signs of abuse, he puts an end to it with proper communication and without anger before it gets out of control. Craig has as much compassion for people as anyone I have ever met; he does not, however, let them bring him down to a lowered state of consciousness.

Reformed Supports are very connected to their surround-ings and only seek safe, healthy situations and healthy people. They identify well with people because they have a good under-standing of themselves, and their desire to support and serve others. RS's don't like forced confrontation, and only partici-pate in it when they are going to teach someone or make some difference in them. They do not argue when there is no chance of a good result for either party. If a communication such as this is necessary an RS will request it to be done by an Entitled part-ner of theirs.

Reformed Supports prefer their friends to choose them-selves before them, and put no undue expectations on them either. They also don't allow demands to be put on themselves above what they already planned for. If they do, they don't keep this kind of relationship. On the other hand, they don't spend time feeling guilt for their actions because they always act ethi-cally and surround themselves with responsible people who do not put guilt on others. Real friends won't expect someone to do something they don't want to and trust if they don't, there is no ill intent. Feeling guilt within yourself is a selfish emotion designed to make you feel better about something you feel you did wrong. It is a waste of energy solving nothing, in artificial relationships.

A Reformed Support is aware they have the potential to be in relationships where people could take advantage of them. They are not untrusting and defensive, but they will not stay in relationships where they have the chance of being abused. A Reformed Support realizes his support is a commodity and does not give it away for free. At the very least, they receive appreciation in return. They also request appreciation when they don't feel it, in order to continue to offer their services. If a Reformed Support is offering support and it is not accepted, they will stop offering it.

Reformed Supports are sympathetic but conscious of the fact that their moods are affected by others. Because of this, they are careful not to "jump in someone else's boat," or emotionally take on their pain. At that point no help, but encouragement to the negativity has been offered and then two people are struggling rather than one. A Reformed Support knows you cannot help someone from that standpoint, only hurt them further.

The Energy of Support

Reformed Supports know that their support is about fulfillment, as opposed to capability. Just because you can support someone does not mean that you should. Endurance is a big factor. When you are supporting someone and you feel tired, you have moved into sacrifice. This means they are taking your energy as opposed to those who give you energy for supporting them. You could support someone to exhaustion, but Reformed Supports know better than to do this. The way you know you are serving the right person is you don't get tired. The right person absorbs what you are saying and gives you the right feedback. Like the chef making food for someone who loves it, they both get energy. When you get burned out, you are not supporting the right person.

Reformed Supports do not try to please everyone or over-support anyone. They are not afraid of confrontation, but prevent it by choosing the right people in their lives. They do not have a hard time saying no to people, unlike Blind Supports.

Abuse might be easy to identify for most people, but identifying sacrifice is more difficult. Sacrifice is when something is being taken from you as opposed to you giving it and it is recognizable by the feeling of your energy being drained.

Sacrifice Versus Support

Supports are good at identifying who needs help. The skill they should work on is deciphering who can *accept* help without putting them into sacrifice. Who is evolving and changing from help they receive, and who is just taking help from others with endless demands? When someone isn't able to accept help, in any area big or small, they only put others into sacrifice. Entitleds usually notice when someone is draining their energy. Notice your value in all exchanges, on multiple levels. All healthy relationships have an exchange. Are you getting enough in the exchange?

If you are having poor exchanges with people, look for a more fair exchange. This goes for intimate relationships, friends, employees, bosses, and family. Often Supports, especially Blind Supports, do not get fair exchanges. Keep in mind however, that the exchange can simply be the person truly accepting your help and changing their life because of it and that, in turn, being rewarding enough for you. This can be any relationship, but often happens in philanthropic exchanges.

Some people feel unworthy of receiving, even with obtaining their own success. This is often over an issue of feeling undeserving. These are often people who are loyal to a fault, too pleasing or reasonable and frequently go into sacrifice. Sacrifice is often a familiar feeling, forced on a person in childhood and allowed to continue into their adult life. When a Blind Supports feels this, they need to break the chain. If this is you, making a commitment to your heart to find your desires will help you to create a fire of your own for you to support. Saying "no" is the place to start to eliminate the ignorant pattern of sacrifice of both parties.

Mahatma Gandhi said, "A 'No' uttered from the deepest conviction is better than a 'Yes' merely uttered to please, or worse, to avoid trouble." To truly be able to support someone, the ability to say no to sacrifice must be present. Sacrifice is dangerous for both people involved because Entitleds develop an addiction to the sacrifice and stop rising to challenges presented in their lives, losing their own vision. In most cases, the more the Support puts himself in sacrifice, the more demanding and dissatisfied the Entitled becomes.

If you are a Support and are working in a service position, recognize when you are in sacrifice. Examples are teachers, doctors, bus drivers, therapists, waiters, and nurses. If sacrifice is a typical behavior of yours, the realization will be enough at first. Once the realization is made, it becomes difficult to continue sacrificing for long, knowing you are not helping yourself or others. Before your energy is depleted, a decision should be made to stop your action and communicate to them about their lack of cooperation in the situation causing you to go into sacrifice. Keep in mind that in the workplace, a greater amount of money can relieve the sacrifice, but often this won't last too long before you need another raise in pay.

I was working with a therapist who felt at the end of her day, that all her energy was drained from working with her patients. The reason this was happening was because she was not getting enough in the exchange to make her feel energized. Her commitment was greater than her client's commitment. She found herself doing most of the talking and that she was more committed, more engaged, and more in pursuit of their change. There was no balance for her, and thus her energy was being depleted. It is important for someone like this to operate on a moment-to-moment basis and realize at what point she feels her energy is being taken by the person she is working with. The other option is to continue as is, doubling her hourly rate, causing the client to raise their commitment, and resulting in her feeling as though she is getting more for her time. However, raising her rates would only be a temporary fix.

Instead of overextending themselves, Supports need to realize when their efforts are futile. This is the case with people who just have a difficult time being happy. This could happen "close to home," such as in the case of a spouse, good friend, or family member. The issue is that they are just not happy on their path and draining others in so many ways is natural for them. Creating distance here is recommended in most cases while maintaining love but from afar. It could be painful, but like an animal cutting off his arm to survive, sometimes it must be done. You cannot force someone to accept help if they do not want it, and if you try, you only diminish your ability to help yourself and others who can accept it.

In conflict Supports are most effective with "killing someone with kindness," or elegantly requesting what they require. A Support is not attractive when they are angry and yelling or demanding something. This is partially because they are not as effective from a position of anger with people, so they should make the request in a way more natural to them. They need to learn how to communicate negative feelings in a healthy way. This is often done by being courageous with their vulnerability, while interacting with responsible Entitleds.

As part of reform, Supports should choose who they are going to support. Many times Supports will, not by choice, but by a default mechanism, offer support to anyone. This includes people they should not be supporting or don't want to support. As a Support evolves, they might feel that they are becoming

Entitled. The truth is that they are still a Support but are now demanding more out of their Entitleds. They no longer accept Selfish Entitleds or abusers in their lives, and they require more evolved partners. Reformed Supports find good leaders to follow: Leaders who have integrity, stability, trustworthiness, and compassion. Supports should have their own checklist of whom they will support. It can be something like this:

1. The person should have my interests, or the best interest of other people in mind, not just their own.

2. They should be of sane mind, not chasing fears or escaping anxiety.

3. They should pursue something I believe in or have passion about.

4. They should give me back energy for my support. That can come either from the satisfaction I get from them bettering their life or the lives of others, or through appreciation, care, or gratitude. It can also come in the form of financial, spiritual, or any other gain.

5. They should have a similar belief structure as I do, including their integrity, humanity, spirituality and whatever else I recognize as important to me.

6. The person I support will make me feel comfortable expressing what I want as well as what I'm unhappy about.

7. Even if I never do, I should not feel afraid to tell them "no."

8. They should not make me feel guilty in any way for my actions, or absence of my actions. Instead, if they require a change, proper and respectful communication should be made.

9. I should feel comfortable with their project, vision, or objective as if it were my own and be able to express my ideas and creativity towards that.

10. They will make me feel I am an important part of the objective and not as a simple employee or dismissed in any way.

This will help Supports think of what they are offering as a commodity and not just something anyone can offer. Supports need to put a value behind what they do whether it is for work, career, love, intimacy, family, friends, or just a person that is a passerby in their life.

Of the Reformed Supports and Entitleds that I have met, all are teachers or inspirers in their own way. They have compassion, but they are not too easy on their students. They do not give them everything they want, but allow them to get it in their own way on their own time and help this process by motivating and instilling courage. They are not judgmental of themselves or others. They also do not restrict people by imposing their values on them and talking about how things used to be. They don't expect anyone to do things their way either, but do expect them to listen if they are teaching and will not offer more unless they feel it is useful and appreciated.

Summary of Ideas for Supports to Do to Evolve to Reform:

- Make a point to say what is bothering you in a communicative way. This prevents being taken for granted, continued abuse, and allows a constant level of respect and appreciation. Being communicative means making requests instead of complaining.

- Be aware when you are making excuses for people. This justifies and allows abuse against yourself and others.

- Identify when someone has the potential for abuse and do not establish a friendship with them.

- Identify the abusers in your life and eliminate them, no matter the cost.

- Get comfortable saying no to people who make you feel tired when you support them.

- Selectively choose who you support and *don't* make yourself available to support everyone.

- Make priorities in who/what you support first and let it be known to people in your life. The people who have a problem with your priorities should potentially be eliminated. Of course, this does not include those people to whom you have pre-agreed obligations to, such as a spouse or children, business partners, etc.

- Ask for what you want. Ask for what you require in order to provide support to the right people. After proper communication of what you require, if the commodity of your support is not received, then it is recommended to move on to the person who will give that to you.

Solutions for Supports looking to find happiness should include the pursuit of physical well-being. Mental issues such as doubt, resentment, and insecurity stop the flow of energy in your body and encourage sickness. Solutions can be exercise, including a martial arts practice to get in touch with their power, independence, and confidence. I strongly recommend meditation to create awareness of when you are anxious and why, as well as what you deserve, why you accept what you do, and how you can get in touch with self. (More on this is discussed at *www.TheArtOfUnity.com*). Acupuncture or other energy healing works also can help move anxiety out of the body and prevent blocks and other illnesses.

Qualities of a Reformed Support:

- Have satisfying relationships with intimate partners as well as friends.

- Experience fulfilling sexual relationships.

- Have a solid sense of themselves, including their own masculinity or femininity.

- Have less radical moods and are able to remain happy when others around them are not – their energy is not stolen from them.

- Are not susceptible to others' guilt, obligations, and other manipulations and have confidence in themselves.

- Have individuality and independence, even in a relationship, making more intimacy possible.

- Are able to be patient, compassionate, and understanding without being taken advantage of.

- Have compassion for self, and forgiveness without holding onto guilt, having no judgment or self-pity.

- Accept themselves for who they are, including their aggression and anger, as much as their happiness and excitement. Emotions are like colors in a rainbow, all have a purpose and make a person complete. Denying one would be denying self.

- Practice healthy activities including exercise and have self-discipline respecting their bodies. Physical self-discipline translates to mental self-discipline. Supports do not naturally face conflict; they avoid it. It takes self-discipline to be aware of being taken advantage of, and goes against their nature not to allow it to continue.

- Work through their discomfort with conflict and speak their mind when a boundary is crossed to avoid an explosion of resentment.

- Enjoy their free time without anxiety or guilt.

- Challenge themselves to create a healthy, happier, more evolved life.

Reformed Supports know even the most negative circumstances have some purpose. Of course, they have negative pathologies, as everyone does, but they welcome the challenge and look for the lesson and how they can use those lessons for contribution.

CHAPTER 16

FINDING YOURSELF - THE KEY TO REFORM

People usually come to self-help seeking a way out of their helplessness. They want to get a feeling of control back in their lives. They realize that the minor changes they have been making on their own keep giving them the same negative results. For example, people think all their problems will be solved if they find a new mate, only to revisit the same problems in the next relationship.

To have success implementing this book or any other psychological work, you will need courage, bravery, and commitment. It takes as much courage to change as it does for a soldier to go to war. The difference is that soldiers undergo intense training, preparation and routine when going to war. Not only is there no predictable training for emotional growth, but we are often entrenched in habits that are the opposite of what will bring us happiness. We are taught to give in to or avoid our fears. There is also a high percentage of failure and bad experiences associated with doing psychological work, mostly because people don't have the courage necessary to see it through. Anyone who has discovered his or her path in life will tell you it is worth all the commitment in the world, and there is never an option to go back. Using this book for awareness of a happier path might be all the motivation you need.

Why is So Much of This About Awareness?

Often when I meet people who are rude, I realize they have too much fear and too little awareness. When couples hire me to consult for them and they have a fight in front of me, they regret it thinking, "Oh great, now he will see how I am at my worst." On the contrary, when a person is at their worst, they know it; they do not need a professional to point that out. It is more important to discover the areas where you didn't realize you were hurting someone, or yourself. If you make a choice to say or do things that are offensive or inconsiderate, it's bad enough, but to treat someone poorly and not realize it, is often more damaging to them and to you. This is why I say people have too much fear and too little awareness. Overcompensating for the fear, or trying to protect yourself from what you think you should be afraid of, often leads to unknowingly hurting someone else.

In reform, the idea is to be in control of your category (Entitled or Support), as opposed to it being in control of you. Many people have no concept of this and continue to hurt themselves and others. They start bad relationships and ruin good ones because of their ignorance. Discovering if your desires are actually more motivated by your fears and committing to act in the most responsible way to yourself and others is a good place to start. Once you know your type, use the most positive attributes that come naturally to you. Supports will find fulfillment exploring their creativity while advocating an Entitled they believe in. An Entitled's contentment will be found initiating ideas, following through on visions, taking risks that others would not, all while taking care of those around them. If the risk doesn't pay off as expected, then altering the method until it does, or finding a different vision, is recommended. Discovery and continued awareness of your best qualities as well as your subconscious fears will clear the path to reform and happiness.

Awareness is the first step to reform. You operate out of fear when you accept behavior that is uncomfortable and abusive, and you don't have to. Accepting abuse relates to a person's fear of abandonment and codependence. These are fears that over-power the discomfort you feel while mistreated. Being aware of your escapes and addictions allows you to move away from continuing to use them to distract you from your fears. Leaving your escapes or addictions will often intensify the anxiety and fear, but it is a necessary part of finding the path to happiness. This is why it often takes a level 10 of unhappiness to give some-one the motivation to make a change. It also takes the discipline similar to that of a pro athlete to maintain it.

Without self-awareness there exists a breading ground for ego and pathology. When you don't have awareness your ego, shame, and fears are left to control your direction. Having self-awareness allows for pathology to be overcome.

It is important to be non-judgmental about what you want to change; otherwise you will replace one unhappy situation with guilt or self-punishment. Self-judgment and self-punishment can be automatic. "Wow, I can't believe I did that. I'm so stupid," "Someone else deserves this more than me," "I wish I were… (something or somebody else)" All this creates is guilt, frustra-tion, depression and other ways of beating yourself up.

Often intimate partners feel threatened about the new land-scape the psychological work will create in a relationship. A lack of understanding of what is going on causes this fear. In order to help your partner feel safe, they have to be well informed that what you are doing will enhance a healthy relationship. If the relationship does not have an ability to be healthy, this work will be the road to ending the relationship. It is critical for your partner to be supportive and join you in order to have success towards reform. With a sense of partnership, the work can be intimate, rewarding, and the spark of something new that many relationships need. Without that support, Entitleds will confuse new strength with an attempt to dominate them, and they will take advantage of the vulnerability this work requires. As the reform to happiness continues, abusive relationships will be exited, as they should.

Dysfunction and Self Realization

Because the dysfunction has always been there, we are often not aware of how destructive we are to ourselves and others. This is especially true with those that we love the most and occurs most frequently in extremes (Selfish Entitled and Blind Supports). If we were suddenly released of our pathologies and were able to find a partner without our dysfunction holding us back, we would think, "Wow, what a terrible ordeal I was in. That had nothing to do with who I really am." It would be like having a nail in your chest for your entire life. When it was suddenly taken out, how much better could you breathe, move and function? Even to try to explain to someone with the nail in their chest how much better their life would be without it would be difficult. Having had the problem for a lifetime, being without it is unknown for them. They would think they were going to die if it were removed. The slow process of removing it would be painful and scary and would require a lot of trust. Until it is totally free, they wouldn't look back and think how uncomfortable and destructive it was. This is why awareness regarding our pathologies and fears versus our nature is important. Most people are never in the moment enough that they can see how dysfunctional they are. They find themselves in an environment that offers similar dysfunction in their choice of friends, so their own seems normal.

The first part of the process is agreeing that we have dysfunctions or pathology. Most people do not come to this agreement without either being extremely unhappy, or making the realization that they are hurting the people they love. Many times relationships are able to exist based on their complementing dysfunctions matching up. So if someone operates with the dysfunction of neediness, and they hook up with someone who is jealous, the two dysfunctions can create a codependent bond. The jealousy will be accepted because it makes the other feel needed. A controller might match up with someone who has a strong fear of abandonment; an addict might bode well with a depressant because they can relate. There are so many possibilities. This is how abusers and those abused or codependent find one another.

Once your dysfunction is recognized, the next step after the discovery is to be aware of when it comes up. Recognize that it is not a part of you but an illusion you have created from fear, and release the dysfunction. This is often very challenging because, like removing the nail from our chest, we might think we will die without it. For example, we might even discover that without our dysfunction, we do not even like the person we are with. If a jealous person lost that dysfunction, suddenly their partner's neediness would become repulsive. For this reason, once you are aware of a dysfunction, it is interesting to see what qualities you have manifested to go along with it. What dysfunction is it partnered to? (Like neediness and jealousy.) More on this is discussed in *co-dependence* later in this chapter.

How Do I Make a Change?

Awareness of your dissatisfaction can inspire you to change. Anger, frustration, impatience and depression are not bad emotions to have as long as you don't stay with them for long. If they are strong enough they can inspire you to make a change you've been avoiding. Beating yourself up is a waste of time that doesn't inspire change. Emotions such as fear, insecurity, self-doubt, blame, shame, and hopelessness also leave you stagnant in negative circumstances.

If you are with someone others perceive as obviously abusive, but it eludes you, you can bet you are not on your path; it is your pathology. To differentiate these, it is important to understand the difference between settling and contentment. True contentment is unmistakable when it is found and settling is just giving into fear. Another clue to misguided contentment is when you feel a need to be abusive to others. People who are content on their path are not motivated for revenge, putting others down to make themselves feel better, needing to be right, one-upping, etc.

Sex can often be a distraction that gives someone the idea they are reaching their contentment, when in fact not much else is working. There are many pathologies associated with sex that can easily attach people. Unfortunately, when sex is there just to alleviate fears, or is the only thing that is working in the relationship, it only provides a temporary high.

The first step to reform is recognizing any dysfunction in your relationships and not ignoring it. If you feel you are temporarily stuck in a bad or abusive situation, learn what you can from it so you don't allow it again in your life. Many problems continue because people are unaware of the difference between their nature/essence and their pathology.

Self Discovery - Your Pathology versus Your Nature

I am often asked if I believe people can change. I believe they have already made a change, often for the worse, and need to discover themselves again. Fears, pathologies, and insecurities take us away from our happy, innocent, fun-loving, inspired self. Rediscovering yourself spiritually or psychologically can bring you back to who you really are. That is the change I believe all people are capable of. The most important thing in becoming reformed is knowing your nature versus your pathology. The point of this book is to help you realize who you are, why you react the way you do, and why you are unhappy or unfulfilled when that occurs. One of the most unpleasant experiences someone can have is to be unhappy and not know why or how to get out of the situation causing it. Knowing your type and who you need to surround yourself with can lead to better awareness of why you feel the way you do.

The Most Important Aspects to Know about Yourself to Find Contentment:

1. *Knowing your pathology or neurosis versus your nature/ essence,* and the difference between them. As part of a person's pathology, they could cross the line to an unnatural category based on fear, anger, self-protection, insecurity, ego, etc. This should be recognized as a pathology and not your nature.

2. *The ability to express your nature.* You want to surround yourself with people that allow this, and also inspire it. Dismantle your fears and insecurities and allow yourself the confidence to express who you are naturally.

3. *Finding people whose nature complements yours.* If you are a Support you want to partner with Entitleds and

vice versa. This will allow you to co-create with others symbiotically. Be mindful to look for a person who naturally receives what is natural for you to provide and vice versa. In reform, you don't spend any time with people who take your energy or take advantage of your good nature.

4. *The ability to receive the nature of people who comple-*
   ments yours. It takes a certain confidence and trust to allow others to support or take care of you.

Many relationships lack substance because people unaware of their nature do not connect with partners who will complement well with who they really are. At the start of most relationships, people build a rapport relating to one another strictly by pathology or the ability a potential partner has to alleviate their fears. This will build a certain rapport until they can no longer hold up the façade of trying to be the person they think their partner wants them to be. Fears rarely, if ever, are overcome externally and need to be worked on within. Discovering your pathology versus your nature, will allow you to identify someone else who has done the same, or has an ability to create healthier partnerships.

It will take some real investigation to learn your nature versus pathology because the pathology often feels natural. From an earlier example, Ryan, like many people, thought of himself as someone who does not, "by nature," like to ask for help from others. In most cases this is a learned pathology, not a natural response. He had an association, learned when he was young, that asking for help is a negative thing. This can be easily associated with a person whose parents called them stupid, or told them that they would never make anything of their lives, every time they asked for help. This is the type of person that will think they "naturally" like to do things without anyone's help because they have such negative connotations associated with asking. That is not natural, it's a hurtful experience carried from childhood into adult decisions. It is healthy to ask for and accept support. When I have trouble, I have a wonderful range of advisors to go to that I respect and can call upon. I enjoy learning from them as well as the interaction, but the very reason they are in place is because I like finding people I can go to for help.

Identifying Shame

Identifying when you escape (explained on page 112) can aid in uncovering your nature because it can reveal a lot about what you unknowingly may be hiding underneath. What are you escaping from? Guilt may have a small role but escaping occurs on a deeper level known as shame; there is a considerable distinction between the two. Guilt is connected to your behavior and shame is connected to self. Guilt tells you that you did something bad, i.e. "I made a mistake," and shame tells you that you *are* bad, i.e. "I am a mistake." You can see how shame is far more impactful and harder to overcome because it is an attack on a person's own character. Shame has a person believe that no matter what the outcome, they are not good enough; and should they overcome that belief, it's replaced with, "Who do you think you are?" Shame camouflages our nature and who we truly are because it tells us we are not good enough to be just that.

The frequency and power of these thoughts is matched with the level of escape a person needs to resort to, in order to quiet them. For this reason shame goes hand in hand with addiction, aggression, depression, violence, bullying, eating disorders, and suicide. Unfortunately these only result in adding more shame, requiring a stronger level of escape, therefore creating a vicious cycle.

The way out of this is having the courage to face the shame. Depending on the level of shame a person experiences, it may require talking to a professional to find the way out. Regardless of the path taken, being aware of the shame, finding your escape pattern, and choosing not to escape is a good start. After which, challenging the shame's validity at every level: Try asking yourself, 'What is the evidence for this worthlessness to exist?' If you have trouble finding evidence against your shame, that is an indication to bring in a professional or someone levelheaded who cares about you. Developing an ability to tolerate it when it shows up without escaping is important, that might include journaling, meditating, joining a support group, or talking about it to bring it into the open and have others reveal how untrue it is. Overcoming shame may include releasing toxic people in your life that perpetuate this shame. Instead of holding on to the shame find ways to release the thoughts as the myth of unworthiness that they are and allow for self-acceptance.

Shame is accompanied and expanded by secrecy, silence, denial, regret, blame, and judgment. Running from those egoistic instincts will help expose the shame. It is also linked to abusers, enablers, and co-dependence, so be aware of who the shame has brought into your life. Other signs of shame are the "protective" ways the ego thinks it can turn it off, such as controlling behavior, perfectionism, procrastination, and being critical of others. The realization that you are worthy of connection, even with your most shameful aspects, will aid in overcoming any aspect of feeling unworthy, and reveal more of your true nature.

If shame or fear is holding you back, realize that you will accomplish your goals when your fear of not going for them overcomes your fear of failure, or your need for success. That requires courage to overcome your vulnerability to whomever or whatever it is your shame is telling to you shy away from. Having had success as a professional kickboxer and dancer, I have learned that the important lessons were not obtained from winning a fight or dancing well in a show. They came from over-coming the unforgettable feeling of humbly returning to the gym after getting beaten over and over again in practice. They came from standing on the sidelines in a dance studio feeling too ashamed to ask anyone to dance for fear of not being good enough or of hearing a polite, "no thank you," for the umpteenth time. I know these lessons exist everyday in the subtlest of ways in both new and old relationships with people who don't ask for what they deserve. I hope my work reflects the message of how to overcome those fears and shame, and offers the tools to create the life and relationship you really want. I have learned that having courage as part of your values far outweighs success, and is imperative for finding your true nature.

Defense Mechanisms

The difference between your nature versus your pathology can be found in exploring your defense mechanism. What do you perceive as a threat and why? What truth lies behind what you are so strongly defending and which you do not want to be brought to light? Feeling a need to defend yourself is caused by a lack of trust in the person that is pointing something out to you. The lack of trust causes you to view what they said as a perceived attack.

The instinct to defend would cause a reformed person to explore where the perceived attack could be true and why they would feel a need to cover something up from the people they are partnered with. When a person defends themselves they are turning away from a situation where they could be vulnerable to their perceived "attacker" by admitting an insecurity and asking for help. The other option, if the accusation is false, is to help the attacker to discover the root of their misinterpreted idea. Choosing to become defensive is a desire to move away from vulnerability that signifies some deeper shame, lie, or pathology, and certainly nothing that would help any healthy relationship.

Your nature would point out where the perceived attack could be true and avoid the situation; or knowing the perceived attack is untrue, it would dismiss the lie. Your pathology, on the other hand, is interested in creating cover-ups for protection. Any cover-ups are good indicators you are moving away from your path or true nature.

Knowing what triggers your defense can tell you where you are being inauthentic and help you discover your pathology. What emotions are triggered by the defense? Selfish Entitleds are often immediately activated to defend themselves. They often feel backed into a corner because they are hiding their insecurity. The emotions associated with it are usually fear/anxiety turned into anger. This is what causes so many Selfish Entitleds to be abusive towards others and often angry.

Blind Supports take the longest to have their defense mechanism activated. When activated, they often defend the relationship shared with the attacker instead of themselves. The emotion associated for them is fear turned to sadness or depression. It often occurs as part of a fear of abandonment. Afraid to say no, to avoid this, they go into sacrifice.

While under stress, Blind Supports tell themselves, "Other people are safe, trustworthy and a good source of support and comfort." This is fine in carefully selected cases, but their bad judgment often leaves them more open to abuse. This unconditional acceptance reflects pathologies that convince them they are unlovable, undeserving, not perfect, they will never find the right person, etc. This is cause for them to give more than they should, and accept less than they deserve. These thoughts steer the person away from their true nature.

The difference with Selfish Entitleds while under stress is that they think, "Other people are dangerous, not to be trusted and will hurt me." "I have to rely on myself and guard against others."

Their pathologies convince them they won't get anything unless they do it themselves, nobody cares about them, and they are deserving of so much more than what they have, consequently causing resentment. This need for self-protection gives them the justification to abuse others, and can turn into revenge and spite, steering them away from their nature.

Knowing your pathology also allows you to notice your unnecessary defense based on misinterpreting something. Misinterpretation is often the result of a lack of trust. The question to ask is, If I don't trust this person, then why are they in my life? If you know they can't be trusted but they do bring value in some way, then it may be okay to have a limited relationship. However, there is no longer a need to be defensive because if you know they can't be trusted, they shouldn't surprise you. If you are defensive with your significant other, then it is recommended to get to the bottom of what the issue really is. On what is your fear based? Explaining to them where you are vulnerable so they don't push those buttons is the first step. If they continue to push them after that, then it becomes abuse because at this point it has been made clear that their behavior is hurting you. If someone you are with is constantly putting you in a defensive position, understanding why you are feeling attacked will reveal a lot about you and your relationship.

Think of the last time you felt the need to defend yourself? There must have been some truth to it; otherwise you wouldn't have gotten upset. For example, if someone accused you of being an axe murderer, you would either laugh or just ignore it. What you perceive as an insult could be the opportunity for an important lesson. If you change your defense to an opportunity, you are left with two lessons: that which comes before (the catalyst) and that which comes after (the response). Here you will find your fear causing the defense and how you responded to it.

For example, let's say that you are naturally very strong. If someone points out to you that you are hurting them when you shake their hand, and what you hear instead is that they think you're hurting them on purpose, that is a reaction from your pathology. Instead, just become aware of your own strength until you have control of it. Most likely though, if you protest their statement, what you are defending is your pathology. In this case, it is beneficial to know what triggered it (the catalyst). It is important to know why you interpret something someone is saying to you one way, when in fact they mean it another way. Are you actually being accused of something, or is someone just making a statement that may be of value to you? Being defensive also causes you to miss seeing another person's point of view.

If you are often on the defense, try to keep a tally of it. Compare the idea to an obese person keeping a journal of what they eat everyday in order to be aware of what they are unknowingly doing. Similar to how overeaters discover they did not know how much they were eating, a defensive person will not be aware of the conflict and abuse they falsely create. Defensiveness is often a sign of dissatisfaction or a lack of trust. Look deeper to find out where you are settling to discover your dissatisfaction in your relationship?

Emotional Prisons

Related to your self-fulfilling prophecy, Emotional Prisons are places you find yourself when unhappy, to the point of tormenting yourself over an issue involving trust in loved ones, friends, or family, over something insignificant or untrue. This includes doubting others to the point of investigation, what you make other people prove to you, and issues which are really yours and not theirs. It could manifest itself as jealousy, thinking your partner is cheating on you, thinking people are making a fool of you, thinking you are unloved, are being used, 'I don't matter to anyone,' etc.

Ellen, a 34 year-old woman I consulted had convinced herself that she'd never have a great relationship because no one could truly love her. You can easily see how her self-fulfilling prophecy here put her in an Emotional Prison. When in a relationship she was constantly looking for evidence to prove the love that her intimate partners offered her was false. The deeper she fell in love with a man, the more she needed him to prove his love, because her fear of being increasingly vulnerable made it more difficult to believe in his love for her. Her Emotional Prison was her act of doubting and investigating whether he loved her, in every detail of his actions.

The realization that she was in her Emotional Prison came when I pointed out to her how much time she spent convincing herself that he was always doing something insincere or dishonest towards her, when none of her theories ever turned out true. Investigating how unloved she was, like most Emotional Prisons, became a place of comfort found in discomfort for her. This is how you know it is associated with some childhood pathologies, not true nature. The comfort came in the familiarity of spending so much time in this place, that she did not feel safe without doing this investigation; she had come to believe that she was actually protecting herself.

How do you know what your Emotional Prison is?

The Emotional Prison is what you most question in people and you most need them to prove to you. It is the negative emotion that you find yourself basking in. It is a place where you try to convince yourself you do not matter, are not loved, are being lied to, or not valued by others in some way. The investigation results in drawing conclusions, misinterpreting conversations, lying to yourself, creating unnecessary fights, and could include checking another's emails, eavesdropping on phone calls, etc., all to prove your Emotional Prison is true.

How do you know when you are going into or are in your prison?

The "logic," behind the EP is that if you are hyper-aware, worry, investigate, and accuse, you will not be caught in the same "trap" you have seen or been in before. It is easy to uncover a person's supposed trap, based on what they talk about that is most important to them, especially when expressed in a negative manner. For example, someone who says, "The most important thing in a relationship (or friendship) is someone who doesn't cheat or lie." For sure, this is their EP, looking for their friends or lover cheating or lying. Emotional Prisons are very active amongst people who are often angry, hold grudges, jealous, untrusting, envious, and who often speak of being disappointed by others.

Another kind of EP is when you find yourself wanting other people to suffer, in the same way you are suffering, especially your intimate partners. Wishing harm on others, especially loved ones, is not a natural state and should trigger you that a change needs to be made. Part of the danger of Emotional Prisons is that you make your partner your enemy, and it gives you a false justification that it's okay to treat them poorly.

Knowing why you are going into your EP is the "key" to getting out. When you break down all Emotional Prisons, you will find they hold only two objectives. It's either a search for love, or trying to prove the love is not there. Once you realize this, the easier thing to do is to just ask for the love. This will stop you from going into your EP or help you get out of it.

Identifying Fear

Anytime we are emotionally uncomfortable we are operating from, or approaching, fear. Discovering your own subconscious fears is a key to discovering yourself. When a person is reacting because of a strong negative emotion, such as frustration, rage, jealousy, etc., the most evolved have what I call a "pathology intervention." This is a sort of alarm that goes off when you are in a place that you do not want to be and tells you to stop (or intervenes) and prompts you to take a different path. To support this intervention, you may just stop and breathe, or go into a different room to revaluate what you want to accomplish in order to come to a more positive emotional state. This can be one process for realizing negative emotions such as this, are not part of your nature but your pathology.

To help find your fears, it is helpful to identify different types of fears and their roots. Every negative emotion or drama can be broken down into three basic fears. The fear of (1) losing safety or control, (2) being alone, disconnected or abandoned, and (3) feeling unworthy. Although these fears may cause a lot of stress they are largely conceptual or imaginary. Real fears help us avoid danger and kick in to protect us from a dangerous threat, such as a speeding car coming towards us or a raging fire.

Often rage, depression, jealousy, hate, shame, and controlling others are based on the feeling of being powerless and part of the fear of losing safety and control. Emotions caused by fear ruin relationships as well as take a person away from contentment. The path to true safety or security is through facing and overcoming this fear.

Fear of abandonment encompasses not just being left by someone physically, but also emotionally, and includes the fear of being alone, disconnection, the unknown, loss, and death. This fear could stem from the experience of a parent leaving for a vacation or work during a vulnerable time in childhood. It could also stem from a parent threatening to leave or send a child away if they do not behave. Any addictions held by parents could result in abandonment of their children. That includes alcohol, drugs, TV, video games, work, etc.

Someone that is overwhelmingly upset at the end of a relationship is often suffering from a fear of abandonment. An important question to ask if you suffer from this fear is, are you with your partner because you truly feel that they are your soul mate or because you are afraid of being alone?

Much suffering is caused from the basis of feeling separate, unwanted or unworthy. One of our most basic desires as humans is that of belonging, and we experience this through friendships, groups, culture, environment, race and relationships. You can easily see in children their desire to give and receive love, even from inanimate objects, such as a stuffed animal.

The fear of unworthiness is one that can encompass many things, such as thinking of yourself as not being smart enough, not important to anyone, not able to make a difference, inadequate, unworthy of love, and unable to make anything of yourself. These feelings of self-doubt and berating oneself all say that you don't measure up. Someone with a feeling of unworthiness prevents good relationships from getting started by pushing people away and also settles for relationships that are abusive, or do not offer any growth. This unworthiness or shame can be started easily enough from simple childhood punishment, rejection, non-acceptance, or just not getting what a person wants. One way to expose this fear is by figuring out how much of what you do is motivated by wanting approval, including from yourself.

Are you in love or are you avoiding fear? Love is the only thing that will overcome the resentment, anger, and frustration that people normally go through in a marriage or any relationship.

Love causes you to overcome your self-righteousness when you are being uncompromising. Letting go of being right defines a relationship as well as the happiness of the individual. If you are in a relationship to avoid a fear of being alone, as opposed to genuine love, when typical challenges of a relationship manifest or some resentment builds, the relationship will not endure it. Often when these relationships split up, each person wonders why yet another relationship of theirs has ended. The truth is, it was not a "real" relationship based on love to begin with, it was instead an unsaid agreement to alleviate one another's fears. Most people don't realize when they are in a relationship to alleviate fear. They just think they are in love because they feel better than they did when they were alone.

Fear comes when you think you will not get what you want and that your only option to getting it is being cut off. With true expectations for achieving something you know you deserve, there is no fear, no negative emotions, and no loss, thus giving you what you want, or the realization that you already have it or don't need it.

Identifying and eliminating fears is a key to discovering your nature and what you can contribute within a relationship. Once you know the fear, you can then discover how it is unfounded. The fear is almost always unfounded and creates unnecessary worry. Creating negative anticipations only increases the problem. An important formula is:

Negative emotion = Fear

Fear = Illusion

To face and move through your unfounded fears, it is necessary to continue to plan, create, explore and prepare despite what your pathology is trying to make you run from. A strong exception to this rule is when you feel someone is being abusive to you. In that case, you are better served exiting the relationship.

Connected by Pathology

People are surprised to hear that our pathologies connect us. Just think about when someone believes they are not enough, they often find someone who will confirm that belief. This is a connection by pathology. There is a give and take here connecting two people by a negative force created from their childhood. It is the same with how someone with neediness or dependency will partner with someone who likes dominance or control. A relationship with these qualities is often fueled by abuse and jealousy. It is beneficial to be aware if, and where, you build these negative connections based on your fears or insecurity.

To understand this, there is something very simple at its root: familiarity. We base our identity on the roles we have always been familiar with because there is comfort in the familiar. If a person's role and identity is to always be in fear, they will subconsciously look for situations to fit that role. No matter what someone might claim in their complaint, familiarity trumps all. Where does your familiarity lie? In *not* being loved? In having to *fight* to get what you want? Or in acceptance and expectation of getting what you want? Does it lie with happiness and harmony, or drama and jealousy?

You can also find this on a smaller level based on where you are afraid to express yourself. We are often drawn to partners that are comfortable expressing an emotion or feeling that we are uncomfortable with. For example, if a woman is shameful about expressing her own anger, it will be comforting for her to partner with someone who expresses anger easily. Her partner will find a link to an emotion she is more comfortable expressing than he, such as neediness. These attractions are links often hidden in the subconscious. So his dependency is somewhat expressed through her neediness, and her anger is expressed through him.

Not expressing yourself is dangerous in many ways. For example, it can be released as a physical sickness, as so much medical evidence is now showing, or it can turn into some other negative emotion you are more comfortable expressing. So, anger could turn into depression or self-loathing/blame. Typical examples of physical illness from the stress of blocking emotions are digestion problems, headaches, ulcers, muscle tension, high blood pressure, heart problems, lowered immunity, and even cancer. If you have any of these ailments, it may be an indication that you are blocking some emotion.

Practicing expressing how you feel, even if that means simply writing it down in a journal will release pressure and stress. At first, it will be challenging, but releasing a little at a time with a trusted partner will help develop more skill and comfort in expression and in the ability to request what you want.

How Pathologies Can Keep a Bad Relationship Together

Even if you cannot completely escape your pathologies, you can be aware of them and not justify, ignore, or fuel them. Entitleds are often seemingly the more attractive or sexier type because they link people to more of their pathologies. If a person is dealing with issues of abandonment, attracted to unpredictability, seeking approval from a leader, they would be attracted to an Entitled's strong personality.

These pathologies people subconsciously carry can be temporarily alleviated through the perceived intimacy and approval of sex. Entitleds also have a certain confidence to lead that people find attractive, even if it takes them in the wrong direction. If you are unhappy in a relationship and cannot seem to get out of it, you can be fairly certain you are linked by pathology, and/or a longtime fear that you feel your partner is alleviating. This is especially true if you are unhappy, and yet strongly attracted to this person.

Repetition Compulsion is the impulse to reenact earlier emotional experiences or traumatic events. This happens with both Entitleds and Supports, but very typical of Blind Supports. The desire is not to derive pleasure from a painful situation like a masochist, but rather an attempt to relive and overcome an unsatisfying situation.

A typical example of this is people who have not been given a "voice" growing up and have the lifelong task of repairing themselves. They choose to do this by getting people to "hear" them, intern giving them a sense of importance. The problem is that not just any listener will do, it has to be someone of perceived importance similar to the one who didn't allow their voice to be heard previously: their parental figure. The listener they prefer is the same neglectful type they are familiar with, such as a Selfish Entitled. Unfortunately, that is the type who happens to also be abusive in relationships, yet they feel overcoming the neglect as a source of validation. This cycle constantly repeats itself because the person knows no other way of making themselves feel important, and thus the subconscious attraction.

This pathology starts because in order to survive intensely negative situations, such as neglect or abuse, children must deny the reality of their predicament, as well as their intense anger, depression, and despair. They cling to the hope that, if only they are good, smart, quiet, etc., they will win over their parent and will finally get the love and approval they've been denied. Because this is what they are used to, it often becomes their reality in adult relationships.

The point is not to be hard on yourself. If the pain is too much to exit the relationship now, then don't. Use it to discover why you pick and stay with the wrong person. Keep a journal of the unhappiness you feel focusing on how often, when, and why it happens. Then explore the pathology that connects you to this person that is unhealthy for you. Questions you may ask yourself during your exploration are:

- Who do they remind you of, and is there a pattern of similar abuse from your childhood or past relationships?

- What are you trying to re-create in order to heal?

- Why are you incomplete without this relationship? Why do you feel unsafe, alone, abandoned, unworthy or need someone outside of yourself to be complete?

- Is this unhappy relationship something you want, or just something you are familiar with?

- Is it possible to heal this issue through this relationship? Or would it be better to heal the perception of what happened on your own, and go for a healthier relationship in the future?

- What negative construct or familiarity, learned from your parents, is causing you to choose unhealthy partners now? For example – your mother may love you dearly, but also emotionally abandoned you, so if a person emotionally abandons you, you seek their love.

- What age are these feelings most associated with when you are feeling them? (For example, do they cause you to feel like you did when you were a vulnerable 13 year-old or perhaps younger?)

Take time observing this. The fact is you could learn a lot from the relationship you are in. This is valuable information to help you avoid this type of relationship again, intimate or otherwise.

Supports can have more of a tendency not to feel whole without a partner. During or after a separation, whatever you miss in your ex-partner, look for in yourself; you probably possess it in abundance. If you are settling for destructive relationships, begin to find gratitude in the positive qualities you have to offer. Know that you are perfect for someone. Look at yourself, not with comparisons, but with love and without fear. When a person seeking approval approves of him- or herself, they will attract the kind of people they can create healthy relationships with. When they feel desperate and fearful, they will attract the same destructive characters they always have.

Co-Dependence

In a dependent relationship, the over-attachment and neediness can be associated with a fear of abandonment, unworthiness, and dependence on someone outside of yourself. Co-dependence is often caused by someone using the other person in the relationship to help cure the issues they have with self-esteem, self-image, self-worth, gender/body/emotional insecurities, motivational issues, shame, etc. When this importance is dependent on another person, their absence will cause the worst manifestations of the issue, magnified. If you need another person in your life to be happy, there is codependence. This also points out the curious issue of people being dependent on someone else being dependent on them.

Codependent behavior is often seen in spouses and children of alcoholics and other drug abusers, as well as people who accept physical or chronic emotional abuse. Dependents have little or no ability to love themselves, so they rely on their partners to do that for them. This is why they take a break-up so hard: they are dependent on the other person loving them because they feel that person is the only one who could.

Having no love for yourself combined with an addictive need to receive it from another person, usually abusive, makes for a relationship roller coaster; temporary highs and awful lows. The highs consist of both sides temporarily alleviating one another from their fear of loss, abandonment, and unworthiness but there is never genuine love or connection. The first step to releasing this is admitting the dysfunction as well as walking away or saying no to abuse and other addictions.

Dependents have expectations that a relationship will cure their anxiety about the lack of love and insecurity in themselves and make life worth living. They expect certain mistreatment, possible rejection or abandonment, as part of any relationship and will do anything in order to avoid that. This could include manipulation, going into sacrifice and accepting abuse in order not to split up with their partner. They have a need to control the other person because their happiness is associated with them. The evidence of this is the emotional roller coaster a person feels in a bad relationship.

What co-dependents call love is really a ball of jealousy, competition, possessiveness, anger and hatred, neediness, domination, and manipulation. When two people are dependent on one another, then they are not choosing to be together; they are choosing to give in to their fears and addictions. Saying they are in love is like saying alcoholics drink because they love the taste of their drinks. They don't do it because they love it, but because they no longer have free will. It is no longer a choice.

Two-thirds of Americans suffer from low self-esteem[1] so there are a lot of potential candidates for dependent or abusive relationships. But to discover the source of how this occurs, we need to look into their life. If we break down what people want

---

1. (**Source:** Gallup Poll quoted in *Self-Esteem: The New Reformation* by Robert Schuller.)

in life into categories, we can see where they are happy or not. Let's take just a few of the major categories, such as:

1. Career – money, power, job, day-to-day life

2. Family – love, acceptance, acknowledgment

3. Friends – love, acceptance, trust, loyalty

4. Relationship – attraction, love, acceptance, trust, companionship

5. Path – contentment/satisfaction in life at a level of your soul, impact on society/world, feeling of fulfillment with your life, purpose

6. Expression – creatively, conversationally, having a voice

Which Is Fulfilling in Your Life?

Many of the co-dependent people I have worked with say they have no happiness in these categories or just some happiness with one or sometimes two of them. In their mind, the easiest solution is to change their intimate relationship. They can usually find someone they are attracted to or who is attracted to them. Then they attach their worth, esteem, issues with body, and other insecurities to that partner. When they do not get exactly what they want, they lose their worth. They then lose their motivations, drive, hope, and opportunity, ending up at the mercy of the abuse they suffer in the relationship. This makes it even more difficult to make improvements in the other categories; yet another reason feeling whole is important prior to entering a relationship.

How Do I Escape This?

Dependency can be described as the lack of mental whole-ness unless under the perceived care of another. The way out is through finding yourself. You might not be able to change your career, family, friends, and path easily, but you can change how you accept or interpret them.

An important realization I made with my own family is that when my mother was saying to me, "You look too skinny; why do you dress like that, etc…" she was actually saying, "I love you and I want the very best for you, more than anyone else, because I would never say these things to anyone else." She cared for and accepted me in every way and knows that I can be better. So every time she started in with her criticisms, I translated them and accepted them differently in my own mind. This made me feel content, and incredibly improved our relationship. It also gave me the inspiration to ask her nicely how I would prefer she express her love to me. The same is possible with friendships, career, or anything you begin to appreciate in ways you haven't before.

This is difficult to do when you are trying to control someone to give you a result within an abusive relationship. Dependents have no responsibility for their own emotions, because they put that responsibility on others. This leaves them completely vulnerable to the other person's moods, actions and ideas.

Co-dependent people need to spend time single to develop responsibility for their own emotions and value their own worth. It starts with being in the moment and acknowledging and appreciating your attributes, talents and all the good in your life. In other words, start from the inside out, not the other way around. The dependence stops when they are no longer using other people as a drug to artificially create worth, happiness, or attraction in themselves. When you feel comfort in being alone, you will no longer live in fear that someone is going to leave you, or you are going to be alone forever and nothing is going to work out for you.

It is also important in any relationship to be aware of your *negative bias*. As a form of low self-esteem, most people forget the positive words and actions offered to them and absorb the negative. In successful relationships as well as in life, happier people remember the positive and forget the negative. This also creates further awareness to notice more positive intentions from people and not focus on negative actions.

If you imagine the problems in your life are too overwhelming to handle with no way out, try to imagine them as perfect. Imagine them as the circumstance you need, to get an important lesson necessary for this stage in your life. Imagine it as exactly what you needed in order to grow and be able to contribute with at a later date. This could apply to anything that you feel is limiting you: not having the job you want, the relationship, the friends, etc. I am not saying you should imagine staying in this situation but if you recognize the present moment as perfect in some way, this will allow you to create something new for your future.

Depression

In order to challenge the negative thoughts that cause depression, identify where you are not living up to typical positive attributes based on your type. Setting realistic goals and not getting caught up in what you think you should be doing, but focusing on what you can do day by day, can turn the tide on depression.

If you are Entitled, stop partnering with or supporting someone who has different intentions or goals than you. You want to support the vision of someone you admire until you can start your own path. Modeling another Entitled will give you the inspiration to learn to do it on your own. If you are a Support, before taking a big risk to start a business, support someone in the business you are passionate about. Use the depression as motivation to change things in your life, rather than escape with drugs, alcohol or anything else taking you away from exactly the life you want. The negative feelings are there for a reason; avoiding them will only give you more of the same or worse.

If you are constantly in discontent stop comparing what you have to what you want. Find contentment in how fortunate you are. One of the most powerful ways to move to the next level of motivation and get out of the depression is by helping others who are not as well off as you. Volunteering your time with needy or handicapped children, the homeless, an animal shelter, or the terminally ill can show you how wonderful your life is. This can provide you with motivation necessary to create or follow through on small visions leading to bigger ones. The key is to force the motivation, or find optimism for the initial steps to find the desired change.

Addictions, Fears, and Justification

How Justification Prevents Positive Change
People in extremes (Selfish Entitleds and Blind Supports) confuse justification with reason. As an alcoholic will tell themselves there is good reason why they can continue drinking, supporting their addiction, someone who abuses, controls, or takes advantage of others will do the same. The same is true for a Blind Support that puts him- or herself in sacrifice. Like an addict, rather than face the discomfort, instead of admitting they are wrong, they confuse their justification with logic or reason to support the negative behavior.

This justification is referred to as cognitive dissonance. For example, a smoker realizes that smoking is deadly but continues to take part in the behavior. So to continue in the deadly behavior, he tells himself things that will make the behavior comfortable for him. "Uncle Mike lived to ninety years old, and he smoked a pack a day."

The idea of cognitive dissonance proves that despite all of our intelligence, humans are not always rational beings. When someone feels a threat to their addictions or fears, they need to justify their actions to avoid change. The dichotomy is obvious to everyone around the person with the negative behavior; such as a gambler saying, "I can make back my house payment in one bet," or a food addict ordering a diet Coke with their unhealthy meal. Knowledge of poor or destructive behavior is always accompanied by justification and false reasoning.

The biggest part of changing for the better is based on self-discovery. In order to make new discoveries, new methods that create awareness are necessary. Justification is in part, a conversation that lightens the blow of a quality you don't like in yourself. Instead, referring to your actions in terms that are repulsive to you, and identifying the truth about them, which you haven't yet considered, will force you to change. So instead of saying, "I have difficulty having patience for others," say, "When anxious, I abuse the ones I love." Instead of referring to your emotion as "anger," call it "fear." "Just wanting to make your point," becomes "I need to be right in order to control this situation out of my own fear." Smoking, drinking too much, overeating and not worrying about your own health in general because, "It's my life," could translate to "My smoking habit proves I have no consideration for my friends and family."

Find out what you've been avoiding by justifying your behavior. This will require the release of control and the need to be right. Needing to be right is the opposite of evolving because it leaves you just where you are. This does not mean beating yourself up; that has judgment behind it. This idea is to look in areas you haven't looked before. For example, I have never seen someone who tries to control others with money have their inner conscious say, "Boy, am I greedy. Creating misery and controlling people's resources really makes me happy." What they actually do is justify: "I'm protective of my family." "If I wasn't careful with my money, my children would starve, and never get an education."

The intention here is to change your motivation, not to think of yourself as "bad." Such as a person being abused saying, "I know I'm an idiot for letting him treat me this way." That just makes them feel bad while they continue to accept abuse. There is a more creative inspiring conversation needed. It often requires asking someone else what you need to work on. A person accepting abuse from a lover or boss often says, "I just give him his way so we don't argue," or "I don't want to make problems." What they are really saying is, "I don't deserve anything more than what you give to me." "I am too fearful to stand up for myself." Changing the justification to truth is the kind of self-talk that can motivate change if the problem doesn't stop.

You can tell a person's prospects for the future based on how they describe the past. If someone is still justifying abuse they've done for years, you can guess they will continue to do the same. I worked with someone who had cheated on his first two wives. About to enter into a new marriage, he was worried he would break down and the same thing would happen. He spoke very easily about how irresponsible and inconsiderate he was and how hurtful it was to the women he loved. Because he recognized the abuse and no longer justified his past behavior, it gave him a strong chance to change the outcome of this new relationship.

I was working with a Blind Support who kept going back to a Selfish Entitled who was abusive to her. Every time she left, he would turn up his charm and get her to come back.

Her justification for returning was that she was, "romantically hopeful and optimistic." This was exactly the opposite of what she was. If she was hopeful and optimistic, she would not have a problem waiting for the arrival of another man who had a chance of being good to her. That term not only justified her walking back into abuse; it actually made her noble for doing so. Not being able to change her mind about continuing to see him, I had her refer to what she was doing as what it actually was. I had her say things like, "I am intent on being abused and will accept it because I am so fearful of being alone." "I refuse to get to know myself during this important transition in order to find another man." "My behavior is romantically self-destructive." This made her realize that she was not being hopeful, but really hopeless. This is why "positive thinking" often doesn't work. Sometimes being open to a different interpretation of your situation will give you the inspiration you need to make a change.

This is not just valid for relationships. Earlier I told you about someone who set up scapegoats saying, "I'm just too busy to pursue that dream." In most of the cases, what people like this are really saying is, "I'm too scared to fail, so I set up very serious blocks to stop me from trying." If this sounds like you, look at the people, the situations, and the work you do in your life that take your energy away from your dream. What convenience do they provide for you? What potential failures are you trying to avoid by having them in your life? Have you convinced yourself that they need so much of your time that it is worth distracting you from your goals?

The key to finding change and your way out of justification is not to be shameful or judgmental. The justification or the words you've been using have allowed you to be in the current state you are in now. If that is not exactly what you want then change the conversation.

Justification Through Friendships

What pathologies are represented by the friends you have? This question includes lovers, and even more importantly, acquaintances. What do you allow yourself to justify by being with, or knowing them? Many times we have people in our lives that allow us to justify our own bad behavior. We often find ourselves in environments with people who have similar or worse dysfunctions, so that ours seems okay.

Someone accepting abuse will say, "Well, it's not like he treats me the way Jennifer's boyfriend treats her." You can see where knowing this person would allow someone to accept more abusive behavior in their own relationship. This goes for friends as well as acquaintances.

This can also be prevalent in all the other categories we've covered. Think of the Selfish Entitled abuser; they definitely have people in their lives that they reference who create more abuse than they do. "At least I don't treat my girlfriend the way Michael does. He doesn't even respect women." The person they use as an excuse might even be one of their parents. "At least I'm not like my father."

Someone who is angry and bitter will cite other angry and bitter people. A cheater will cite other cheaters worse than themselves. Gamblers, alcoholics, overeaters, etc., find others that represent a less evolved person than themselves. They may not even do this consciously or out loud but just part of a natural justification process that happens within them. A good place to start is to look at the less reformed people in your life and what they represent to you.

Being committed and around committed people is the key to creating positive change in your life. I've seen people after a heart attack, despite being scared, not create much real change and continue to live an uncomfortable life until their next ailment, which usually kills them. It is the ones that commit to a lifestyle change that transform themselves in a way that is unrecognizable to their old self, creating new comfort and happiness. With all the people I've worked with, the ones who commit to the lifestyle changes in this book in this same way transform their relationships or find healthier happier ones, unrecognizable to their previous self.

CHAPTER 17

A CATEGORY DOES NOT DEFINE A PERSON

Every person has qualities of both categories, and as with being predominately right handed you will use your left hand when you so desire. Without that flexibility, your abilities are limited to almost half. In order to find balance in your life, part of moving towards reform requires not defining yourself as the simple attributes found in each category. This is to keep, but not *define* yourself with the positive qualities, and eventually contribute with the negative.

Defining yourself with an attribute will cause you to lose your identity in situations where those attributes are not necessary. If you *define* yourself as a leader, that limits you from learning something new because you will find it difficult to follow other leaders. Thinking of yourself as only important in one area causes you to never want to leave that arena. This limits your creativity for, and discovery of new positive attributes.

The same is true if someone defines themselves with a *negative* attribute, such as "not that smart." In this case, anytime a situation arises where they must do some real thinking, they would not even attempt it. Therefore, positive or negative, attributes should be recognized as just one of many qualities people have and just specific to different situations. This allows a person to be open to contributing or learning in other areas where those attributes may not apply.

Bad judgment also turns a positive attribute into a detriment. If someone has the positive attribute of protecting their friends and family, but they were to attack everyone they thought might be a potential threat, their ability to protect would go from an attribute to a detriment. Every positive contribution has its proper time and place.

For example, if a great therapist, who is a Support, serves his clients until he is mentally drained in their issues, that becomes poor judgment on his part, turning an attribute of support or concern into a detriment. A good therapist must be responsible to those he can truly help and not to those he cannot. This will prevent becoming burnt out or exhausted to the point of not being helpful to anyone. It is vital to discover your most important attributes and to then be responsible to yourself and to others with them.

A Selfish Entitled I worked with had a natural ability to lead and a great attribute to get people to do things for her. Her poor judgment, which turned this attribute into a detriment, was that she kept asking everyone for far too much. After having been burnt out, they were not interested in doing anything for her again. She had bad judgment in not recognizing the signs that people were depleted. Overestimating how much people were willing to serve her drove them away. Her attribute of leadership and confidence then turned into unending neediness.

Finding your best qualities and being aware of when they become a detriment to you is a simple path towards more happiness and reform. Some examples include:

- **Protection** – Are you aware of when you become overprotective? This also includes overprotection of oneself, such as in the case of a person who is always defensive or arguing with others.

- **Leading others** – Are you aware of where your leadership becomes reckless or irresponsible? This happens when a person moves towards leading in directions where they are unfamiliar or do not respect others' abilities.

- **Generosity** – Where are you too generous with your time or resources? When being generous, do you feel as though your energy is being taken?

- **Compassion** – Are you sometimes too compassionate with others? Do you see their side to the point of putting yourself in sacrifice, welcoming abuse?

- **Acceptance** – Are you sometimes too accepting of others? Do you allow others to push you further than you are comfortable without telling them?

- **Open-mindedness** – Are you too open-minded? Do you find yourself in dangerous situations because of this?

- **Trust** – Do you put too much trust in others, putting you or your resources in jeopardy?

- **Loyalty** – Are you loyal to a fault? Does your instinct to be loyal put you in harm's way? Do you live your relationship paying more attention to what your parents, society or religion says you should do, over your better judgment?

Without balance, any good quality can turn into a detriment. Be aware of whether or not you are overcompensating to try to prove yourself.

The most well-rounded, healthy and happy people have many of the best qualities found in either category, Entitled or Support, and move freely in and out of them, especially if they are not in a relationship. Getting in touch with good qualities of the category not typical of you can be very challenging because you have to overcome fears, but can also be very fulfilling.

How to Get in Touch with Good Qualities of a Category Not as Natural for You

— Entitleds Wanting to Be More Supportive (Especially Helpful for Selfish Entitleds)

You can be more supportive if you get in touch with your ability to trust in others and their leadership. Lose your need for control, and resist thinking that you have to do everything. Work to give the Supports around you confidence to take the lead; then relax and enjoy their care. Release your need for perfection and the idea that things can only be done one way. Release your need for recognition. Get in touch with your insecurities and fears about why it is important to be attractive or powerful to others. Make a list of times when you are reactive and not proactive, times when you are defending your "principles," rather than being compassionate to others. Enjoy your successes and accomplishments, live more in the moment, and realize it may not be as important as you think to get to the "next step." When meeting a new person ask yourself, "What talents of mine would be helpful for their life?" instead of "What can this person do for me?"

— Supports Wanting to Be More Entitled

If you are looking to have more follow through/leadership on your vision, then start trusting yourself and your ability to lead and take educated, well researched, and informed risks. Trust in your abilities, talents, leadership, and others' confidence in you. Know that if your vision or follow-through goes awry in any way, from choosing a restaurant to starting a business, the risk may not be as great as you are concerned about. From all great failures come great learning experiences, as long as you can move on from them and continue to try again. Realize your insecurities and fears and how they have held you back up to this point. How different will your life be when you face your insecurities? Think about the effect confidence will have on you emotionally, spiritually, financially, as well as physically. How will your relationships change? Go into the future six months, five years, ten years from now. Where will you be if you don't make changes?

Also, be more selective in your support; when meeting someone new, instead of always thinking, "How can I support them?" wait and see what common interest you have that would be beneficial for you to be in support of.

— Avoiding Polar Extremes

We all have temporary bouts of extremes (Selfish Entitled and Blind Support). This usually happens when we feel threatened or out of control. From this place, we might either lash out against someone, or accept too much out of fear. A person's happiness is in direct relation to how much they feel they are in control of their own life. Anger, frustration, and sadness are all a result of feeling threatened in some way. Happiness is also in direct relation to how healthy a person is. A simple fever can destroy anyone's mood, let alone a debilitating disease. For this reason, our website (*www.TheArtOfUnity.com*) has lessons regarding relationships as well as nutrition, meditation, and overall wellbeing.

The deeper truth is that a person's happiness is in direct relation to how they internally interpret what happens to them. So what makes one person feel threatened, another might interpret differently allowing for happiness in an otherwise uncomfortable situation. People who are in extremes try to gain control based on external forces. They try to create circumstances, take actions, and cause situations that give them control of everything around them. People who are reformed realize that the only way to maintain real control is by controlling how you interpret circumstances, actions, and situations from within yourself.

Releasing Control

Becoming aware of how reactive versus proactive you are, will be a good indicator if you are trying to control the outside versus the inside. If you are trying to control the outside, you will get mad, frustrated, make drama, and be abusive to others. This often results in unworthiness and depression because you are trying to force a change that is not happening. Reaction, as opposed to response, stems from the past. It is a force of old habits and is absent of any awareness or compassion (polar extremes react often).

Proactive responses stem from the present moment. To be responsive is to be totally alive in the here and now. Being proactive means taking leadership and is non-aggressive towards others. Being proactive means monitoring how you accept something. Do you see things people say as something personal, as them trying to control you, or as them just seeking love in their own way? This realization is seeking acceptance from the inside, and in turn gaining control.

Commitment is the Key to Change

Transformation is more than just a change in your behavior, it comes from within; causing a certain contentment with no further energy wasted on the old behavior. A change of behavior without transforming could just mean suppressing fears. There is a difference between holding fears at arm's length and recognizing them as an illusion. The idea is to find love in others intentions despite their actions. Even an expression of anger can be translated as love.

Since this is all about awareness, I invite you to become a witness; a witness of your own life, all your thoughts, including insecurities, frustrations, judgments, control tactics, shame, and your happiness. To find true joy, you will want to get to know who you are at the deepest level. To do that you need to witness all the things created by your ego, your fears, and your environment that is different than who you really are, underneath it all. Once you do that and so has your partner, you will find your true happiness, your bliss together, and that you are in fact "right" for each other.

I believe we are creatures of love, connection, and belonging. We need companionship to survive as much as food and water. Those who are not good at expressing love, or who have the propensity to hurt others, are the most hurt themselves and often don't even know it. At all times, people have the ability to choose, give, and accept love, even if that means simply loving themselves; and when you have love for yourself it overflows.

In taking actions to show appreciation towards others, everything including our relationships, businesses, and friendships will consistently get better. In 1946, The Labor Relations Institute found that the number one thing employees said they want from their employers is appreciation[2]. Employers thought it would be higher wages, but that came in at number five on the list. Since then at least five studies have produced the same results. Appreciation can heal so many problems found in relationships, and it is much easier to control than anything outside of you.

The information I've shared in this book has improved my life greatly and all the relationships around me. I have great appreciation for all who read it and hope it does the same for you and the ones around you. Right now, you might not have the relationship, the business, or even the friends you want, but I believe if you start appreciating what you have, it will build the foundation and the readiness to find all that you want. I offer all my love and support to those searching for a more joyful path.

---

2. (**Source** - This survey first came out in 1946 in Foreman Facts, from the Labor Relations Institute of NY and was produced again by Lawrence Lindahl in *Personnel* magazine, in 1949. This study has since been replicated with similar results by Ken Kovach (1980); Valerie Wilson, Achievers International (1988); Bob Nelson, Blanchard Training & Development (1991); and Sheryl & Don Grimme, GHR Training Solutions (1997-2001).

GLOSSARY

Abuse (63-68, 74, 80, 98, 104, 111, 178, 193-199, 214, 279) - Any improper treatment, often to unfairly gain benefit to one person while hurting another. Abuse in relationships can come in many forms, such as: physical, verbal, psychological, emotional, or sexual. It includes bullying, where perceived imbalance of power with the more powerful attacking the less powerful, including subtle methods of coercion, manipulation, dominating and/or intimidation.

Some examples are:

- Physical aggression, including pushing, shaking, restraining or throwing objects or threats thereof.

- Financial abuse (withholding money or controlling, threatening another via some financial means, such as not paying for a necessity of theirs.)

- Social abuse (restricting access to, insulting or threatening of friends or family.)

- Controlling, domineering, intimidating, pressuring or manipulating.

- Stalking.

- Passive/covert abuse (neglect)

- Gaslighting - Any actions taken to manipulate your partner into thinking they are insane; including withholding information, lying, or having the gradual effect of making someone anxious, confused and less able to trust their own memory and perception.

Acceptance is a person's assent to the reality of a situation. It is recognizing a condition (often a negative or unwanted situation) without protest, or escape from it. Acceptance can also be described as a "surrender" or "voluntary submission" to the current situation. This is in no way synonymous with Tolerance. Acceptance can be defined as the desire to submit to the struggle instead of resisting it.

Acceptance of self as well as your partner is the basis of harmonious and positive relationships. Self-acceptance is being loving and happy with who you are *now*. It's an agreement with yourself to appreciate, validate, accept and support who you are at this moment. There is the misconception that accepting self as is, will result in a lack of motivation to move towards positive change, this is not true; you don't have to be unhappy with yourself to desire and motivate change of the things you don't like. Acceptance can be considered the first step in change

Appreciation (182-186, 207, 257, 317) - Any form of gratitude, acknowledgement, or thankful recognition. It can be expressed in many ways including non-verbal and is often the start of mending non-harmonious relationships and further strengthening good ones.

Awareness (278-282) - The state or ability to assess, feel, or to be conscious of actions, events, or sensory patterns currently occurring. In this level of consciousness, an observer can identify sensory information without necessarily implying understanding. This is not to be confused with self-consciousness, where a person's analyzes self, usually negatively. Awareness for the purpose of this book is the consciousness of internal reactions from occurrences of the external world.

Awareness is the ability to bring attention to one's thoughts, emotions, memories, ideas, ideals, belief-systems, actions and reactions. In having awareness a person can experience a state of freedom, giving him or her the ability to act with consciousness rather than react in defense or self-protection causing potential regret. Awareness is the key to change.

Benevolent Entitled (30, 34-35) - A subcategory of Entitled, A Benevolent Entitled fulfills his or her part in a healthy, harmonious relationship as an Entitled. These are responsible Entitleds that are not "Selfish Entitled" or yet "Reformed." The differences in subcategories are related to how responsible an Entitled is within his or her type. Benevolent Entitleds carry all the responsibility an Entitled should, such as leadership, vision for the relationship, care and protection of their Supports without controlling them. People move in and out of selfishness depending on fears and emotions, it is important to move back to a more positive place especially in an intimate relationship (often the hardest place to do that). The chapters on reform show how.

Blame (186-188) - The act of holding another responsible for negative or irresponsible events or actions that have occurred. Blame is the opposite of praise or appreciation. In blame a person feels they are taking the responsibility away from themselves but are unknowingly making themselves a victim. Blame is a way of discharging pain and discomfort.

Blind Support (BS) (Chapter 4) – Subcategory of Support, characterized by dependence, sacrifice, and attachment. A Blind Support is supportive in more than 90 percent of all instances continuing to support despite ongoing abuse.

BS – Blind Support (See Blind Support)

Codependence (85, 300-303) refers to the dependence on the needs or control of another. It is a psychological condition or relationship in which a person is controlled or manipulated by another who is affected with a pathological condition, such as an addiction to alcohol or drugs. It involves being excessively preoccupied with the needs of others and placing a lower priority on self. This can occur in any type of relationship, including family, work, friendship, and intimate.

Like many addictions codependency is often characterized by denial, low self-esteem, and control patterns. Narcissists as well as both Selfish Entitleds and Blind Supports are considered to be natural magnets for the codependent.

Cognitive Dissonance (305-306) is used to describe when a person knows of something to be detrimental to their well being yet take part in it anyway. It is the state of holding two or more conflicting ideas, such as wanting to smoke, despite knowing it is unhealthy. This is always accompanied by justification in order take part in the detrimental behavior.

Commitment is the state of being dedicated to a cause, activity, relationship etc. Commitment does not happen by default but by choice. You cannot default to change, it must occur consciously.

Communication (200-217) - Derived from the Latin word "*communis*", meaning to share. Communication is the ability to share thoughts, ideas, and create an understanding with another. Communication is the most basic and perhaps the single biggest separator that occurs between partners in relationships that when corrected can solve most relationship problems. Without commitment to proper communication problems can spiral out of control causing an inability to have resolution. Proper communication is not complete until the receiver has understood the message of the sender.

Compassion (177, 197-198) - Concern and understanding for another's circumstance or well being in order to see their point of view; empathy for the suffering of others. Compassion is the key to resolution and the connection with one another depends on it. Compassion has the power to stop all suffering.

Compatibility (226-233) - The ability for two or more things to exist together harmoniously.

Connection versus Attachment (45-47) - Connection is a feeling of understanding and ease of communication in a relationship while attachment is a dependence on another.

Constructive Support (43) – A subcategory of Support, a Constructive Support is person fulfilling his or her part in a healthy, harmonious relationship as a Support. Constructive Supports offer support to responsible, appreciative partners and not to people inconsiderate of others, such as a Selfish Entitled. This category is for supports not offering "Blind Support" or yet "Reformed." A Support moves away from being Constructive when they go from service to sacrifice. Supports can move into sacrifice depending on the situation, so it is important to hold back their support until they are more appreciated or with a more evolved Entitled, especially in an intimate relationship (often the hardest place to do that). The chapters on reform show how.

Control versus Care (35, 42, 55, 82, 87) - Control involves some authority over another and includes manipulation and/or deception and expectations. Care is compassionate treatment given to those in need without obligation attached. Care is offered in healthy relationships but is often misconstrued for what is actually control in unhealthy relationships.

Criticism (63-65, 93, 98) - A value judgment of another's ideas, actions or values. It can have constructive or destructive intentions.

Defense Mechanisms (179, 287-290) provide refuge from anxiety or fear and lie in what a person perceives as a threat and why. Brought by the subconscious mind, they manipulate deny or distort reality.

Having awareness of when you feel you need to defend yourself often can point out unreal fears.

Dependence (47, 57) – See Codependence

Depression (304) - A state of being, or mood where a person feels hopeless or extreme sadness. In depression people feel out of control of their own circumstance. A state of depression can be accompanied by too much sleep or inability to sleep. Feeling anxious, worried, helpless, worthless, loss of appetite or interest are just some symptoms of depression.

Emotional Prisons (EP) (290 - 292) are the emotional places you find yourself in when unhappy, even to the point of tormenting yourself over an issue involving trust in loved one's, friends, family or even yourself over what is usually nothing. It includes what you doubt in others to the point of investigation, what you make other people prove to you, issues which are really yours and not theirs. Could be jealousy, thinking someone is cheating on you, thinking people are making fun of you, people don't love you, people are using you, you don't matter to anyone, etc.

Enabling (85-88) is behavior that is intended to help but actually perpetuate a problem. Synonymous with addiction, enablers take blame for, allow, add fuel to and mistakenly encourage those addicted to negative behavior. A common example is the relationship between an addict and the codependent spouse. The spouse either "minds their business," makes excuses for, or cleans up the problems made by the addict. Blind Supports are very commonly enablers because of weak boundaries or low self-esteem.

Entitled (chapter 1) - For purpose of this book, "Entitled," is one of two main categories in a relationship dynamic. A person in this category naturally takes the initiative, the responsibility, and has the vision for the couple's actions. A healthy Entitled provides care and protection in a relationship, as well as follow through on his or her vision. An Entitled naturally thinks of his or her own vision before considering that of another.

Entitled Masquerading as a Support (Chapter 9) - People in this category feel they need to pretend they are a Support when they actually are Entitled. This often occurs in the subconscious and is usually caused by shame and insecurity.

Escapes (65, 112-113, 285) - Any mental diversion used as a relief from unpleasant thoughts about daily life, guilt, or shame. They are actions people, often subconsciously take to relieve or avoid persisting feelings of depression, sadness, fear, anxiety or the like.

Evolution (62, 100, 180, 200) - Moving beyond, and not passing the same negativity, pathologies, fears, shame, and insecurities you received from your parents onto your children. Not wanting other people, especially loved ones, to go through the same pain that you went through or are going through. When you are hurt, not choosing to hurt others. Evolution is the gradual process of something changing into a better form.

Expressed (146, 185, 213) - The feeling that your ideas or feelings have been heard, accepted, or understood by your partner.

Fears – Imaginary versus Non-Imaginary (44, 293) - Non-imaginary fears are those that animals are equally afraid of, such as burning yourself or rushing to avoid getting hit by a car. Non-imaginary fears are anything putting a person in harms way.

Imaginary fears are those caused by our pathology such as most of what causes the three most common. That is the fear of losing safety or control, fear of abandonment, and the fear of unworthiness. Although these fears may cause a lot of stress they are largely conceptual or imagined.

Justifying (45, 99, 111, 262, 305-310) - What a person tells themselves to avoid guilt when feeling bad about behavior they know to be outside of compassion or benefit towards others. The same is true about people who justify another's abuse, not having compassion towards themselves or the person or persons being abused.

Judgmental (63, 198) - See Criticism

Mirror versus Complementary Relationships (232-235) - "Mirror" relationships are those that which both parties have similar traits. Rapport and understanding for one another is formed quickly based on familiarity. "Complementary" relationships are those in which both have quite different traits. The risk here is a lack of understanding of two people together with little similarity to one another, however when they intermix well the relationship provides much growth for both with each fitting together perfectly like two different pieces of a puzzle.

Narcissism - Beyond a healthy self-approval, narcissism is extreme egotistical behavior, vanity and selfishness. Selfish Entitleds are often narcissists. Narcissism is often related to defenses against shame.

Neediness (84, 296, 300) - Beyond ordinary need of another, neediness defines a dependency, addiction, or unhealthy attachment outside of self. Blind Supports are often needy.

Pathology (36, 282-290, 296-299) - A negative behavior pattern that is developed from childhood. For the unreformed, their pathology is the go-to, reactive response, even when it doesn't feel healthy or fulfilling. Pathologies occur from the ego as a form of self-protection or familiarity despite them only having a negative impact. The result of acting from pathology often gives a person the opposite of what they truly want. Awareness of pathologies is an ongoing process and the key to change. Jealousy, drama, dismissing self, not accepting love, shame, choosing unhealthy relationships, most fears and anxiety, giving or accepting abuse all constitute pathology and not a person's true self.

Procrastination (93) - The process of putting important tasks off to a later time. Procrastination is characterized by a lack of commitment and follow through. Procrastinators are often escapist.

The Profile (Chapter 8) is a test taken to know which category you fall into and by what percentage.

Psychological Abuse - also referred to as emotional abuse or mental abuse, is a form of abuse characterized by a person subjecting or exposing another to behavior that may result in psychological trauma, including anxiety, depression, or post-traumatic stress disorder. Such abuse is often associated with situations of power imbalance, such as abusive relationships, bullying, and abuse in the workplace. Examples include, denying access to money, harassing, threatening, belittling, damaging property, and preventing the victim from eating, sleeping, or leaving their residence.

RE – Reformed Entitled (See Reformed Entitled)

Reformed (44, 52, 57, 99, Chapters 14-16, 283) - Self-improvements by the awareness and avoidance of our faults or abuses while bettering conduct, behavior or morals. A reformed person is someone working on evolving themselves for a happier more harmonious way of living.

Reformed Entitled (RE) (Chapter 14) - The healthiest category of an Entitled, and goal Entitleds should strive for. A person with high moral values characterized by leadership, care, contribution, and protection of those around them.

Reformed Support (RS) (Chapter 15) - The healthiest category of a Support and goal Supports should strive for. A person with high moral values and strong self-worth, characterized by supporting those responsible towards others.

Repetition Compulsion (162, 298) - The impulse to reenact earlier emotional experiences or traumatic behavior in a subconscious attempt to overcome them.

Resentment (84, 115, 274) - The experience of a negative emotion felt as a result of a perceived wrongdoing. Not expressing yourself in this situation only causes the build up of resentment, anger and spite leading to the destruction of a relationship. Because they rarely express their feelings Blind Supports often are prone to resentment. Relationship combinations of two Entitleds together need to be careful of resentment (see chapter 12).

RS – Reformed Support (See Reformed Support)

Sacrifice (35, 43-45, 80-83, 268-270) - The point in which service or support of another turns negative. Sacrifice is characterized by a drain of energy and lack of appreciation in return for the support given and an endless amount of more support expected. This is typical of a Selfish Entitled.

SE – Selfish Entitled (See Selfish Entitled)

Self-Esteem (85, 301, 304) is a person's evaluation or appraisal of his or her own worth based on beliefs. People often mistakenly base their self-esteem with success they have in what they desire. The problem with this is that failure can occur at any time, therefore destroying their esteem. Esteem effects the way we act in the world and how we relate to everybody else. Low self-esteem is the cause of many psychological disorders, weak boundaries, dependence, and other pathologies.

Self-Fulfilling Prophecy is a prediction that directly or indirectly causes itself to become true, by the very terms of the prophecy itself. It is based on a strongly held belief declared as truth when actually false, but sufficiently influences the believer, to take actions of precautions against it, causing it to happen.

Self-Righteousness (59-61, 190-192, 263, 295) - The idea that you are "right" in an argument, circumstance, situation and your partner is "wrong." Often it is inclusive of moral superiority. The ability to give up self-righteousness defines a relationship and is directly related to a person's ability to be happy, let go of past issues, have harmony with self and others, openness, and ability to adapt.

Selfish Entitled (SE) (Chapter 3) - A subcategory of Entitled, "Selfish Entitleds" are people thinking of what is best for *them* more than 90 percent of the time, leading with unjustified entitlement, abuse and control.

Support (Chapter 2) - For purpose of this book, "Support," is one of the two main categories in a relationship dynamic. A person in this category prefers to support the initiative or vision mapped out by their "Entitled" partner. A Support naturally thinks of others before him or herself.

Support Masquerading as an Entitled (Chapter 10) - A category of people who are more naturally a Support but act as if they are an Entitled. This usually occurs in people who overcompensate for insecurity or are in fear and feel they need to protect themselves rather than submitting to others such as their intimate partner.

Unreformed (243, 257) are those not changing or evolving at all but staying in their complaint, upset, or misfortune.

Vision (31-33, 92-93, 184, 237, 241-243, 254) – In terms of the role of an Entitled, vision is the knowledge of what they want specifically, inclusive of a plan to move forward to follow through. (*Follow through* is the ability to actually move the plan through to its fruition.) When following through the vision will include adapting to unexpected circumstances and surprises along the way.

INDEX

Made in the USA
San Bernardino, CA
24 September 2015